MEHER BABA

THE AWAKENER OF THE AGE

Meher Baba at Longchamps Restaurant in New York, 1952.

Meher Baba
The Awakener of the Age

Don E. Stevens

1 9 9 9

COMPANION BOOKS
COMPANION ENTERPRISES

By The Same Author

Some Results
Man's Search For Certainty
Listen! The New Humanity
The Inner Path in the New Life
Listen, Humanity
(Editor and Narrator)

CONTENTS

LIST OF PHOTOGRAPHS

ACKNOWLEDGMENTS

I f the work you are about to read hangs together and makes for enjoyable, connected reading, then you must thank a close friend of mine from Latin America, who wishes to remain anonymous. In the early days as the ideas seemed to flood from nowhere onto the computer, it was she who read carefully through the first chapters and made key suggestions on content and styling which proved invaluable as the story took shape. And when the flood had spent itself and the hard work of reworking the manuscript had to be undertaken, it was Heather Nadel and Meherwan Jessawala who absented themselves from other pressing duties and spent the long hours discussing, recounting and encouraging, which helped immeasurably by filling in many vivid observations and historic occurrences in the life of Meher Baba.

Some time later, Ward Parks contributed his thoughts in great detail on many points of structure, and about then, that priceless couple, Susan and Emory Ayers, came into the practical side of the picture in a hundred different manners, including writing the Introduction. Faultless companionship also played its key role of unobtrusive backing at every turn. Claude Longuet stayed on the production scene from beginning to end, and Dick Duman added his own bright insights and suggestions.

My special gratitude goes to Bhau Kalchuri and Lawrence

Reiter for permission to use many important stories from *Lord Meher* by Bhau Kalchuri. Sufism Reoriented also contributed greatly by allowing the use of material from *God Speaks* by Meher Baba, as well as the fine photo of Baba used on the cover. The Avatar Meher Baba Perpetual Public Charitable Trust in turn has allowed us to use portions from the *Discourses; Listen, Humanity* and *Sparks*, all by Meher Baba, *The Wayfarers* by Dr. William Donkin, as well as material collected by various mandali in *Tales from the New Life*. In addition to these, we are grateful to Charles Haynes and the Quarterly Newsletter of Berkeley, California for their permission to use "Surrender to Meher Baba," to The Meher Baba Association of London for quotes from *Much Silence* by Tom and Dorothy Hopkinson, as well as to the Meher Spiritual Center, Inc. of Myrtle Beach, S.C. for quotes from Charles Purdom's *The God-Man* copyright © 1971. Used by permission. Lastly, the fine collection of messages and documents from the New Life of Meher Baba, made by the Meher Vihar Trust in their *Messages from the New Life*, has been invaluable to our efforts.

Although the list is already long, we wish especially to thank Lawrence Reiter for permission to use several photographs of Meher Baba, and Mehera, whose personal choice and gifts of some of her favorite photos of Meher Baba also grace this work.

Who else? Obviously, Meher Baba. Not since that memorable day at the end of January in 1969 have I known him to produce so many breathless and even hair-raising incidents such that at once it became obvious who was doing the necessary molding of the total project. Baba, I hope it is pleasing to you.

D. E. Stevens
Cagnes-sur-Mer, France
January 29, 1998

INTRODUCTION

There is a wave of increased interest in spirituality in the West. Evidence of this can be seen in the statistics that 95% of individuals in the United States believe in God, and the publishing industry offers over 10,000 new spiritual book titles each year. Interest and belief in miracles and spiritual healing is also widespread. The idea that one can tap something beyond human laws in order to achieve a better life is a view held by many. Within this surge of interest there are differing viewpoints about the meaning of spirituality, and thus the attempts to describe God are numerous and varied. At one extreme is the belief in God as an impersonal cosmic intelligence; at the other extreme is a highly committed group of fundamentalist Christians, who believe that God is personal and manifested himself as Jesus Christ, and consider this a one-time event. There are also the fringe groups which are drawn to occult leaders. It is also interesting to note that in their search for God, some have gone beyond getting something for themselves and are seeking God for the sake of love alone.

Meher Baba, The Awakener of the Age tells of one who put in perspective all views about God and went further to reveal the secrets of Creation beyond anything previously disclosed. Meher Baba's life was one of Mastery in Servitude. He mingled with famous celebrities of the world and the unknown poorest of the poor. His love and work with the downtrodden of India was extensive. His close followers were willing to sacrifice all just to be in his company. His message of love and compassion saved many from the drug scene in the West. Record is made of the mysterious, universal work done by Meher Baba during his long periods of fasting and seclusion. There were many miracles that occurred around Meher Baba, but he taught that he did not come to perform miracles; and in fact that interest in miracles could be a distraction in one's search for Reality. Meher Baba revealed that he was the Avatar, God incarnate. He maintained silence as an aspect of his universal ministry, from 1925 until he dropped his body in 1969. Meher Baba communicated through the use of an alphabet board and hand gestures.

Meher Baba is written by Don Stevens, a retired, international oil executive, who has been a life-long spiritual seeker. Don became a member of the Sufi Movement in the United States in 1945. Some months later its leader, Murshida Martin, recognized Meher Baba as the great spiritual master of the Age and asked him to guide her and the Sufi Movement which was under her charge. This Meher Baba accepted, and thereby Don came under the spiritual guidance of Meher Baba in a manner that became increasingly direct as Murshida Martin's health failed and Meher Baba assumed progressively his spiritual promise to the Murshida. Don is one of the few Westerners alive today who had close and frequent access to Meher Baba. His probing and skeptical mind is the ideal vehicle to introduce the Westerner to Meher Baba. Don reveals his original uncertainty of Meher Baba's divinity and how this doubt dissolved from the learning situations and universal intimate care that he experienced at Meher Baba's feet. Don Stevens offers rare glimpses into life with the Avatar through recollected moments spent in his presence. Don now lives in Cagnes-sur-Mer, France, and he devotes full time to writing about Meher Baba, arranging translations of Meher Baba's writing, and working closely with several Meher Baba groups in Europe and the United Kingdom.

If the Western reader is to capture the essence of the secrets revealed by Meher Baba, an open mind on three major concepts is necessary. First, that God *has* manifested himself in the human form. Second, that this manifestation occurs periodically in history (a belief held by many Hindus and mystics). And third, that Meher Baba is the most recent manifestation, the Christ, the Avatar of our current age (a conviction held by thousands of Meher Baba followers in both the East and the West). For one to accept these concepts blindly is not likely; however, an absolute treasure awaits the reader who has an open mind to the concepts contained in *Meher Baba* and who reads for understanding.

The book is divided into two sections. Part I presents a biographical sketch of Meher Baba's life, the last seventeen years of which Don had an opportunity to be in his contact. For the earlier part of Meher Baba's life Don draws upon a vast resource of material. In fact, almost every day of Baba's life is documented from the time he received the awareness of his divinity at the age of 19. Reading of the quite "human" day-to-day activities of Meher Baba, one is constantly awestruck by his wisdom, energy, focus and compassion - one learns of Meher Baba's Divinity.

Part II of *Meher Baba* elucidates Don's understanding of Meher Baba's words. Contained here are such concepts as The Whim (the origin of Creation), Sanskaras (the impressions that determine our mode of being in life), Love, Surrender, Meditation, the Individual, the Occult, and the Master. Part II is brimming with delightful, pertinent examples that apply these concepts in a meaningful way to the practical issues of daily life. These examples provide a dynamic vehicle for understanding the fundamental Truths contained in them. In *Meher Baba* Don Stevens writes: "I believe we are living in the full flood tide of the manifestation of love of the Avatar." To satisfy this new wave of interest, Avatar Meher Baba's advent left us with new forms of seeking the Truth, and unique concepts heretofore not available. Springing from his love for Meher Baba is Don's very unique, strong incentive to recall, record and make these concepts available to as many individuals as possible. The reader will find these concepts beautifully described.

Meher Baba's message is universal and can speak to all regardless of age, sex, race, education, economic position, or social standing. *Meher Baba, The Awakener of the Age* provides one with a fresh way to understand life and gain a great confidence in the ultimate good and glory of all. It awakens us to the new bright dawn.

Emory and Susan Ayers
Mystic, Connecticut
July 1998

CHRONOLOGY

Key dates in the lifetime of Meher Baba

EVENT	DATE
Birth, Poona, India	February 25, 1894
Kindergarten, Padamji Gujarati School, Poona	1899
Zoroastrian School, Poona	September 1902
Government English School, Poona	August 1903
St. Vincent's High School, Poona	January 4, 1909
Deccan College, Poona	December 1911
Babajan removes the veil	May 1913
Merwan meets Narayan Maharaj, the Perfect Master, near Kedgaon	April 1915
Merwan meets Tajuddin Baba, the Perfect Master, near Nagpur	April–May 1915
Merwan meets Sai Baba and Upasni Maharaj, the Perfect Masters	Late 1915
Upasni Maharaj hits Merwan on the forehead with a stone	April 1915
Formation of the Circle, the mandali; first ashram in Bombay	1922
Foundation of second ashram at Meherabad	1924
Meher Baba begins observing silence	July 10, 1925
Stops writing, starts using an alphabet board	January 1, 1927
Traveling. Kashmir, Persia	September 1929
A seclusion cave is built at Meherabad	October 1929

Develops cervical spondylosis	1963
Last Eastern darshan program, Guru Prasad	May 2–6, 1965
Last walk at Guru Prasad, darshan for Poona lovers	1967
Last intense seclusion starts at Meherazad	June 1967
Seclusion continues at Guru Prasad	April–June 1968
Seclusion ends "to my complete satisfaction"	July 30, 1968
Health deteriorates	November 1968
Wedding of Dara and Amrit	December 19, 1968
Stops coming to mandali hall	January 12, 1969
Drops the body at Meherazad	January 31, 1969

Some words used in the text:

avatar: the direct descent of God into Creation in the form of man.

karma: the law of cause and effect in the totality of Creation. Its fundamental characteristic is that it requires the balancing out of all action and experience before the individual can finally realize his nature as being that of God.

Perfect Master: one who has completed the long journey of perfecting consciousness by removing all traces of identification with the physical, subtle and mental domains of creation and who has in consequence realized his identity with God, then returns to consciousness of all levels of Creation in order to assist in various tasks of assisting the ongoing process of perfecting consciousness in other individuals.

reincarnation: the rebirth of the individual into a new physical body after having left his previous physical form and passed a time of relative repose and reflection in the so-called astral world before adopting a new physical body. Meher Baba exposes the fact that these reincarnations continue until all of the sanskaric residues are exhausted and removed and the karma of the individual is completely balanced out.

sanskara: an ancient Sanskrit word which Meher Baba has endowed with further specialized meaning to denote the residues of experience within Creation. These, he says, are stored in the mental body of each individual being and hence continue their existence even when the physical body is worn out or left behind at the end of an incarnation. They are of great importance, he clarifies, as they are the cause of consciousness identifying with objects and events in Creation rather than with Reality, which is infinite God.

PART I

1. THE BEGINNING

The life of Meher Baba, born Merwan Sheriar Irani, in Poona on February 25, 1894, is inextricably intertwined with the subject of his clear and repeated statement that he is the Avatar of the age. Before giving even the bare details of his early childhood, it would be best to clarify immediately what this term's significance is. At the present time the word "avatar" is used quite loosely, and in common parlance corresponds perhaps most closely to what the Indians used to term a "mahatma," meaning a person of considerable spiritual attainment. But as so large a percentage of current humanity still associates this word with the man Mahatma Gandhi, it was necessary to find a new term to designate a person who is spiritually advanced. The word avatar dates back to the Sanskrit and the concept that God sends his son (the first human to complete the cycle of the generation and perfection of individual consciousness, terminating in God Realization) into Creation from time to time to catapult humanity from a stage of increasing spiritual paralysis, into a further push towards Reality. But now the term has begun to be used in a broad and quite general manner.

Remaining for the moment with the original usage of the word avatar, Meher Baba has laid out in some detail the mechanism by which the Avatar is brought into play in Creation during these periods of spiritual and moral stagnation. According to him, the ancient tradition that the Avatar (avtarna means literally *to descend,* being the direct descent of God into Creation) returns periodically among mankind is a fact, and it is always the same soul who does this, although in a different body form each time, and often into quite different civilizations. The timing and the mechanics of this return, however, are left to the five Perfect Masters[1] in Creation to judge, and when they consider that the progress of mankind's spiritual development has slowed markedly, these five Masters evoke the Avataric presence.

The Avatar is born into an ordinary family and goes through an ordinary development until one of the five Perfect Ones takes on the responsibility of removing the "veil" that covers the avataric nature from the individual himself. In effect, he does not know himself as anything other than a completely average and "normal" human being until the veil is removed. There inevitably follows a period of readjustment, in Baba's case some seven years, to return the level of consciousness to that of physical creation, a very painful process. From that point the individual knows himself as the Avatar and takes on himself thenceforth the role of quickening the spiritual development of mankind.

Therefore to speak of "an" avatar, as is so frequently done nowadays, is already to bastardize the term. There is only one, and he is always the same one, according to ancient tradition. To make the claim to be the Avatar, therefore, is a very serious statement bound to create a storm of conflicting opinion. This is exactly what happened in the case of Meher Baba, and the storm has not died down yet. To complicate matters, there is a sizable crowd of individuals scattered across the globe at the present writing who claim either to be an avatar, or in some cases, the avatar.

Having defined the heart of much of the public argument

---

[1] The term "Perfect Master" (*sadguru*) denotes one who has realized God. Meher Baba has clarified that at all times there are 56 God Realized beings in Creation, five of whom are charged with supervising Creation in conjunction with the Spiritual Hierarchy of spiritually advanced beings and agents. Baba has also pointed out that the Avatar, in his work, attends to all details, while the Perfect Master does not.

concerning Merwan Sheriar Irani, later to be known by his close followers as Meher Baba, we return to his birth and early childhood. Sheriar was the first name of his father, and Irani the family name, indicating a tie to Iranian ancestry. In fact, Sheriar the father was born in Iran, moving to India as a young man. Merwan's mother was born of Persian parents who had migrated to India shortly before her birth.

In his mid-twenties Merwan was renamed by his close friends as Meher Baba, meaning *compassionate father*. In this change of name, by which Merwan was known universally for the rest of his life, lies the kernel of our story. It will be an intensely personal story, unlike the classical biography which stands to the side of past events, judging them frequently after the passage of many years, and from an impersonal and objective point of view. But this newly born man-child was destined to become, at the least, one of the great spiritual masters of his time. It is for this reason that, to give any true account of the man, it is necessary to abandon in large part the objective approach and enter deeply into the subjective and the personal aspects so central to his aims. All the more so in this instance, as I had such a personal relationship with him, and I intend to write as I saw the man and his impact on the deepest layers of being in both myself and those I observed about me.

It would be hard to imagine starting one's early life with three greater handicaps than taking a vow of silence, which Baba did as a young man, and which lasted (interspersed with frequent pronouncements by him that he intended to break that silence) to the end of his life 44 years later, plus declaring publicly and repeatedly that one was the Avatar of the age, and finally, saddling oneself with the absolute responsibility for numerous devotees from both East and West. With these Meher Baba lived and participated intimately in their development for over forty years.

There are several really fine biographies of Meher Baba which treat at length his youth and the spectacularly normal manner in which it unfolded.[2] He was a really typical boy, interested in sports, especially cricket, with some leanings at an early age to poetry. Often he was referred to by his comrades as the arbitrator among them when knots of dissension arose. But nothing extraordinary set him aside from others until he was 19 and attending the Deccan College in Poona.

Merwan had a habit as he returned home after classes to stop by the spot in the Chabarvdi (literally, The Four Wells Gardens) in central Poona where a very ancient Sufi, Hazrat Babajan (who was in fact one of the five contemporary Perfect Masters) sat under a neem tree. This was her de facto home. Usually at that time of day she was surrounded by soldiers from a nearby encampment, and Baba arriving would look on from outside the circle. But one day Babajan beckoned to him and, as he approached, the ancient woman stood up with her arms spread wide and embraced him with the fervor of a mother finding her lost son. With tears in her eyes she cried out loudly, *My beloved son.* Merwan felt something indescribable, as if an electric shock passed through his body from head to toes.

Merwan, the usually bright, outgoing and diligent student, lost all interest in the world and his surroundings, after this and his only interest was Babajan, whom he would visit every evening for several hours. On one late night after several months of this, as Merwan rose to leave Babajan, he kissed her hands. In turn, as she held his face, Babajan looked into his eyes with all her love and kissed him on the forehead. Turning to her followers nearby she declared, *This is my beloved son. One day he will shake the world, and all*

---

[2] C. B. Purdom, *The God-Man* (Myrtle Beach: Sheriar Press Second Edition, 1971), and Tom and Dorothy Hopkinson, *Much Silence* (London: Victor Gollancz, 1974), are two of the most readable and well researched. A third monumental work, Bhau Kalchuri, *Lord Meher* (North Myrtle Beach: Manifestation, 1980) is already up to Volume XIV and at this point just completing the year 1956 in Meher Baba's life. It is a treasure house of intimate detail.

humanity will be benefited by him.

Merwan somehow returned home in a totally dazed condition and lay on his bed. Suddenly the earlier experience of electric shock returned with infinitely greater intensity. A great terror gripped him as he felt his identity disappearing and merging into the ocean of bliss of Godhood.[3] As could be expected, his state shocked and disturbed his family greatly. Despite all they could do to try to alleviate the problem the disorientation continued for days, then weeks, and finally months.

Eventually, in April of 1915, after confiding his intentions in a close friend, Behram (Behramji) Irani, Merwan set off alone by train for the little village of Kedgaon, about 50 miles from Poona, in search of an individual who was another of the five Perfect Masters, Narayan Maharaj. While for the greater part the Perfect Masters live very simply or even totally without possessions, the case of Narayan Maharaj was significantly different. He lived in a style befitting a minor potentate, with fine clothes and in rich surroundings.

Despite his dazed state, Meher Baba managed to get to the temple associated with the Master, only to be told that he was presently in his palace giving spiritual blessings. Again Merwan managed to find the place in which the Master was carrying out his work. Seeing Baba, Narayan sent all the crowd around him away and led Baba up to the throne to sit beside him. The two conversed for a long time and Baba stayed overnight, returning by train the next morning to Poona.

After several more short adventures, Baba made his way to the place where the third of the Perfect Masters, Tajuddin Baba, was staying near Nagpur in central India. On this particular occasion Baba was accompanied only by Behramji. Nearing the site of the

---

[3] *Lord Meher*, pp. 196, 198.

Master's presence, they were warned not to bother him, as he was in a very bad mood that day. But Baba insisted that Tajuddin was waiting for him, and so it actually turned out. Tajuddin greeted Baba and his companion as honored guests and, the smell of roses filled the air. After some hours the two young men made their way back to the train station and returned to Poona.

Two of the five Perfect Masters had still not been included in Baba's contacts. Some days after meeting Tajuddin Baba, Meher Baba in the company of a friend called Khodu made his way to Shirdi where Sai Baba, one of the most esteemed of the five Perfect Masters lived. We know from Baba's later elucidation that Sai Baba was the head of the spiritual hierarchy at that time and one of his closest followers was Upasni Maharaj, the fifth of the Perfect Masters.

Sai Baba at that moment spent relatively little time with Meher Baba, and almost at once Baba left Sai Baba's presence and made his way to Sakori where he found Upasni Maharaj. Maharaj promptly greeted him by throwing a stone at him. His aim, as it should be, was the best, and the stone hit Meher Baba square in the middle of the forehead. The workings of many spiritual mechanisms is, and no doubt will remain, a mystery to most, but the consequence was that a small reintegration of consciousness of physical surroundings penetrated Meher Baba. From that day, and over a period of about seven years, Maharaj and Baba continued in periodic, close contact. Finally, to all intents and purposes, Meher Baba was restored to consciousness of the physical world around him.

Meanwhile, both Maharaj as well as Babajan pronounced on various occasions their assessment of the spiritual importance of Meher Baba. These pronouncements are duly recorded, and in truth amount to the fact that Meher Baba was to be the great mover of the spiritual world.

It was during the period in which the reintegration of his consciousness was taking place that Meher Baba began to renew relationships with old schoolhood friends. Rapidly these individuals seemed to come under the spell of a new quality in their old chum. Rapidly also a natural guru-aspirant relationship developed, although there is no indication that it was recognized as such at that early stage.

The period of reintegration into physical consciousness that had now occurred Baba later described as a time of the most intense torture and pain. This he explained simply as being due to the fact that the kiss on the forehead from Babajan had given him instant realization of his godhood, and this was attended by the qualities of Infinite Knowledge, Power and Bliss, the triune attributes of Infinite God. The descent back into the realm of the duality of Creation had been, in consequence, a source of the greatest pain which caused him unbelievable suffering.

2. EARLY DAYS

Through the haze of trips back and forth to Upasni Maharaj's residence, life still lived in greater part with his family in Poona, and indications of what might be involved in his spiritual responsibility towards humanity, the pattern of Baba's renewal of old relationships with earlier schoolmates and friends continues and becomes central to his life. A detailed account of this period has been collected from original sources by Bhau Kalchuri, one of Baba's close later mandali, and is published in an epic collection entitled *Lord Meher*[1]. It is well worth the effort to plumb this resource to establish the flavor of the life and the increasing demands Meher Baba placed on those around him. It was not to be a time of simple inspiration and great happiness lived within the garden of spiritual enlightenment.

In May 1922 Baba took his followers to Bombay to live in a property called Manzil-e-Meem. It is here that I propose to stop for the moment and examine several basic concepts that rapidly become so fundamental to Meher Baba's thought and actions that it is almost impossible to absorb the biographical portion of his life without understanding at the beginning several of these precepts.

---

[1] See footnote 2, Chapter I.

*Many of those who have been reared in the Christian
faith and its traditions come unthinkingly to consider the
spiritual life as being one of enlightened personal relationship
permeated by deep, understanding love. Anger, aggression,
criticism, physical violence are all cast aside and associated
often with a diabolic element. Yet, in the Orient, there is a
strong and persistent tradition that admits and values a
variety of different approaches to the final goal.*

*During the Manzil-e-Meem stay Meher Baba frequently
chastised and often struck the close ones who lived there with
him. To one familiar with the methods used by historically
renowned mystic masters in the Far East accredited with
great spiritual development, above all those generally termed
Perfect Masters, this would come as no surprise. Nor would it
be considered unusual within a classic spiritual discipline.
Such masters have frequently resorted to severe chastisement
of the aspirant, including beating them physically.*

*To tie some sort of logic into all this, especially for the
Western mind, this might become tolerable if one describes
here a basic new consideration introduced by Meher Baba,
essentially for the first time. This new factor that Meher Baba
added to our understanding of the mechanics of the
unfoldment of creation is that of the importance of habit
patterns in each human's daily life. This may well be
considered as a disappointing pronouncement, as one can
point out immediately that habit has been recognized since
the beginning of humankind. Quite true. The existence of
personal habits and the importance of their role in human
action and living must have been seen as a fundamental fact
of human existence since the first human began to reflect on
his own nature.*

*Yet, it was left to this age and to Meher Baba to elucidate
the key role that these simple habits in daily life play in*

man's search and return to his origin, which is God.

Meher Baba's term in referring to them is just as ancient as human culture, being the Sanskrit word "sanskara." The concept it embodies is so important that the entirety of Chapter 10 is devoted to the subject. Here we will give no more than the skeleton of the matter in order to establish some understanding of a term that will occur constantly in the recounting of Baba's life.

Within this concept, part of which is placed in its detailed complexity by Baba, and much of which is part of our mystic heritage from ancient sources, the original state of Reality is described as that of simple, tranquil, undivided, infinite Oneness. This Oneness was totally unconscious of itself, but latent within it was not only the urge to become conscious of its nature of Infinite Being, but also Infinite Consciousness, which would become manifest no sooner the urge to be conscious manifested. This innate potentiality to know Infinite Being stirred[2], and the motion created inevitably a disturbance, which also inevitably included contrast and the possibility of the idea of separateness. These are the basic conditions within which consciousness is manifested. These are also the basic conditions which underlie the nature of all matter.

In one amazing stroke, in the movement of God's possible wish to know His own divinity, both the beginning of consciousness as well as of the matter of Creation, are brought into being.

Perhaps one may comment that it is all a bit too simple. But there is nothing here that is out of step with the thinking and discoveries of present day scientists and psychologists. I remember as a young man reading the words of Carl Jung in which he compared consciousness to the current generated

---

[2] See Chapter 9, The Whim.

*between the two opposite poles of a battery, with our
surrounding world of contrast and opposition representing the
poles of the battery. The current generated[3] between the poles
of contrast is the consciousness which is created.*

*Meher Baba sets out positively and unmistakably that
two things happen each time that two imagined separate
entities in Creation come into relationship with each other.
The first is the generation of an iota of consciousness induced,
like Jung's electric current between the poles of opposite
energy, but now through contrast and apparent separation in
a "physical" medium. Baba does not stop here, however, but
adds that there is also recorded in some way the pattern of
the event, and of greatest importance, that this pattern
contains within itself a factor pushing towards repetition.*
***Once something happens in a certain way, a "form of
conduct" as it were is established, and whenever the two
bodies come into contact later, they tend to reproduce the
contact in the original manner.***

*The essence of Baba's point is that there is a memory
storage mechanism in Creation, and this pushes later actions
into similar patterns. It takes no great leap of imagination to
see the similarity of this to the more complex habits that
human beings manifest constantly. All these Baba calls
sanskaras, a word which even in its early origins included a
loose concept that each action produces a residue which
influences later action, and must eventually be erased.*

*Baba however goes much further. He says flatly that the
iota of consciousness that has now been produced associates
"reality" with the incident which occurred between the two
separate objects. The iota of consciousness thus does not*

---

[1] Strictly speaking consciousness is not generated nor produced nor formed in Creation. It is the latency within God to be infinitely conscious of his Godhood that is manifested in the complex process of Creation. For a discussion of this, see Chapter 9, The Whim, footnote 2.

function at all in the manner that it was originally destined to do, which is to be conscious of the reality of the Original One. Hence, for now, a complete subversion of the original intent has occurred.

In Creation there is nevertheless the saving grace that the beginning and the inevitable end are all contained within the reality of the Original One. Thus there is nowhere else finally for it all to go, so it is like a mouse in a maze, and regardless of the possibilities of wrong turns and repeated wrong turns, finally there is only the one exit, which is the return to the Original One. So, a long battle ensues, and the only solution is to unravel from the start the impressions of habit, the sanskaric record, which mistakes the generating source for the reality.

Baba says that from the first human incarnation, in which complete consciousness has already been attained, the kernel of spiritual progress consists in the dissipation of these sanskaras or habit patterns, which are wrongfully identified by our consciousness as reality. The day that the last misidentification has been wiped off the slate of one's being is the day when Reality will be seen where it always was–inside oneself. But all that is for a bit later.

Manzil-e-Meem is still to be seen standing in a somewhat decrepit state in the heart of Bombay. What went on there was a classic of discipline: setting up projects, abandoning projects, not infrequent physical violence, and great emotional outbursts. All this does not sound too much like the classic Western ideal of spiritual contemplation and advancement.

Now, for possibly the first time, Meher Baba's detailed description of sanskaras, their nature and their importance on the path to spiritual enlightenment, may have given the key after thousands of years to understand why so many spiritual masters of the highest repute have used physical violence with their devotees. It is already a great deal to accept that there is a road of discipline and development which returns the individual to the One Source from which he sprang. It is still further a very great challenge even to contemplate that this discipline and development should center around something as prosaic as our everyday habit patterns.

Without trying to argue the logic of this last, suppose for the moment that Meher Baba did indeed know what he was talking about, and that these habit patterns or *impressions*, as he also often terms them, are the root of the problem of the return to the Source. If this can be accepted on a temporary basis, then it will be possible to construct a logic that could explain Baba's manner of treating the mandali at Manzil-e-Meem.

To start, it needs to be clear that sanskaras may be physical, subtle or mental. The first are the most ancient in our evolutionary heritage, and Baba emphasizes they are the most difficult to eradicate - almost impossible, in fact, without the aid of a Perfect Master.

Here then in all probability lies the clue to why the Perfect Master often treats the disciple roughly, even to the point of physical violence. The cure is adapted to the illness. It is rapid and effective. This was frequently used by Baba during the residence at Manzil-e-Meem, and through the 20s and 30s and even beyond. This is why I have come to use the term Perfect Master Period for this portion of Baba's ministry.

The term is not new with me, having heard it employed many years ago by a European who had spent much time with Baba during the 30s. Interestingly enough in his "Biographical Sketch" to *Messages of Meher Baba* edited in 1945, Adi K. Irani, a close follower of Baba who appears frequently in this work, states that on the completion of the seven years Baba spent coming down to normal consciousness of Creation, he "became a *Perfect Master*." Also one notes Purdom's choice of *The Perfect Master* as the title for his first biography of Baba published in the 30s.

While speaking of Meher Baba's use of techniques usually associated with a Perfect Master, one should avoid any confusion that this manner of functioning implies that his spiritual status was that of a Perfect Master rather than of the Avatar. Everything that Meher Baba describes of his own experience with Babajan, as well as his detailed explanations concerning the roles of Perfect Masters as distinguished from that of the Avatar, leads inescapably to the conclusion that from the moment of Babajan's embrace, he knew himself as the Avatar and functioned within the norms of that office unless, as we are suggesting, he may have chosen specifically in a given instance to act as would a Perfect Master, or even as a conventional human being.

Obedience is another highly charged spiritual word. Baba emphasized this above all else, on many occasions. A small section from Bhau's major biography of Meher Baba, *Lord Meher*, is illuminating in this respect. The incident described occurred just before Baba led his small group from Poona to Bombay, on May 22, 1922.

"Beginning that very night, an incident occurred which forced Meher Baba to emphasize this aspect of strict obedience in living with him, whereby the men mandali were made keenly aware of their responsibility toward him as *their Master*. The first lesson came shortly before they left Poona.

"Meher Baba decided to call for refreshments for all and sent Ghani, Adi and Slamson to bring tea, bread and cream from a nearby hotel. When they placed the order, Adi started feeling hungry and was wondering if it would be all right to eat his share then. Seeking Ghani's advice, because he was an elder, Adi was told it would be all right. However, his snack made them late in returning with the refreshments. When asked the reason, Adi admitted that he had eaten in the restaurant, and Meher Baba was extremely displeased. Adi explained that he suddenly felt hungry and asked Ghani if it would be permissible. Baba turned to Ghani and asked him if that was true. Ghani denied it! Angry at this lie, Baba then slapped Adi across the face!

"Baba became irate at all three men and told them to get out of his sight and never come back! They were shocked and started walking off, but he called them back and demanded, 'Never again be unmindful of what I wish. Learn what I want and what I don't want!' "[4]

At no time before in their association had Baba reacted in this manner in his treatment of them nor laid down such a severe rule concerning their observance of his preferences. A new day and a new course were dawning. Skipping over adventures in Bombay, we take up the story and the author's observations again around the end of July.

"Due to his meager diet and prolonged fasting while staying in the Manzil, Meher Baba was very thin. Although frail in appearance, he claimed to have the physical strength of a 'lion,' and one day demonstrated his strength to Adi. He told Adi to wrestle with him with all his might. Taken aback, Adi did not know what to do, but began lightly grappling with Baba, who said, 'No! As hard as you can!' Baba looked so frail that Adi did not wish to hurt him, but he had to obey and exerted his full strength against Baba. He was, therefore, greatly startled when Baba, without much effort, picked him up and threw him on the floor!

"On another occasion, to convince them that he had *superhuman* strength, he once challenged all the mandali to a tug-of-war contest. Even forty of the men, using all their strength, could not budge him an inch!

---

[4] *Lord Meher*, pp. 374–375.

"Meher Baba had inherited certain characteristics from each of his five Masters.[5] It is known that Hazrat Babajan, Tajuddin Baba and Sai Baba would at times slap people, or use abusive language if someone displeased them or displayed arrogance. Narayan Maharaj had a high pitched, squeaking voice and was as meek as a child. Narayan had a gentle, *jamali* personality, and it was rare if he abused anyone in front of others. Although Upasni Maharaj could oftentimes appear meek and humble, his foremost characteristic was *jalali*[6] – divinely glorious and awe-inspiring, and his beating of disciples was frequent. Such a beating was considered a true blessing.

"From the time Meher Baba began staying in Manzil-e-Meem, he would sometimes exhibit this jalali trait–a fiery or violent mood. It is said without exaggeration that he was *fire*! At such times, every man would be terrified of him, and it was difficult to remain in his presence; some would even run away and hide in their rooms. When in that *jalali* mood, Meher Baba's voice would roar and he would pick up and throw anything at anyone nearby. But this fiery mood would always subside as swiftly as it had flamed."[7]

For one not familiar with some of the traditions of mystic groups in the Far East, the picture presented is a daunting one. I cannot claim to have escaped without experiencing one or two of Baba's jalali moods. But I reserve this recounting for its proper place chronologically. I do say here, though, that it was an experience never to be forgotten and one of the most powerful during my various stays with Meher Baba. However, I feel this is the point to recount an experience which I had on my first visit to India in the 1950s. Although the episode occurred much later than the events

---

[5] These are the five Perfect Masters with all of whom Meher Baba had established contact shortly after Babajan had removed the veil.

[6] Sufi terms used generally to characterize the two major categories of saints: the fiery, and the loving.

[7] *ibid.*, pp. 396–397.

now being described in Meher Baba's life, it formed for me one of the most important bridges in making intelligible many of the things that I witnessed throughout the years in the conduct of the Indian in situations that would have brought on either rebellion or frank stupefaction in the average Westerner.

Having missed a great occasion to which Baba had invited a number of Western men the year before, he invited me along with the Australian poet, Francis Brabazon, to attend in November 1955 the "Four Language Groups Sahavas." Here, about two hundred men (this was the budget Baba had laid out for Padri, one of his earliest disciples) from each of the four major language areas were invited for a week each to be in the company of Baba at Meherabad.

At one point, Baba decided that I should go in the company of Francis and Adi Irani Sr., of Manzil-e-Meem days, to Aurangabad to see the Ellora Caves. This was a glorious opportunity, as normally Baba made the rule that one should never arrive for sightseeing and, after seeing Baba, should go directly home. To have a chance for a tour set up by Baba himself was therefore completely unexpected.

We set out, and my stomach being still queasy from the change in hours after a long journey as well as the unaccustomed spicy diet, I sat in front by the driver and dozed as we rode along. The habit in India is to stop for a tea break in mid-morning and again in mid-afternoon. It now being the latter, we duly stopped at a shoddy little restaurant. I could not face it, so I told my friends I preferred to sit and relax.

Some minutes later I became aware that someone was standing outside the car looking in at me. I opened my eyes, prepared to shoo off someone begging, and was chagrined to see that the beggar was in fact a very old man, dressed in clean but completely shredded rags. He looked at me; I looked back at him, waiting for the extended hand. It did not appear. I continued my waiting game.

Then the old man reached down inside his collection of rags and fumbled around his legs. Finally after some moments, and as I expected him to bring up a trinket to try to sell to me, he brought out instead two beautiful oranges. This surprised me, as it was a wrinkle I had not yet been subjected to by the wily beggar clan in India. I was touched by the novelty of the approach and the cleanliness of the oranges, but I was not hungry. The driver was still in the car with me and understood just enough English to understand my wish to tell the beggar that I did not want to buy his oranges.

The driver was instantly horrified by my rejection. "No, sahib, he not want to sell, he want to make gift to you!"

This touched me more, and then I realized that here was indeed a crafty one. He knew I would not accept them as a gift and that I would undoubtedly offer him some money instead. A truly clever fellow!

It took all of my patience and all the driver's small stock of English to get the idea over to me that the ragged old man did not want money. He had simply seen something in me as he had passed by and wanted to offer a small gift to what he had seen.

About this time my friends emerged from the tea shop, and I recounted the entire story, the old man standing meanwhile at dignified attention. "I can't just accept these from him. It is probably all that he has to eat for the entire day. I have to give him some money so he can eat."

"No, never!" both friends said in the same breath. "That would ruin everything. Don't you see? The only thing possible is to accept and give him the pleasure of your acceptance."

This I did, and we drove away. I never forgot my first experience of this uncanny sensibility and appreciation of the inner man that is so deeply rooted in the knowing of India.

It is a base of great antiquity of this sort which allows especially the Indian to see value and to steel himself to crisis in searching for that value, whereas the Western mind would either see nothing or go into rebellion in the first trying minutes. What could there have been in a schoolhood chum relationship or casual later friendship to cause grown, intelligent men to undergo such bouts of temperament as Meher Baba generated? There is no logic that one can set forth easily, and what can be constructed is inadequate to allow the Western temperament to withstand the negative emotions aroused by actions which he regards instantly as both uncalled for and totally unacceptable. One should also remember that at this time Meher Baba had no particular standing as a philosopher or mystic teacher. These men around him were simply persons of roughly his own age who for unexplained reasons were deeply attracted to him.

Having already asked the near impossible of the reader, one may as well continue by making several even more difficult observations for digestion concerning Meher Baba's life style at Manzil-e-Meem. It is not just physical violence and arbitrary obedience that need to be reflected upon in considering this early stage of Baba's life. There are also such tendencies as a penchant to make plans, set en route complex projects, make promises that appear very firm, and then toss them all into the ashcan. Sometimes a project would reach completion physically and be put into action, but it was rare for one to last very long.

Isn't this the very opposite of what one commonly regards as honorable dependability? Usually one is taught at an early age that one of the greatest tests of the character of a person is how he follows through on what he has said he would do. Nevertheless, is it possible to conceive a manner by which such actions could be tied back into a method by means of which the eradication of habits might be effected? Or, alternatively, of use in setting up important universal spiritual work? This is such a constant theme in Meher Baba's life, especially in these years of the 1920s and 30s, that it must be laid out clearly and dealt with straightforwardly.

On April 19, 1923, Baba left Manzil-e-Meem with those who had remained with him. It had been a hectic and tempestuous year. Of perhaps all the periods of Meher Baba's life, I personally have the suspicion borne of some years of reflection that it was probably the most valuable time spiritually for those who had been able to endure it. But I am still thankful that I personally did not have to experience it.

It was at this time that contact was made by Baba with the property soon to be called Meherabad, near Arangaon village and not far from Ahmednagar, a small city about 75 miles northeast of Poona. It was Meherabad which shortly became home for the group, and later the place for meetings, and finally the place for the reposing of the physical remains of Baba. At this time Adi Irani's mother, Gulmai, and her entire family became the surrogate family of Meher Baba.

It was in this atmosphere, and shortly after Meher Baba's arrival in the area on a semi-permanent basis, that those pillars such as the Dadachanjis, the Jessawalas, and a whole complex tribe of inter-related Iranis and people from different religious backgrounds began to flock around him. At this time also the first contacts were made with Westerners.

It was in this period, in fact on July 10, 1925, that the silence Baba was to continue the rest of his life began. Of all the subjects that have been brought up repeatedly for at times fierce argument, this is perhaps the most tempestuous of all. At the same time, in many ways, it has remained one of the most inspiring of deep reflection as well.

Meher Baba started his silence at Meherabad without great fanfare. He gave special instructions to everyone about the manner in which they should carry on, but above all, life was not to have any special upsets or new rules. It was just that he would not be speaking for awhile–so he gave to understand. Such periods of silence are quite common among spiritually-minded people in India, and it is always assumed that the person carries out the discipline for inner reasons associated with his or her spiritual progress or responsibilities. And then one day the silence ends. But in Baba's case, it was neither for spiritual progress nor did it end outwardly.

What did Meher Baba himself have to say on the subject? In fact, many things through the years, but the following have been selected to give a fair sample:

"I come not to teach but to awaken." "Things that are real are given and received in silence." "If my silence cannot be heard, of what avail words?"[8]

On many occasions Baba said quite certainly that on such and such a day, or in such a circumstance, he would break his silence. He also grew in later years to associate momentous events in creation and in his spiritual manifestation with the breaking of his silence. At one point he even said he would start to speak again over the radio at a special ceremony to be observed in the Hollywood Bowl. Despite the fact that by that time he had already broken his word a number of times on this score, and one would have thought that everyone would have been quite fed up with the subject, all still seemed to take him quite seriously. Several of the Western women who were now living near Baba in India even took the occasion to buy new "realization" dresses, as they expected to get God Realization on the occasion.

Meher Baba's younger brother, Adi Jr., went so far as to remonstrate Baba in private asking why Baba was doing this, as Adi

[8] Meher Baba, *Discourses* (Myrtle Beach: Sheriar Press, 1987 seventh edition), p. xiv.

knew he would not do what he had promised. Baba replied with a sharp slap to Adi's cheek and told him to mind his own business and to just obey Baba.

Of course, he did not break his silence, and yet nobody seems to have been particularly disappointed. By the time I came to know of Baba in 1946, the subject of his silence was pretty well commented upon around the world through two or three books on Far Eastern spirituality written by well-known authors. In fact, even during the brief introduction to the subject of Meher Baba that I originally underwent during Murshida Martin's presentation of his existence, I managed a fearful case of mental indigestion on the whole subject of silence. I could not see what good a silence did in the first place, and for someone who by then directed in rather intimate detail the lives of some thousands of people, this seemed to me the height of inefficiency. In fact, to myself I used the term "idiocy," but I did not dare use the term publicly.

To make matters worse, to say that you would break the silence on a particular day, and not do it, was the crowning touch. I could not fathom how a person who did such things could be trusted. Yet. Yet. Yet.

Strange how inner knowledge comes unexpectedly. Only a few weeks after making this flat judgment on Meher Baba's silence, I inherited the responsibility of caring for a middle-aged woman with terminal cancer, her aged mother, two cats, and about seven hangers-on in their late seventies and eighties. Besides this, I had a job as a process chemist in one of the more important laboratories in the West of the United States. It was a fearful combination to try to keep afloat. I slept one or two hours a night if I was lucky.

One day as I arrived at my desk, I was so tired that I did not think I could possibly go through the morning mail, let

*alone spend the whole day working. Then suddenly, Meher
Baba and his silence spun through my mind. Crazy, but why
not try being silent for awhile and see what would happen to
my crisis of having no energy? I drew my chair up close to my
desk and hunched over it as if I were in deep thought.
Nobody bothered me. I spent a good half hour like that and
then "woke up" to my surroundings.*

*To this day I don't know exactly what happened. I felt
wonderful and managed to get through the whole day
without collapsing. Whenever in the course of the next several
weeks I felt completely exhausted, I tried my same quiet half
hour hunched over my desk. After some days, the cancer
victim died, her mother and the cats moved in with me, the
other hangers-on found new nests, and I got through the crisis.*

I cannot say that this is at all similar to what Baba was
accomplishing through his silence–probably nothing to do with it–
but my enthusiastic condemnation of his actions ran out of steam.
For some reason I felt like a fellow accomplice rather than an uptight
critic. In later years, I began to have many other thoughts about why
it could make sense to be silent, even for long periods of time. I will
come back to this later. But for now, can you imagine a much better
method for breaking up a complex of habit patterns and
expectancies embedded in a large number of people than taking a
vow of silence, then making pronouncements about it quite
frequently, which you then completely ignore? Very frustrating, but
the great fact that emerged is that nobody close to Baba ever
complained about all this. They all went on blissfully as if nothing
had ever really happened. Which was exactly the case externally, but
the inner facts were far different.

While it is my preference to connect Baba's unpredictable and
seemingly chaotic activity to his function of clearing up the

sanskaras of his devotees, there has long been another very worthy hypothesis advanced by a number of his followers. This relates especially to projects such as centers, schools, hospitals and the like, which were started and often even carried to fairly advanced stages before being abandoned. This second hypothesis suggests that Meher Baba was setting out certain forms which would continue to exist in the thought levels of Creation, to be picked up and carried on to completion at a later date. In other words, something akin to the Platonic thought form was placed in existence, and this acted in turn as the mold for the eventual project or like the scaffolding of a building under construction, which is abandoned after the edifice is completed. In this manner presumably a great spiritual figure might leave a heritage of already formed projects for the future good of humanity.

This corresponds fairly accurately to some of the hypotheses of the reality of thought form, current especially in the 1920s and continuing to the present day. While in the case of Meher Baba and his puzzling abrupt termination of projects, there is nothing inconsistent with such a creation of forms for later accomplishment; it is perhaps only my liberal Scandinavian ancestry that causes me to prefer to link the puzzle of Baba's actions into the high priority subject of the erasure of personal sanskaras. But why not a combination of the two, or possibly even other reasons not yet dreamed of? When one is dealing with a highly developed spiritual master, one finds often that his actions are aimed simultaneously in a number of directions. It is the old story of killing two birds with one stone, except that the spiritual master seems able to increase considerably the target and the eventual kill.

3. STILL EARLY DAYS

T he subject of miracles is almost always tightly interwoven in most people's minds with the spiritual path and the actions of spiritually advanced souls. Such is also frequently the case for persons drawn to Meher Baba; but while he seemed in the early days to perform at least minor wonders, his attitude towards the subject veered rather rapidly into one of almost bare tolerance. This change may be upsetting to many seekers in our times, as the ability to perform astounding feats is generally considered to be an absolute necessity in order to qualify as a great master. In fact, often the first question a newly interested person asks about Meher Baba is how many miracles he performed that have been verified. When one admits that it might be hard to identify even one well-authenticated case, the level of interest frequently suffers a sharp drop. Then one wonders if it would not be best to stop the interchange, as the principal point of interest for the inquirer appears already to have been totally and *un*satisfactorily covered.

On this subject there is another wonderful little story from Bhau's epic biography. It takes place in the early part of 1922 shortly before Baba brought his brood of followers to Bombay to establish Manzil-e-Meem.

"Lateef gave a new bicycle to Meher Baba and a lottery was proposed to decide to whom the Master should give it. All the tickets were sold to followers and it was decided that the drawing should be held during a picnic at the village of Chinchwad.

"Meher Baba met there with his followers on Saturday, March 25th, and in the evening the lottery was held. Nervous[1] won the new bicycle. But then the Master gave a strange order. Nervous' old bicycle was taken in exchange and Baba ordered it to be broken into pieces and thrown into a nearby well. Shortly after this, Baba asked Nervous if he felt uneasy about his bicycle being destroyed and thrown away. Nervous expressed no regret; however, the other men were at a loss to understand why this order had been given, since Nervous' bicycle was still in good condition.

"After Meher Baba returned to Poona from Chinchwad, Baily informed him that while Baba was away he had inadvertently fallen into a well near the hut but was miraculously rescued from drowning by a stranger. When Baily was questioned what time the incident had occurred, the other men found out that it had happened at the exact hour when the pieces of Nervous' bicycle were being thrown into the well! The men then realized why the Master had given such a strange order, and later he explained, 'Instead of allowing Baily to drown, I sank the bicycle in the well. It was simply an exchange of gross mediums.' "[2]

Bhau does not note any further discussion of the subject, Baba's explanation apparently having sufficed. Some persons might confess however to being left with more questions than Baba's simple comment has explained. But no doubt that is why it takes so much time for the majority of humanity to see the simplest things.

Let us take another brief comment from *Lord Meher*:

"Many things about the Master impressed the early disciples

---

[1] Baba had a delightful habit of giving very colorful nicknames to most of those who became his disciples. One of the most inventive was "Barsoap."
[2] *Lord Meher*, p. 350.

as they came to discover who their Baba really was. Three recurrent things in particular impressed all of them about Meher Baba, whom they would refer to as Baba or Master. He would read the minds and hearts of those around him, and he would express their thoughts in one way or another, making them feel that 'Baba knew everything they were thinking.' Without their asking, the Master would reply to questions that were troubling them. And lastly, Baba would often make predictions that at a certain time, a certain person would be coming; or at a certain time, a certain event would take place. Invariably, these predictions would come true."[3]

Years later, when I met Baba and on numerous occasions thereafter, it was always completely clear to me that Baba knew everything about me and everything that I was thinking. And yet in my actions, I always discounted this, as I soon came to realize that there is a strange but reassuring ethic in the great spiritual master's use of this capacity. He does not use it against you. He awaits your invitation to enter. He may prod you to invite him, and he may even ask you to sign a legal paper giving him certain spiritual rights, but the rule still holds true: he does not enter unless he is invited.

To give a concrete example, there were two departments in my personal life which I automatically withheld from my relation with Baba. He knew it. He did not intrude until I had made such a mess of trying to resolve those areas myself that I prayed out loud one day that he take them over. Needless to say, from that moment the race horses were unleashed and I could barely keep up with the speed of events. And they were constructive!

[3] *ibid.*, pp. 355–356.

In his later life Baba began to say with increasing frequency that he did not perform miracles. But why the big change from the early days that Bhau records? What caused Baba to turn about on the subject? Was he lying to those around him but in fact continuing to perform the sort of minor, or even big, miracles that happened in his early manhood?

To give another illustration in this field, one of the most frequent and unvarying experiences I had on various visits was to be sitting in mandali hall, Baba in his armchair near the door beside the small window with almost no one around except for some of the close ones (termed the "mandali") who were always present. Unexpectedly Baba would interrupt what was going on and look inquiringly at Eruch. There must have been some sort of telepathy between Eruch and Baba, as Eruch always seemed to know what Baba wanted to know even without the usual hand gestures.

Then Eruch would explain to Baba that such and such a person had come unannounced. In some instances Baba would tell Eruch to send the person on his way. On other occasions Baba would indicate that the person should enter. "And what brought you here when no one is supposed to bother Baba?" *(When this was set out, I always asked myself exactly the same thing, and then hurried to forget that I had a magic pass.)*

Frequently the person was an old disciple of many years' standing. Many times it was a great crisis, usually of health, in the family, that had caused the devotee to ignore the injunction against trying to contact Baba during a period of seclusion. Usually Baba would explain that because of the devotee's long years of great love for the Avatar, the rule was being waived. "So now tell Baba what it is that is on your mind."

Almost always it was a child or uncle or grandmother who was at death's door. "And Baba, as I know you are God, I know that you can cure my (whomever) of this condition." Baba would look very thoughtful for a few moments and then respond, "Yes, I am God, and I have the power to do what you ask of me. But do you know that this is happening because of the karma of your (whomever), and so he must undergo it? Yes, I have the power to change the karma, but it was I who put the law of karma into motion in Creation and I am not about to break my own law. But, because of your love for me, I will lower this karma," and Baba pointed to his head, "from here and place it here," pointing to his shoulders. At other times when Baba was asked to help someone who was suffering, Baba would remark that that it was best for the person to suffer while he, Baba, was around, as it would speed up the progress of that individual.

This says a lot very simply, doesn't it? And the man (never was it a woman; one wonders why) would leave consoled. The outcome of the brief interview was seldom known, but one could judge what may well have occurred by a counterpart scene also frequently observed at similar times. It would again be a little old man who would rush to kiss Baba's hand or to embrace him, and then the words would flow out that the (whoever in the family) had been at death's door, when they had prayed to Baba, and suddenly and miraculously, the (whomever) was cured totally. Baba had performed the miracle!

Baba would look nonplused and smile. Then the hand gestures: "No, Baba did not knowingly do this. If a miracle occurred, it was your love for Baba which performed the miracle. Baba did not knowingly do this for you. It was your love which did it."

As I have been writing this section on Baba's life and reflecting once more on his manner of insisting that he did not perform miracles and yet, in the next moment, being embroiled in events that seemed to belie his very disclaimers, I have received news of the death of one of his dearest devotees. Her real name was Mani, but to differentiate this person from Baba's younger sister, also named Mani, the first and older Mani became known for the rest of her life

as Mansari. Her early days with Baba include a moving example of
what happened quite often in this domain in those days, and how
Baba handled events in his own unique and imponderable manner.
Let us listen for a few moments to Mansari's story as transcribed
from a tape recording in her late years.[4]

"Sometimes I say that I sat in the train and I came to 'Nagar,
and I came to Baba! But now, the real thing—how I came to Baba. I
was born in Bombay and lived there for 15 years. My aunt raised me
because she loved me and she had no children. My parents used to
stay in Navsari.

"Until the age of 5 years, I was very healthy–skinny, but still
very healthy. Then I got an awful skin disease, on the feet and on the
hands. It spread from my feet up to my knees, and from my hands
up to the elbows. The rest of the body and face was completely
intact, but where the disease was I was scarred, I thought for life. My
dear aunt took utmost care to cure me, and every medicine was tried
but failed. When I was 12 years old, somebody suggested a skin
specialist, so I was taken there by Kaikobad Dastur, a close family
friend and the one I liked and trusted most. When that doctor saw
me, he said, 'Really, I don't know why the other doctors didn't cure
her, it's a very simple case.' Well, the poor doctor tried his best, for
months, but he could not cure me. He tried everything. He gave me
75 injections in one day! But it did not work at all, and at last, he had
to say, 'I'm very sorry to say that this child has to suffer for the rest
of her life, because I have never seen such an obstinate disease.' I
heard that, and since by nature I'm obstinate, this just added to my
obstinacy. I decided not to go to any more doctors and concluded
that all doctors were hypocrites. From then on, whenever my aunt
would suggest a doctor, I would refuse.

"In 1925 my aunt died so, naturally, I had to go to my parents.

---

[4] "Mansari's Special Disease," *Quarterly Newsletter* Vol. 26, Spring, 1997 (Meher Baba
Center of Northern California, 2131 University Ave., Berkeley, CA 94704).

My father had been following Baba for two years at that time, so my parents tried to persuade me to go to Baba. They said, 'Baba will cure you.' I was so disgusted, I said, 'When all doctors fail, what will your Baba do?' I refused to go. So they wrote to Kaikobad to take me to Baba because he followed Meher Baba too. At that time, if I would listen to anyone, I would listen to Kaikobad. He was very kind to us, very kind. He wrote to me to come to Bombay and go on a picnic to 'Nagar, saying that I would be pleased to see Baba. Kaikobad wrote, 'I promise that I won't say anything about your disease to Baba.' If it pleased Kaikobad I felt I could do it, as long as he was not going to say anything to Baba.

"Then I came here, to Ahmednagar. At 8 o'clock I saw Baba for the first time. He was in the rickshaw (the one now in the Meherabad museum), and was being drawn, probably by the Prem Ashram boys, from Meherabad Hill to Lower Meherabad. I was standing in a queue when I saw Him. At that time there were no restrictions on visiting Meherabad, and many lovers used to come for Darshan, for an interview or for advice. I saw Baba coming out of the rickshaw. From the beginning, I took Baba as a great personality, but not more. I did not consider Him even a saint or a perfect master, so the idea of His being God was very far away. I saw Baba as I saw any ordinary person but, for Kaikobad's sake, I folded my hands.

"Baba went in the room and started giving Darshan and interviews. I was just standing there, and then my turn came. Baba was in the old bungalow, with a small window, and He peeked through and beckoned me to come. I was undoing the lace of my shoe and, just for half a second, I stared at Baba. To this day I don't know how or why, but I cried. I almost sobbed. I cried like a child, and I went to Baba with tears. Baba asked me why I was crying. I said, 'I don't know.' I had Baba's Darshan and I stood, sobbing. Then Kaikobad told Him everything about me and my disease. Baba said, 'For that you are crying?' I said, 'No, I don't know.' Then He asked me again, 'Tell Me your complaint. Tell Me what you suffered with your disease, in your own words.' But I could not. Then He dictated on the board, 'Don't worry, it will go permanently.' He signed the message to emphasize it, *Baba*. I read the board, I heard Him, but I had been told the same by so many doctors. When the interview was finished, Baba gave me a little dhuni ash in a bottle and told me to take a pinch in the mouth before tea in the morning while saying 'Baba.' I said, 'Yes, Baba.'

"All my obstinacy was washed out. I went back to Navsari and I started taking the ashes. For one month, without any hope, I just took them. Then, to my amazement, I was completely cured. Even my scars vanished. I was so happy to be out of the clutches of the disease that immediately my view of Baba jumped from 'great personality' to 'God' because only God could have done that. I began to love Baba, and I had much, much respect for Him. I wrote a letter to Baba thanking Him and He got Chanji to write to me, 'Baba is glad to receive your letter, but He says He hasn't done anything. Your faith and love has done the work.' At that time He might have been aware of my faith and love, but I felt that I had not, at that time, had such faith.

"Then for a few months, I was very happy, very, very happy. Kaikobad used to come to Baba often, and He wrote to me, telling me about Baba's moods, how He cracked a joke and everything. After months, he wrote a letter to me about how happy he was to be with Baba and how happy Baba appeared, but the last line in the letter was, 'This time I saw on Baba the disease that you had.' That line made me completely upset, so upset that I could not put my mind on anything, and the very second I read that line I hated myself. I said to myself, 'If I had not gone to Baba, and if I had stuck to my obstinacy, this wouldn't have happened, but now it is too late.' Now I began to pray in my mind, every second, 'Baba, give it back to me.' I wanted to see Baba personally so I could make the matter clear, because I was shy to write and I didn't want anyone else to read the letter.

"For months I had to wait, but after some months my disease

came back in a small form and I was happy. I could not hide it. My Baba lover relatives saw it, understood the story, and said that they would tell Baba. I didn't want that, so I said I would tell Baba and no one should interfere. Then, again, I was waiting and waiting to see Baba, and one day Kaikobad's letter came, saying that Baba was coming to Bombay on His way to Iran. I immediately dropped everything and went to Bombay. Kaikobad saw me and said, 'A relapse? We will tell Baba.' Again, I said that I would tell Baba and He should not.

"The next day we went to Baba for Darshan, and Kaikobad told Baba that the disease had relapsed. Baba appeared very indifferent and said, 'Try some sulphur.' My whole mind was on how to speak to Baba directly about it, but there were too many people and I was too shy. After Darshan, we left. That same day, at four o'clock, feeling inspired, I went the few blocks from Kaikobad's house to where Baba was staying. Baba was sitting with 25 or 30 boys, playing carom. He gestured, 'Why did you come? You were already here in the morning.' So I said, 'Yes, Baba, I came.' He said, 'OK, sit down. Do you know how to play carom?' I said, 'No, Baba.' Then He said, 'Why did you come, then? Is there anything to say?' I said, 'Yes, Baba.' 'Then say it now,' He said. 'No, Baba,' I said, 'I want to talk to You privately.' He beckoned Chanji to come to the inner room with the alphabet board. I then said, forcefully, "I have nothing to *hear* from you Baba, I have things to *say*. And I don't want Chanji either!'

"Baba took the alphabet board and called me. He was sitting on a couch, spinning His board. He asked me, 'Say what you want to say.' I said everything, and stopped. He said, 'Are you mad? You are mad. Who could do that? Who could take anybody's disease on their person?' I said, 'Baba, any ordinary being could not, but God can and You are God.' He said, 'You are stark mad.' I didn't say anything. He said, 'Let it be as it is now.' I said, 'Baba, You know my plight. I cannot be happy at all until You just give it back to me.' He didn't say anything right away. 'Then what to do?' He asked. 'That is up to

You,' I said. Then He said, 'I have one result. Would you like it?' I said, 'How do I know Baba? What is it?' He said, 'Neither you nor I would suffer. Would you like it?' I said, 'Yes, Baba, I would like it very much.' I liked it, but I felt that Baba was getting rid of me, like getting rid of an obstinate child by promising it a piece of chocolate. So I said, 'Baba, I like it, but it doesn't appeal to me here,' and I pointed to my heart. He said, 'Give your hand to me,' and slapped my hand in the gesture for a promise. He looked at me and said, 'Is it all right now?' I felt that it would be OK. I knew that He would keep the promise, but still I said, 'Now, Baba, stick to that please, OK?' Baba said, 'Didn't I promise you?' Then He clapped, called all the boys into the room and Baba asked them, 'Have you ever seen a mad woman?' They said, 'No,' and Baba pointed to me and said, 'See, she is stark mad.' I laughed over that for months. I was completely cured, and have remained cured up till now.

"I came to live with Baba permanently in 1938. One day He asked me, 'How long did you suffer from your disease?' I said, '14 years.' Baba said, '14 years? That is the time-honored period for a penance. And suffering is very good. It brought you to Me.' Then He asked me all sorts of questions about the medical procedures and asked, 'Why didn't the doctors cure you?' 'I don't know, Baba,' I said. Then He said, 'Science is advancing by leaps and bounds, but what did they accomplish? It was my key to draw you to Me. That's why they didn't cure you. Now you are with Me, so be happy.' He did this because this mulish person would not have come, perhaps, but here I am."

Baba has said many times that he is the slave of the love of his lovers. A lovely, heart-warming statement, one obviously based on much factual truth and obviously related to Mansari's experience. A typical story that illustrates the point occurred during a drought many years ago in Ahmednagar. A disciple of Meher Baba, in desperation, was digging a well, finally investing all his available resources, and still with no show of water. Lamenting to Baba, he was told to dig three meters further. Behold, a miracle! There he encountered freely flowing water!

Rustom Irani, long charged by Baba with finding more water at Meherabad, hearing of all this stormed in to Baba and resigned his post, pointing out that Baba had helped a simple farmer, but devotees of years of service and obedience he appeared to help not at all.

Baba calmly pointed out the vast difference between the spiritual objectives of the farmer, and those dedicated to Baba and the final goal of Realization.

Meher Baba also repeated on almost every occasion in which miracles were front and center that he had not consciously performed one.

The subject is complex, and also important because of the status we give it in our present day evaluation of "spirituality." But we cannot delay further our story of Baba's temporal life. The subject is given a fuller treatment, however, in Chapter 11 on Love, Surrender and Meditation.

Baba began establishing schools, one of the earliest being named the Hazrat Babajan School. This however essentially disappeared on one of the occasions when Baba had the principal buildings razed. But shortly afterwards, a new institute for boys was started on December 31, 1926. After a series of confusing changes in its composition, Baba and several of his devotees visited the National School in Ahmednagar on February 26. They chose on this occasion to announce the opening officially of what was named the "Meher Ashram School."

Several of the students now began to show special interest and attachment to Baba's love, gradually coming to prefer meditation to their studies. They were separated from the other boys and were transferred after five days to another portion of the hill at Upper Meherabad where Baba was staying. This new grouping became known as the Prem Ashram, or the Abode of Divine Love. Baba himself seems to have been chiefly responsible for the teaching of these special boys. It is recorded that for a month and a half he would give them discourses about the Creation, the different worlds, suns, universes, and about sanskaras and the evolution of forms.

The Prem Ashram was a unique project in education, it being the heart that received the attention, and with the result that on occasion the hearts of all the boys burst into uncontrollable tears. Not that they were being beaten or mishandled in any way, but just that this continual close contact with a great spiritual master was too much to absorb without such an outward reaction. For an account of this unique educational project it is necessary to find a copy of Ramjoo Abdullah's *Sobs and Throbs*. Ramjoo was up to the task of capturing and conveying in writing the deep emotional wells that were tapped and filled to overflowing. It is a rare person who can remain unmoved when reading of the times that Ali, perhaps Baba's favorite among the boys, was removed repeatedly from the school by his fickle father, and how Ali made his way back to Baba each time.

Even the Prem Ashram, however, was not safe from the frequent changes of plans. Baba soon began hinting of a "great march" that was to take place. Eventually this did occur and on Sunday, June 3, 1928, Baba and all those transferring to the new site made their way in a cortege of vehicles to Toka, some 80 kilometers from Ahmednagar on the Aurangabad road. This is considered an important religious spot, being the confluence of the Godavri and Pravara rivers. One often sees on the road leading to Toka small groups of pilgrims with brass jugs hung at the ends of poles carried over the shoulder, designed to be filled with water from this holy site. Strangely enough, or perhaps not strangely at all in India, many of these are young businessmen who have taken several days from work to accomplish this important pilgrimage. Often they walk barefoot, a part of the devotion, for hundreds of miles on the round trip.

Here at Toka the Englishman Meredith Starr and his wife, Margaret, after quite some earlier correspondence and planning of the trip, met Baba for the first time. It was to be Meredith who would act as the conduit for so many of the key early English people who were attracted to Baba. But it was also to be Meredith who had his own deeply-seated ideas on spirituality and the manner in which it should be conducted. After a long and sad gradual drifting away on his part from that essential abandon of self in love for the Master, Meredith finally disappeared into the haze of life; and it was his close associates and friends who became the pillars of Baba's love in Western Europe.

Several months passed in Toka with periodic visits by the father of Ali, the hero of *Sobs and Throbs*. Ali would be removed to his father's home, and then run away and come back to Baba, and so it went on. By November, Baba was starting to complain of the climate at Toka, and some of the boys were sent off to other locations. The portents were becoming ominous that the days of Toka were numbered.

The roll call of the school at that time makes interesting reading:

"Meher Ashram, which had started with only ten Hindu children, gradually increased in number until by November 18th, 1928, the total number was one hundred and two boys: forty-nine Hindus, fifteen were Harijans, fifteen Marathas, eleven Brahmins, five Cobbler caste, two Tailor caste, one Goldsmith caste, one Jain Marwadi and one Pardeshi. Of the thirty Iranis, six were Parsis. Of the twenty Muslims, six were Moghals, five were from Persia, five from the Deccan, two were Bhris (Sunnis) and two Kutchis."[5]

After various health problems among the students as well as the teachers, the decision was taken to abandon Toka. On the 26 of

[5] *Lord Meher*, p. 1116.

November the buildings were dismantled and everyone returned to Meherabad. It was not the final end of the schools, but from that time on they played a constantly decreasing role in the activities surrounding the Master. It was now that the days of travels began.

Before leaving Toka, however, one should quote a phrase Baba spelled out on September 23, 1928, during his residence there: "My plan here is to forge links,"[6] a simple, innocuous phrase, without further elaboration. For a real extension and clarification of what Baba was driving at by this cryptic statement, one has to wait until the 1950s and his last statement dictated on the alphabet board. Then the importance of this word "links" becomes abundantly clear. It is worth the effort to retain this seed for some pages still. It is an extraordinary example of the manner in which Baba prepared long in advance many of the key elements of the human and philosophical structures that he intended.

It was also at this time that Meher Baba began a systematic search for what are termed *masts*, who are the intoxicated of God who have lost much of their conscious contact with their physical surroundings. They live within the magic spell of their vision of God. Baba spent many months over the years searching out these very special human beings, who are carefully distinguished from the emotionally insane. The particular dilemma of the mast, Baba explains, is that he is caught in his enchantment and, as a consequence, unable to progress further in his spiritual development. It requires the touch of a spiritually advanced person to move him from this point of paralysis.

This was the function Baba performed for hundreds of these God-intoxicated. In turn they will become in their next lifetime a spiritual treasure for humanity, which has been unavailable during the present time. Baba clarified on one occasion that the force of the

---

[6] *ibid.*, p. 1094.

masts' spiritual experience causes them actual brain damage, but after the push of a master to restart their spiritual progress, this will not be a block in a next lifetime, as it will be lived with a new physical body and a new brain.

A classic account of this activity of Baba has been written by Dr. William Donkin called *The Wayfarers*.[7] Dr. Donkin became a disciple of Meher Baba shortly after graduating from medical school in London and spent all his life as a close mandali. It was he who, with Dr. Goher Irani, set up so many free dispensaries in so many of the different spots that Baba inhabited all over India. One of these still functions very close to Baba's tomb near Meherabad, and another operates within the property of Meherazad.

The Wayfarers, as well as sections of *Lord Meher*, contain scores of fascinating tales of Baba's arduous and extended searches throughout India to contact masts, as well as the extraordinary pains he took frequently to bathe and clothe them. This was often followed by long hours, sometimes over many months, spent in their company carrying out inner work, the nature of which is known in most instances only to him and the mast in question.

Although this was one of the major activities carried out by Baba, we will limit our discussion here to short histories of only two masts: Mohammed, who has lived continuously with and near Baba since 1936; and Chatti Baba, who was brought to Baba in November 1939 and was returned to his native Negatapatam after almost two years of constant contact with Baba.

Mohammed, a potter by trade, had been living in Bombay, married, and reputed to have two children. The circumstances of his spiritual experience, as is so often the case, are not known. When he was brought to Baba in 1936 he was irascible, stubborn, often in

---

[7] William Donkin, *The Wayfarers* (Ahmednagar: Adi K. Irani, 1948).

Meher Baba with Mohammed, 1938.

very bad humor, and constantly inspecting the ground about him and often digging into it to find what only Mohammed knew he was looking for. Baba said he was stuck between the third and fourth planes, and after some time with Baba, he was reported by Baba to have been boosted to between the fourth and fifth planes. In any event, his humor improved, and now, still living in what is known as Lower Meherabad, he continues his search for unknown treasure in and on the dirt about him, and is considerably easier to live with and to handle.

In 1937 Mohammed was brought at Baba's command by several mandali to Cannes by passenger liner. The stories told to me long ago by two of those involved in accompanying Mohammed cause me to wonder that the feat was ever accomplished without their all being thrown into a lunatic asylum. The flavor of Mohammed is beautifully conveyed by Dr. Donkin:

"Whatever may be one's intellectual estimate of this strange blend of child, man and saint, Mohammed somehow commands one's affection. In short, despite his impossible behavior, one loves him, and through the chinks in his distorted personality one discerns, now and again, a beauty of soul that makes the shortcomings of his character unimportant. In this way, of course, he is much the same as any mast, for either by an irony of the love of God, or for some specific divine purpose, the spiritual state of these God-intoxicated souls is veiled from our eyes by the dense folds of a cloak of eccentricity."[8]

Chatti Baba was said by Meher Baba to be a sixth plane mast, that is, just short of the perfection of God Realization. His native town of Negatapatam, located not far from Bangalore, was in a flood area at the time he was being searched for by Baba's mast team.

---

[8] *ibid.*, p. 50.

The story of the floods and the incredible misadventures of those trying to reach Chatti Baba are an epic in themselves. But finally they reached their goal, and after the usual refusals by the mast to budge and go to where Baba was located at the moment, Chatti Baba finally accompanied them and spent almost two years with Meher Baba. His was a delightful combination of humor and winsome attractiveness. Baba's first greeting to Chatti Baba was literally to give him a bath, which was done with fifty buckets of water used in the Indian "slosh" fashion. The number of buckets was later increased to 150, and then 250. After almost every bath, Chatti Baba would revel in dumping handfuls of loose earth over his head, and apparently this was the state in which he stayed until the next torrential bathing.

Chatti Baba was said by Meher Baba to be closely connected with the destiny of France. In any event, during the period of the fall of France to the Germans in 1940, Chatti Baba became almost ungovernable in his despair, despite the complete absence of any means by which he might have been informed of the events taking place. And as the events in France became more normal, so did the behavior of Chatti Baba.

Dr. Donkin in his characteristic manner captures the essence of Chatti Baba:

"The moods of this great man were extraordinary, and would fluctuate from a sunny expansiveness to a truculent attitude, without apparently much provocation. He was like a child, quick to change for a very little thing, but he had a bewildering enchantment about him that made him loved by all. The other important masts have all had their charm, and some sort of disposition that made them attractive, but there has been no one who has so unanimously commanded the affection of others. In his way Chatti Baba was unique, and today, years after (1947) he has been separated from Baba, the mandali, and Baba himself, often recall with delight his little ways, and especially the lightness and captivating spell of his laugh."[9]

Returning briefly to the subject of Baba's frequent changes of plans and his scrapping of projects early in their course, and often even before their physical initiation, a further review of this recurrent and important aspect of Baba's life needs to be made. It was suggested earlier that Baba's habit of planning or even initiating major projects and then suddenly, without apparent reason, discarding those plans may well be connected with his taking on the responsibility of the elimination of sanskaras or habit patterns in his devotees.

In this important area I must weigh the experience of my own life of over twenty years lived in frequent physical contact with Meher Baba and my own assessment of the impact of his presence on the inner problems that obviously needed solution. There were many inspiring as well as hilarious episodes that occurred in connection with Baba's presence in my life. These went on constantly, even when I was in a far corner of the globe. He had a way of tying all events in one's life back into his presence, into courses of action that in one way and another he had set in motion. From the first time I set eyes on his physical presence, the manner in which the main currents of life and even the smaller streams tied back into his being, his presence, his words, his humor, showed that he was the master and that he had taken on a major responsibility for the working out of the important patterns of my life. I will describe how this happened shortly.

The second and more popular hypothesis concerning

[9] *ibid.*, p. 65.

Baba's constant changes of plans set forth briefly above is
that great spiritual masters are responsible for laying down
patterns for later action in creation.

A third aspect of Baba's unexplained actions is likely to
be just that of efficiency. It was not that Baba set out to be
puzzling or to pose a challenge to the follower. One must
simply reflect on the fact that in the final analysis there is just
so much time and energy available to be expended. Baba did
not work outside the laws of Creation–which include those
which govern time and energy–in whose formation he had
been the participant.

When the Avatar arrives in Creation to carry on the job
of reawakening humanity to Truth and speeding up the rate
of progress in achieving it, he does not magically suspend for
himself the requirements of physical law. He works within
those laws. He may occasionally utilize some levels that are
not readily accessible to many human beings, but the laws of
balance and compensation, of energy input into product
achieved on the physical level, remain the same for the
Avatar as for all of mankind. He respects those laws. If he did
not, God might just as well have said at the beginning of
Creation, "Well, on second thought, this will all become a bit
too complex and tiring, so I will just use my divine power and
cut through to the end instead."

The observance of the rules of Creation was one of the
most constant themes of my personal contact with Meher
Baba–no magic wands, or muttering of secret formulae. Get
on with the problems of life within the principles laid down in
the beginning for the functioning of the universe. In this
regard, one of the most impressive facts that flows down
through the centuries is that the Avatar takes on himself a
weighty part of human and universal suffering each time he
comes. Both are accepted by him fully within the principles of

*human, physical suffering experienced in daily life by
everyone. He does not use his divine attribute of Bliss to avoid
this burden or its agony in his sharing of our burden within
Creation.*

*One of my earliest recollections of being with Baba was a
sense of relief that he was not constantly explaining himself. I
admired someone who had the guts to do a completely non-
understandable act without turning around each five seconds
to ask if everyone understood what he was doing and why.
Isn't this consonant with his comment on why he does not do
miracles for those really close to him? In a truly respected and
valued friendship, inevitably one of the things the friend will
have to do on occasion is to offer the benefit of the doubt. Is it
not becoming evident that we must reinvent this ancient due
inherent in real relationship: that of accepting the friend's
actions for a few moments or hours or even days without
jumping immediately to judge and ask questions? There is no
time for all this constant questioning in progressive, vital
living within the challenges of real life. Because real life is
the format of spiritual learning and discipline, where
understanding has to give way to faith and love. "Don't try
to understand me, just love me."*

Let us take up again the narrative of Meher Baba's life in the
late 1920s and early 1930s, the period in which he began to travel
all over the world, meanwhile searching out in exhausting voyages in
India the intoxicated in God's love (the masts), founding and closing
schools for boys, erecting hospitals and building ashrams for
followers from all over the world. This intensive and arduous
combination of activities continued until the start of the New Life at
the end of the 40s. Meanwhile, on August 29, 1931, Baba boarded
the *S.S. Rajputana* from Bombay bound for Marseilles. On board
was Mahatma Gandhi.

"On the night of September 8th, at nine o'clock, Mahatma Gandhi came to Meher Baba's cabin with his secretary Mahadev Desai. After Gandhi was introduced to Baba, he looked at Baba and then said, 'I have read much about you and wanted to see you one day when God willed it; but I never expected it to be so soon.'

"Baba expressed how happy he was meeting Gandhi and dictated from his alphabet board, 'Do you have the time to stay?'

" 'Yes, I have come to sit and listen,' Gandhi replied."

There followed an exchange of personal information, including Baba's description of his contact and relations with both Hazrat Babajan and Upasni Maharaj, as well as Sai Baba. The conversation then turned to "The Book" Baba had written,[10] and which was being carried along on this particular trip. Gandhi wanted to read the book. Baba managed diplomatically to sidetrack the conversation. However, before Gandhi left, Baba confided the box with the book locked inside it to Gandhi, saying that the key had been forgotten in Bombay. Gandhi said he would have it opened by an expert. The account continues:

"Concerning his activities, Gandhi remarked, 'Whatever I do, I take upon myself the responsibility for it. Though in the end, internally I leave everything to God, I cannot shirk my responsibility. Except for God, it is my conviction that I cannot disavow my responsibility.'

" 'But that thought should not be there,' Baba explained to him. 'I do'... 'I think'... 'I renounce'... 'I suffer'... 'I do everything for others.' These thoughts should not be there. If to the detriment of others, one tries to know and understand God, it creates terrible sanskaras.' "[11]

---

[10] "The Book" was also frequently referred to as Meher Baba's "Bible." He had written it by hand while secluded in a tiny box-like structure still preserved at Meherabad. When he had completed it, he often said that many of the secrets of Creation were contained in this writing. After its completion, he gave up writing by hand and used thereafter the alphabet board and, more and more, hand gestures.

[11] *Lord Meher*, pp. 1388–1391.

Despite this rather unpromising beginning, the contact between Baba and Gandhi continued and flourished. During the voyage the box with The Book inside was returned. There is no record of any comment made by Gandhi at that meeting on either having had the box opened, or his having read The Book. On a subsequent meeting on the ship, Baba gave Gandhi some pages he had selected from The Book as well as other things written by Baba, which he was planning to have reworked by K. J. Dastur, a close follower of some years. Gandhi now made extensive comments on the need for Baba to preserve his own natural style, but went on to say that some of the terms Baba used in The Book were difficult or impossible to convey in words. So apparently Gandhi did read some portions of The Book.

There is no record of any other person having been given this opportunity by Baba. I have seen the box in which The Book was stored at the time, but not the contents. It was last reliably reported (and even this is disputed) to be in a safe deposit box in Bombay, but subsequently no one knows where it went. Years later Eruch was asking Baba an abstruse point on philosophy, and Baba impatiently replied that he should not be bothered with such questions, as all this was recorded in The Book and that he, Baba, had personally confided the work to someone along with instructions as to when it should be restored to humanity.

All this remains to this day one of those delightful and often exasperating mysteries that crop up regularly in Baba's life. But this is still not the end to the intriguing tale of Baba's relation with Gandhi.

Throughout the negotiations that Gandhi continued subsequently in London with the British, there was a constant exchange of notes between Gandhi and Baba. On one occasion when Baba and Gandhi were meeting face to face in London, at one point

Gandhi exclaimed impatiently that India absolutely must have its independence, and his exclamation contained the implication of asking what Baba intended doing about this. Baba simply replied, "Granted." But then Baba followed up with an invitation to Gandhi to give up all the press of worldly events and come to live with Baba, to live the life of a seeker of the Truth, which Baba had maintained to Gandhi that he was, in reality. Gandhi promised Baba that when he had continued in his present role until independence was achieved, he would come and join Baba.

Time passed, independence was formally promised, and both men were back in India. No news from Gandhi. Baba sent one of his closest mandali to Gandhi to say from Baba: Now that I have kept my promise to you, what about your promise to me? Gandhi asked that Baba be assured that he would keep his promise when all had been properly established for the newly independent country. This was the last exchange between the father of his country and the Father of all mankind. Shortly after, Gandhi died at the hands of an assassin.

Now we return to the arrival of the *S.S. Rajputana* on that early 1931 trip to London. Baba was met by several persons who were destined to spend the rest of their lives in close contact with him as well as to become bywords of devotion and simple wisdom. Kitty Davy, Margaret Craske and Delia DeLeon lived into their late nineties and, in Kitty Davy's case, just over the 100 mark. Charles Purdom, editor of *Everyman* and planner of modern cities, was also among them. It was in the middle of these encounters that a telegram was received from India telling of Hazrat Babajan's dropping the body, reputedly at the age of 125 years. And then Baba set off on another side-trip to the Middle East.

After a brief excursion via *The Orient Express* to Istanbul, Baba returned to Italy and took the *S.S. Roma* from Genoa on October 27 bound for New York. There too he was to meet others who also stayed with him inwardly and often outwardly for the rest of their lives: Malcolm Schloss and his wife, Jean Adriel; Princess Norina Matchabelli, Anita de Caro (later Vieillard), and Elizabeth Patterson. Each of these contributed a lifetime of care, love, endless energy and great wisdom to the flocks of persons of all descriptions that were attracted to Baba. Almost all have written at least one book in which they recount their personal adventures in the company of the one who has rested for an entire lifetime at the center of their being.

It would be an unpardonable omission to go further in the enumeration of people already drawn close to Baba and who would stay with him for a lifetime, without making special mention of the key woman disciple who already had drawn close to him in India, Mehera Irani, as well as Mani, Baba's sister, the youngest in the family.

One day I will trace back for my own curiosity the exact lineage of Mehera Irani. For now she is one of that maze of persons named Irani, a number of whom were actually close relatives of Meher Baba.

It was all too much for me when I met most of them, and still is. It was only a very short time ago that I found out for instance that one of the most beloved of Baba's mandali, Pendu Irani ("Pendu" because his head waggled like the pendulum on a clock as he did the early morning meditation. Pendu would be standing in order not to fall asleep, but he swayed, so Baba called him "Pendulum," then shortened this to Pendu.) and Naja Irani, who made the world's greatest herb omelets, were actually brother and sister as well as first cousins of Meher Baba. I had known them for years, and yet these little facts had never pierced through my skull. But being around Baba was like that. The focus of one's attention was always inevitably on Baba, and the universe about one

Mehera holding Kippy, late 1930s.

*could fold and collapse and form again while one rested in
oblivion. He just commanded that attention. There was no
way to concentrate on anything but the top priority. However,
let us return to Mehera Irani.*

*If it were possible for Meher Baba to experience
competition within the hearts of humanity, it would be due to
the grace and beauty of this, his closest woman disciple.
There is a tradition that the Avatar always has his close
woman consort. Mehera is compared to the traditions of
Jesus's Mary and Krishna's Radha and others of legendary
qualities. Certainly it would be very difficult to imagine a
woman more attractive than Mehera Irani. Further, her
devotion to Baba was total, and Baba's love for his Mehera
was unmatched. Long after Baba's dropping of the body,
Mehera continued in life to fascinate those who had the
unmatched privilege to contact her.*

*While during Baba's lifetime she was guarded from any
contact and, almost without exception, from any view by
males other than Baba himself, at the end of Baba's life in the
physical body she began to be allowed to see and be seen by
selected men close to Baba. She was often referred to as one
of the Four "Perfect" Women.*

*Just what this was all about is another of the seemingly
endless riddles associated with Baba's life. One part of the
riddle, though, is not difficult to interpret. To have met these
four perfect ones was to have a supreme experience of
individuals of such grace and warmth as to lend new
meaning to the word "perfect."*

*Mani, Baba's sister was adorable. There is no other term
that describes her physical appearance and her actions.
Petite, smiling (her eyes could flash anger, though, like her*

brother's), *highly intelligent, the center of her life focused on
Meher Baba.*

*I had the lovely experience of long years of close contact
with her, when she would often appear around the corner of
Mandali Hall and the shelter for the blue bus with a message
or often even a gift. Once when I arrived in November she
had a large manila envelope in her hands containing, I
immediately supposed, some manuscript that Baba intended
for some literary project. But then why were her eyes dancing
like a little girl's about to go on a picnic?*

*"This is a present from Baba. It is the sadhra he was
wearing on your birthday, January 14. He gave it to Mehera
to give to you on your next visit."*

*Dear Mani, you have joined your big brother now, but
what a treasure trove of memories you have left–of fun, of
serious questions while editing so many of Baba's words, of
scenarios for motion pictures of Baba that you and Mehera
egged him into enduring as the hero-actor when I arrived
camera in hand. (I detest photography, but it brought whole
hours of my most treasured experiences of Baba with Mani.)*

*It was Mani who shouldered the responsibility when Baba
left his physical form of presiding over the Avatar Meher Baba
Trust, an arduous, demanding job that she fulfilled with great
competency, balance and delightful admixtures of humor.*

After a month of very busy days on the East Coast of the United
States, Meher Baba finally set sail again on December 5 on the S.S.
Bremen for the port of Le Havre. After some excursions in Paris and
then down into Venice, Baba's party boarded ship once again and
arrived back in Bombay on January 1, 1932.

This was, of course, only one of the many intercontinental trips
that Baba made during the 1930s. Others took him on to California
and the predictable encounters with the stars of Hollywood. Despite

the excitement, and the famous misfire of breaking the silence in the Hollywood Bowl, nothing too much ever came of those contacts. One, with the director Gabriel Pascal, turned into a long-enduring project to make a film. In fact there have been a number of projects through the years to make a film on a theme proposed by Baba, but to date none has ever gone beyond the planning stage. One might call this a monumental foul-up, but no doubt Baba employed this as a superb mechanism for erasing several million very potent sanskaras along the way.

4. THE MIDDLE PERIOD

I t is now 1932 and Meher Baba is almost 38 years old, about the average life expectancy of the Indian male at that time. Life was moving along. As if in recognition of what remained to be done and the probable time left in which to do it, Baba's travels and projects increased both in number and in speed. This was true not only of how much was crowded into each day, but also the sheer rate at which Baba moved physically. Many have commented on the difficulty which one walking with him had to undergo just to stay at his side. This remained true even into the later days when the first of two auto accidents had taken its physical toll.

Obviously there was a great deal of work remaining to be done. The itinerary of the next two years gives one an idea of the dizzying external pace maintained by Baba throughout his earthly sojourn:

Bombay to Nasik and Navsari: January–March 1932
London and Devonshire: March–April
Lugano: May
New York, Hollywood, Hawaii, Japan, China: June–July
Santa Margherita, Assisi, Venice: August
Nasik, then back to London and Zurich: September–November
Egypt, Ceylon: December 1932–January 1933
Westerners come to India: February
Portofino, Rome: June–July

Nasik, Hyderabad: August–September
London, Avila, Madrid, Barcelona: October–November
Return to Meherabad: November 15, 1933

Meher Baba had arrived back in Bombay at the beginning of 1932. On February 17 his birthday was celebrated in Nasik. On March 24 he boarded the Italian ship *Conte Rosso* for Venice. He was responding to an invitation sent in January from London by Kitty Davy asking Baba to return there for a week in the spring to "pay Baba back" for the week he had given them in Paris on his previous visit to Europe.

It was in London in the spring of 1932 that the Paramount Film Company arranged to meet Baba for an interview. Baba gave them the slip for reasons he did not explain, but finally relented and on April 8 gave them the interview including a classic message which has lasted through the decades as a keynote of his mission. He said to the world in Paramount's film:

"My coming to the West is not with the object of establishing new creeds and spiritual societies and organizations, but it is intended to make people understand religion in its true sense. True religion consists in developing that attitude of mind, which would ultimately result in seeing one Infinite Existence prevailing throughout the universe; when one could live in the world and yet be not of it, and at the same time, be in harmony with everyone and everything; when one could attend to all worldly duties and affairs, and yet feel completely detached from all their results; when one could see the same divinity in art and science, and experience the highest consciousness and indivisible bliss in everyday life.

"I see the structure of all the great and recognized religions and creeds of the world tottering. The West particularly is more inclined toward the material side of things, which has from untold ages brought in its wake wars, pestilence and financial crises. It should not be understood that I discard and hate materialism. I mean that materialism should not be considered an end in itself, but a means to an end.

"Organized efforts, such as the League of Nations, are being made to solve the world's problems and bring about the millennium. In some parts of the West, particularly in America, intellectual understanding of Truth and Reality is attempted, but without the true spirit of religion. It is all like groping in the dark.

"I intend bringing together all religions and cults like beads on one string and revitalize them for individual and collective needs. This is my mission to the West. The peace and harmony that I shall talk of and that will settle on the face of this world is not far off."[1]

After several visits and adventures in England, Baba observed that the weather was too cold for him. Someone had the bright idea of going to Switzerland to warm up. (Could this have been an Englishman who made the suggestion?) The logic of going to Switzerland from London to get warm is difficult to follow, but it does lead to a further observation. One cannot escape the suspicion that these followers of Baba in their youth were just as madcap as any of the best products of our present days of great individualism.

Shortly after arriving in Lugano, a cable from India advised Baba of the death of his father, Sheriar. In fact, on the night of Sheriar's death, Baba had called his brother Adi Jr. to his room by a handclap, but Adi could not understand Baba's gestures. Now Baba explained to him just what had happened on that evening.

Baba spent some days more in England, where the author Rom Landau met him. Landau's subsequent book added to the skepticism about Baba that had already been aroused by Paul Brunton in his controversial book *A Search in Secret India*. On May 14 Baba boarded

---

[1] *Lord Meher*, p. 1554.

the *S.S. Bremen*, bound again for New York. The little week's "return visit" was turning into a much more lengthy and important venture.

After three days and a dinner party in Greenwich Village for three hundred people, plus interviews covering among other topics Baba's marital status and his voluntary remarks on corollary sex life, it must have been all a bit too much even for the Avatar. Nevertheless it was at this time that another lifetime devotee met Baba for the first time, Nadine Tolstoy, the daughter-in-law of the world-renowned Leo Tolstoy.

Perhaps as an antidote to the days spent in New York, Baba drove with the Schlosses to the quiet subsurban town of Harmon, where it was said that Baba would be staying for a full year. Apparently there had been some confusion in the transmittal of messages, for he stayed just two days. Fortunately, Jean (Adriel) Schloss had not taken the house on a long-term lease.

On May 25 Baba left Harmon by train and continued to Chicago. After a stop there and in various other cities in Kansas and Texas, he finally reached Los Angeles on May 29. By some coincidence, the Olympic games were being held there at just that time. Nevertheless, press and films were well in attendance at Baba's arrival. Baba stayed "seven hectic days" in Hollywood. The schedule was jammed. It included a reception at Pickfair by Mary Pickford, the queen of Hollywood, dinner with Tallulah Bankhead and lunch with Marie Dressler.

The Hollywood stay also included a sensitive problem when Meredith Starr arrived and insisted on staying in Baba's bedroom. Finally, Baba said to Meredith, "There is a *bad* influence here in Hollywood for one as spiritually sensitive as you." He then suggested that Meredith spend the time in a town called the Dunes along the Pacific Coast, and there Meredith should meditate. The Problem of a sticky customer was accordingly resolved, an example of Baba's divine humor and humanity. And then he was off to Hawaii and the Far East. En route in Honolulu Baba sent a message back to Los Angeles saying that he had decided after all on the postponing of the breaking of his silence in the Hollywood Bowl. This he let be understood as having been an intentionally calculated body blow to the sanskaras (habit patterns) of his close ones, who had had to undergo a rugged combination of embarrassment, disappointment and loss of face.

After a racing journey through the Far East, obviously laying cables for the future, and a bare two-week stop in India, we find Baba and his small group of traveling companions headed back to Europe. On July 29 they arrived in Marseilles to be met by Kitty Davy and her indefatigable brother, Herbert. The next day they took the train to Santa Margherita which, along with Portofino, forms one of the most beautiful stretches of coastline in all the world. Baba returned there several times for good, relaxed (?) stays. If one had the opportunity to see these various properties, one could not but admire greatly Baba's taste both in the choice of scenic area as well as the residences he selected. Those in which he stayed, and especially the now razed villa "Capo di Monte" in Cannes, are some of the loveliest sites one could wish to see.

Being the Avatar presumably does not necessarily mean that one must always choose to holiday in the most thread-bare and forsaken sites in the world. On the other hand, making similar inspections in India, one would be hard put to think of trying to sleep one hour in many of the spots where he stayed. Neither extreme concerned him in the slightest. He had marvelous taste, and at the same time he was not bound by that taste.

The period spent in Santa Margherita was one of relaxed companionship with the Master, certainly what each of the small group of Europeans who stayed with him had hoped might happen one day. And here it was happening. Each person who stayed with Baba found some manner to express his or her sense of the love and sparkling warmth at being with Baba. So it went on, and one day Baba announced that he wanted to spend twenty-four hours in seclusion somewhere in Italy. He chose Assisi because of the association with St. Francis. And it was in Assisi that Herbert Davy turned in a sparkling job of research, finding the caves in which the early Franciscan monks had prayed, and in particular one in which St. Francis himself had often remained.

Years later at a gathering in Myrtle Beach, South Carolina, Baba explained that the four really great saints of the Christian tradition were St. Francis, St. Theresa of Avila, St. Catherine of Sienna and St. Augustine of Hippo. Of these, the one to achieve God Realization had been St. Francis through the intercession of Khwaja Khizr as God's direct representative. Baba urged that all from the Christian tradition study diligently the lives of these four truly great saints. Baba would also remark on occasion to a group that when they too would love Baba as St. Francis had loved Jesus, they also would be granted God Realization.

In Assisi Baba carried out his meditation in the cave that St. Francis had used, meeting inwardly, as he explained afterwards, with the present and past Perfect Masters and saints, charting out the course that Creation was to follow for thousands of years in the future. This cave has become a place of pilgrimage for many people devoted both to the Christian tradition and to Meher Baba.

Two weeks after their return to Santa Margherita, the entire group packed up and made once again for Venice. There Baba managed to impress on them the importance of obedience, but gently, very gently. One day for example, the group accompanying Baba went off for a swim. When they returned, he quietly chided them for having gone off and left him completely alone. It is hard for the Western mentality to digest the key role that such events play on the spiritual path. Nevertheless he posed patiently for photographs with several of the women, each sitting individually with Baba at the base of the column in St. Mark's Square while the doves flitted about and the women smiled blissfully. They should have.

Meher Baba with Western and Eastern lovers in India, 1937.

Late on August 20 with Kaka and Chanji in tow, Baba boarded ship for Alexandria, arriving there three days later. After five days of what appeared to be typical sightseeing of the major local Egyptian wonders, Baba and his companions set sail from Port Said on August 29 for India. The entire idyll had occupied just six weeks.

I have dwelt at some length on these early trips that Baba made to the West to give some idea of the manner in which he began setting up the close personal ties to key disciples in those areas. There are many charming and also fascinating episodes that occurred constantly in the trips listed above in the inventory of travels, and these are only the trips he took between March 1932 and May 1934. But I will not go into the further activities of this period except to mention that in 1934 Baba began having the Westerners come to India for stays of varying periods. These visits gradually assumed the proportions of rather large contingents for whom special plans and accommodations had to be made. The stories of the crises of adaptation and personality conflicts would fill a separate book in themselves.

I am anxious now to get to what I term to myself as the "continental divide" in Baba's life, the time and actions which it seem to me separate the earlier period of his activities from the publicly declared Avataric portion of his spiritual ministration. This occurred in fact after World War II and is termed "The New Life" period by Baba and all those around him. Jumping now over something more than ten years, I will recount briefly the circumstances that led to my first indirect contacts with Meher Baba that occurred in 1945, five years before he went off into this "New Life," and which I describe in the next chapter, devoted in its entirety to this subject.

After graduation from the Johns Hopkins University I started into my professional career in the sciences, but almost immediately found myself facing some unusual experiences in my personal life which I could not explain even by the excellent educational background I had obtained. I set up therefore my own course of esoteric study. After about a year and a half of intensive investigation of all available resources, of which there were many in California, I decided that the tradition which offered most promise for my purposes was that of the ancient Sufis.

My initiator for the course I had decided to take was Murshida Rabia Martin of San Francisco, the head of the Sufi Order in the Americas and Australia. She had been the first initiate of Inayat Khan on his arrival in the Western Hemisphere to carry out his Chistia master's injunction to found Sufism in the Western world. After some months of study with Murshida Martin and watching with apprehension the growing involvement of the United States in World War II, I was called up for the draft and rejected because of a kidney infection. When my own doctors searched exhaustively for the cause and found neither infection nor clues to the problem, I went back to my draft board and advised them that I was fit for service after all. They asked me the source of my authority. When I replied with some pride that they were the best in the field in the San Francisco area, they looked sadly at me and said that their own doctors were their base for their decisions and, essentially, I should leave them alone. Years later my doctors found I had an abcess on the right lobe of the prostate, and this flared on occasion when I was under stress. But what odd timing.

Not too long after starting my classes with Murshida Martin she announced one day that she had major news to give us. A few days later all those who could be reached in the near area assembled in her living room. She told us that since the death of Inayat Khan in 1928 she had, according to classic Chistia tradition, been searching for her new master to continue her spiritual development. After all this time, she had now finally found two women in New York who told her of their master, who lived in India and was called Meher Baba. For two years she had taken every opportunity to travel to New York to listen to their words on Meher Baba and his qualities.

Finally, Murshida Martin continued, she had decided that Meher Baba was the one intended to be her master and, mind the words, she had also come to the conclusion that he was the great Spiritual Messenger of this age. Therefore she had asked him to accept not only her as his student, but also the guidance of the Sufi Order for which she was responsible. Meher Baba had accepted both requests. Now Murshida Martin was giving us, her mureeds as we were termed, two weeks to decide whether to accept her decision and follow her under the spiritual guidance of Meher Baba.

I am typical of the Western mentality which cherishes individual rights and responsibilities. To give a vow of allegiance to a spiritual master had already been an enormous challenge when I became a Sufi. Now I was being given a deadline of a few days to follow the murshida off into some God-only-knew what perilous and conceivably mined field of search under a man about whom I knew absolutely nothing.

But Meher Baba, I soon found out, was not entirely unknown. Both Paul Brunton and Rom Landau, who were read by many in those days, had written chapters on Meher Baba. Friends loaned me the books, and the parts concerning Meher Baba contained descriptions of the puzzling actions he took, as mentioned earlier. Oddly enough, it was all the impossible background of Baba's silence and breaking the silence that threw me into the worst dilemma of judgment. I could not digest what I read in those short works. I asked Murshida Martin for an appointment.

Trying to be diplomatic but honest, I outlined my problem. Murshida Martin looked quizzically at me. She did not get angry, which incidentally she could do very well on occasion. She simply smiled at me and asked, "Don, how can the drop measure the ocean?"

There it was. By that time I at least knew somewhat of what I knew and a very little bit of what I still did not. Murshida Martin was very thorough in placing one's ego where it belonged, without being at all insulting in the process. I knew I didn't know, and that was the essential fact. I took the Bay Transit back to Piedmont and I realized that I had no other choice but to follow the one person in whom I had the faith to follow along into the complete unknown. There was no other way. I did. I then spent the next seven years gradually learning from many events in my own personal life that all the things I had mistrusted in the accounts I had read of Meher Baba were potentially resolvable and not necessarily to be condemned. I was slowly put into neutral, but I still did not know.

Murshida Martin was told by Meher Baba that he would shortly travel to America and meet the new Order of which he had accepted the charge. We set about cleaning up the Sufi School quarters in Fairfax to receive and house him. I painted. We all cleaned walls and windows. There was an air of the greatest expectation. Months went by. Baba wrote, postponing the trip. This happened several times. Francis Brabazon arrived from Australia to be on hand to meet the new Master. Again delay. Murshida Martin contracted a cancer and eventually died of it. Ivy Duce was appointed by Murshida Martin shortly before her death to be her successor. The new murshida stayed on the East Coast. We waited. Meanwhile we began getting circular letters outlining something called the New Life that Baba had embarked upon, and if I understood correctly what I read, it was almost certain that Meher Baba would never return to public life. What a grim situation.

This was the continental dividing line of which I spoke above, but at that time I had no idea really what it was all about. Little did I know that I would spend virtually the rest of my life mining out the implications of the events that were taking place at that time. I will not try to sketch yet the known record of that period, which lasted for two years from late 1949 until the beginning of 1952. On January 1, 1949, Baba sent out a circular to his followers commenting on the start of the New Life, "1949 marks the artificial end to an artificial beginning, and the Real Beginning to the Real End." He then went on to warn his lovers that "1949 will be a year of tests and trouble for all, and a great personal disaster for me."[2]

One day in early 1952 the news arrived from India that Meher Baba had terminated his New Life and the Manonash period that followed it and was now living the Complicated Free Life. For the moment he had re-established himself at Meherazad, the charming collection of buildings on the side of Ahmednagar opposite to that in which Meherabad is located.

Meher Baba had lived principally in Meherazad for a short period before the start of the New Life, and in fact it became his primary residence for the remainder of his physical presence.

Baba indicated in his letters to America that he would stop in Europe to see his old devotees there, most of whom had not glimpsed him since the outbreak of the war. A very few Westerners had continued to live with Baba during the entire conflict, and some

---

[2] *ibid.*, p. 3381

of these continued to do so for the rest of their lives. But several others had been sent back to Europe and America during the early days of the war.

After a fairly short visit in England, Baba advised that he would continue to New York and to Myrtle Beach, South Carolina, where Elizabeth Patterson had established and built a center for Meher Baba and his activities. In this she had been constantly helped and advised by Norina Matchabelli. This most marvelous property is thus the result of the combined taste of two of the most devoted followers of Meher Baba, and certainly will be for a very long time a living memorial to their wonderful qualities. The center breathes peace and love. It was used for several weeks in 1952 by Baba and those traveling with him, and again in 1956 and 1958. Except for the properties in India, it has the distinction of having been used by Baba for the longest period of time of any one site.

> *How many times did Baba say to me, "Don, do you know what Elizabeth did? She knew I had always slept on a bed with ropes intertwined instead of a mattress, so she had this rope bed shipped over from India so I would feel comfortable." Baba would say this as if it were the first time in his life someone had been so thoughtful concerning his comfort. Elizabeth was like that. She could think of the smallest thing and make certain it was done for Baba.*

After New York and Myrtle Beach, Baba intended to drive with the group in two cars to Los Angeles and then San Francisco. However, if there were any on the West Coast who wished to come early to meet him in Myrtle Beach, they could do so. The Sufis on the East Coast could see him both in New York and Myrtle Beach. And so the trip started and all proceeded normally until the party left Myrtle Beach by car en route to California.

Chaos! Consternation! The news jolted those waiting in the

West: Baba, driving through Oklahoma, had been in a serious automobile accident, and he and several of the mandali were in a tiny hospital in Prague recovering. While none was in danger of dying, their injuries were severe and painful. Baba himself had sustained a broken leg and very heavy lacerations of the face. Mehera had had a serious skull injury, and in fact the indentation from it was visible on her forehead for the rest of her life.

The news was sickening. No one could believe that it had happened. How could such a painful event occur, and just as they were all setting out for the glorious visit to the West Coast? Rather quickly Baba reminded all that he had predicted some time before that it would be necessary for him to spill his blood one day in America. He never did elucidate further the exact mechanics and reasons for all this, but again one must recall that it is an ancient tradition that the Avatar during his physical life takes on himself the living of a portion of the pain of humanity. This is his contribution to what all have to go through in Creation, and his rule is that he will live part of this with humanity in full experience of the very pain that each suffers.

After some days in the Prague hospital, Baba and the rest of the injured were driven in ambulances from Oklahoma back to Myrtle Beach. Following several weeks of recovery there, all on the West Coast were advised that Baba would travel in August to New York and spend about one week receiving those from the West who still had had no opportunity to see him. I planned at once to spend a weekend in New York for this long anticipated meeting. What was to occur was one of the two cardinal lessons and experiences Baba afforded me. I recount it in its entirety, although I have set it out before in slightly shorter form in the "Introduction" to Meher Baba's *God Speaks*.[3]

---

[3] Meher Baba, *God Speaks* (New York: Dodd, Mead, 2nd edition, 1973).

It was still not the age of the jet, at least in commercial travel. I was to take a United Airlines DC-6 from San Francisco airport at the end of work on a Friday afternoon, with a stop in Chicago, arriving in New York early on Saturday morning. My schoolhood friend Bob Porter had invited me to stop at his apartment for a shower and a shave, and then I was to go at once to Murshida Duce's home on the west side of Central Park to see Baba. This all went exactly as programmed, and despite the short sleep I had managed on the plane, I was too excited to feel tired.

Arriving at the familiar entry to the apartment building in which the Duces lived, I went up in the elevator and rang the bell. Charmie, the Duces' daughter, opened the door for me and asked at once if I would like to go up to her bedroom to wait, as Baba was not yet ready to see me. Several people were with him at the moment.

I went up the rather narrow stairs and into Charmie's bedroom, which I saw at once had two girls already in it. I knew them, not well, and was disappointed that obviously I would have to make small talk instead of being quiet, which I longed for. To my surprise they nodded and went back at once to a busy discussion that I had obviously interrupted. Or at least they pretended it that way. In any case, I was thankful.

As I sat on Charmie's bed my mind went completely blank. I thought of none of the things that I would have to be sure to bring up. My mind refused to function. But what, what is this–the beginning of a cold? My throat suddenly felt sore and scratchy. No doubt I had picked up a bug in the plane overnight. And what a hell of a time for this to happen!

A few seconds later the soreness of my throat became almost unbearable, and I wondered at the rapidity and the force of this commencing infection. Damn, damn, damn!

The next moment I felt tears running down the side of my

nose. I had never had a cold set in like this before. Then it hit
me. For some unexplainable reason, I was crying. I hadn't
cried since I was fifteen and my old collie dog died after
being with me for fourteen years. What under the sun was
going on? I had absolutely no reason to be crying. It just was
completely outside my nature.

My first reaction was to look over towards the two girls,
to see if they had noticed these completely uncharacteristic
goings-on of staid, stable Stevens. No, they were still busily
engaged in their chitchat and not even looking in my
direction. With a superhuman effort I controlled my emotions
and tried to get rid of the tears without obvious gestures or
noises. Not very easy, but I did it. At least, the girls still gave
no indication of having noticed what was happening.

I was no sooner controlled than Charmie appeared at the
doorway. "Baba's ready to see you now," she said cheerily.
The two girls in the room still seemed oblivious to any and all
events other than their gossip. I think it was for real.
Sometimes girls get like that.

Down the stairs I went and Charmie threw the two
library doors open. There in the small but tasteful room
decorated in soft yellows and gold was a strange assembly of
humanity and kitchenware. The centerpiece was a chaise
longue on which I recognized Meher Baba stretched out,
facing generally towards the opposite windows. On that side,
with their backs to the street, were several obviously Oriental
gentlemen, and just in front of them was one of the big, old
classic tin washtubs of the day with a large block of ice in it.
Just towards the window was a normal sized fan blowing
across the block of ice in the direction of Meher Baba's chaise
longue. This was the air conditioning for this oppressive New
York summer day. It did not work very well.

But I had little time to test the barometrics. Murshida

*Duce was on her feet and approaching me, with her warm
embrace. I caught sight out of the corner of my eye of Meher
Baba making a monumental effort to rise from his chaise
longue, and this at once broke my heart. Imagine, the Avatar,
trying despite a broken leg to get up and greet me on his feet!
I suppose I should really stop the story right here, because
there it all is in that one simple act. This is the way God loves
and takes care of us. It was not an effort. It just was. It has
always been that way, too. The most unfathomable sensitivity
and oneness in all things. I do not know if Baba taught me
one thing after that. Yes, perhaps a few embellishments and
variations on what he did and established at that moment.
All my years of learning and finding out possible bases of
different unexplainable actions were annihilated in one
instant. Here was reality, and nothing else of any importance
existed.*

*A bit strong? No, not at all. Once in a long time,
something happens in life which you know at once to be
cardinal. I knew it at that moment, and I knew the man, and
I knew also that he knew me completely. Incredible–no?–to
have such deep instant knowledge of such important things?
But it is like that. Some knowledge comes gradually and with
great hardship attached. It is important, yes. But the cardinal
arrives at once and with no apparent effort. Maybe I had
been spending lifetimes leading up to this moment, and
perhaps I had earned it all way back then, and what I was
conscious of now was the great wave that broke through the
dam of consciousness. I don't know, really, and I don't really
care. It was, and I was.*

*At any rate, I at once protested loudly to Baba that he
must not rise and risk his injured leg. Tell it to the winds.
Baba waved his hand and smiled and he was standing and
supported by two of the Oriental gentlemen. I just felt foolish,*

but also, so happy and full.

"Baba, this is my boy, Don," Ivy Duce started the conversation. We had known each other for quite a few years already and had come through quite a bit together.

I was not even conscious of the fact that it was Baba doing the gesticulating and someone else doing the speaking: "What do you mean, your boy Don? He is my boy. We have been together since the dawn of time."

Well, that is quite a statement to be coming from the Avatar, but even before I could speculate on the mechanics of all this, my typical American mind said, "Good heavens, what a pun Baba pulled." Because, of course, dawn is pronounced just like my first name.

Baba never gives you much chance for reflection. At once he asked about my travel, and how long I was staying, and where I worked. I don't know what else, but the truth was that I was back to being a little boy again, and the cat had got my tongue. I could not say a word, only "huh," and "yes," and "not long," and a few nonsensical things of the sort. I did have the good grace at least to be ashamed of myself and wonder what under the sun Baba must be thinking of this dunce from San Francisco. But oddly, I didn't care.

I had just made an incredible discovery, and I knew this to be completely true. Baba knew me completely, everything about me, and in fact, he knew me better than I knew myself. But that was not all. The most incredible fact was that he accepted me totally for just what I was. Now this was what I realized I had been searching for all of my life, one person who just knew me and accepted me without reservations. And here he was in front of me. It was the last thing I had expected. A great spiritual master should know a lot about you, but inevitably that must include a lot of bad spots, and obviously the rest of life would be spent trying to get rid of those bad spots that he knew and that I knew he knew.

But it wasn't like that at all. He just loved and accepted me as I was. And it was and is and will always be like that. Why is it that we cannot imagine that this is the basic characteristic of one who is One? All the philosophy in creation will not produce this, nor substitute for it.

Finally Baba woke me up from my indulgent daydreaming. His gestures, another's voice: "And we will see each other tomorrow morning in Harmon, no?" I had almost forgotten that there was a full day ahead, and that I would see Baba both in the morning to discuss Sufi affairs with Murshida Duce, and again in the afternoon in New York when Baba had promised to discuss honesty with the Sufis. "Yes, I will look forward to it," I managed to mumble. Baba gave me a radiant smile for this gem I had managed to utter, and I was whisked through the library doors and back into the high-ceiled living room. I had met him. He knew me. He accepted me totally as I was. What an incredible event I had lived through in such a short time. I sat down on a small chair against the far wall and tried to recover my sense of orientation. Literally, it was like living in a new world. All the old standards of importance had disappeared and a new world with totally new structures had taken its place. I reflected. Fortunately, again, everyone had the good sense not to talk to me. I stayed in my universe that had just been created. I was not alone in it, but I really did not know anyone in it yet.

Eventually I realized that it was noontime and that I ought to get a bite of lunch. I drifted out and down. I went somewhere and bought a sandwich. I ate it somewhere. I came back to the apartment and rang the bell. Someone opened for me; they did not seem surprised to see me. I think they may have said hello. I am not sure I did. It was like that. I looked at my watch much later and it was after three. I supposed I ought to go back to Bob's apartment and take a nap. I resisted the idea. Suddenly Filis Frederick threw open the doors to the library. "Baba's going to tell us a story." I suddenly knew that this was what I had been waiting for.

Perhaps ten or twelve of us were still in the apartment at that point. We assembled ourselves in a crescent around Baba's chaise longue. I was at the extreme upper tip of the crescent just in back of Baba's right ear. He started gesticulating and someone translated into words. For me it was not necessary. I was lost in the beauty of the gestures of his hand. It was the most graceful story I have ever witnessed. Murshida Duce later repeated it to me twice. I forgot it each time. I still see and hear only the grace of the gestures.

Baba's story was coming to a climax. The manner in which he held the attention of his small audience was magic. I had never witnessed anyone capture so completely the attention of a group. Involuntarily, as if sleep walking, I started to raise my right hand behind Baba's head and my thumb and forefinger made a circle, the symbol of perfection. As I did so, Baba turned slightly and naturally in his chair and gestured back to me the same symbol. My heart was deeply warmed by the sensitivity and perfect timing. I watched. The story continued quickly.

How come? Suddenly my mind started up. How did Baba know when to do that? How did he do it? Intrigued by the mathematical probabilities of the situation, I raised my hand again, this time as Baba was staring completely away from me. Again, as if by magnetic response he turned in his chair and gestured the same to me again. Good heavens, he can see through the back of his head! It couldn't be mathematical chance this time.

Finally the story was at an end, the doors were thrown open again and I went back to my wall. Time went on. It was five o'clock, the chimes were ringing, and again the doors opened, this time for Baba to roll in his wheel chair to the elevator and to be driven to Harmon. The wheel chair must have been found specially in a museum, an ancient wooden contraption and very narrow. In it Baba was all squeezed up, and pushing it was a huge hulk of a man whom I later knew as Sarosh, the mayor of Ahmednagar and one of Baba's closest lifelong mandali. Sarosh looked five times as big as Baba and completely hid him from the rear. I jumped up and got right behind Sarosh as he rolled Baba towards the front door. I raised my right hand again in the gesture of perfection, and again Baba, but with great effort in his cramped chair, twisted about and looked in back of the great hulk of Sarosh to make the same gesture back to me, with a big smile, as if we had a secret between us. What the Avatar has to go through to satisfy our whimsies!

The next morning was Sunday, but we started early for Harmon and found Baba ready for us with Adi Irani to translate his gestures. There were financial questions on which to ask Baba's advice, and Murshida had some very rare philosophical points to clarify with Baba. I sat through it and could only marvel that an Avatar could also be a quicker and clearer thinker on financial questions than the best experts I knew on the West Coast. He was not only quick and clear, but also always dead-on. The same for Murshida's philosophical questions. Most thinkers would have taken pages to suggest what Baba clearly stated in a few moments.

Finally Baba looked at me. "Don, you have some questions for Baba." A statement. Not a question. In fact, I had jotted down five on a paper and put it in my wallet.

*I was ashamed of myself for having done it. They seemed so
trite and unimportant. I said I had none. Baba insisted.
Again I said I had none. Baba insisted the third time, and
offered to shoo Ivy and Charmie away since it was obvious
that the questions were personal. I said no. Baba insisted
again, and out they went. I asked two. Baba gave simple and
short replies, and I followed his suggestions. They were really
just right.*

In the afternoon Baba had promised the Sufis to discuss
what Baba means by honesty. In his charter for Sufism
Reoriented he had included five points, one of which was one
vowed to do one's best to try to make an effort to put into
practice. Of course, we all interpreted this to mean
immediately. No break-in period. One of these was absolute
honesty. Of course, within two weeks everyone was in the
middle of full-blown crises, either with the boss, or the family,
or both. What to do?

Baba's comments on this were unique. He pointed out
that honesty is precipitated above all when someone asks you
a question, often for information they want. Baba said that
the fact that they asked did not mean that you were
committed automatically to reply. In fact, it was your
responsibility first of all to decide whether the person had any
right at all to the information you had and they wanted.
Perhaps your decision would be completely in the negative.
Baba said this was not dishonesty.

The more frequent situation, however, would be when
you decided finally that the person had the right to know,
and could understand and creatively utilize part of what you
knew, but not all. It was your responsibility then to decide
how much. But, here was the big point. It was necessary in
giving, say the 60% you might have decided they could use,

*a just balance between the positive and the negative, the
pleasing and the displeasing, and not a weighted portion just
to please your own ends in the matter. This was what Baba
said he called honesty. A very unusual analysis, and one I've
spent a lifetime trying to apply equitably. It is a huge
challenge but finally the only way. It has been one of the most
creative principles I have ever encountered in daily life.*

*Late that Sunday afternoon I took a taxi out to the
airport and was soon airborne for San Francisco. My mind
traced over the incredible two days. Nothing like this had ever
been crammed into my life. It was an entire new experience,
and I knew that I had indeed been in the presence of the
great Master. As I continued my thoughts, gradually I started
to reflect on what awaited me at the office the next morning.
There were problems aplenty, and some involved serious
personnel questions. They are the most difficult of all. But I
was surprised to note that I suddenly saw how to handle the
most serious of the human problems. Intrigued, I brought
another to mind, and I saw here again a potential avenue of
attack. Then I went on to the financial field. No solutions, but
for some reason I couldn't get worried about them. The same
in some of my own household snarls. Then I realized that
for some reason my great capacity to worry had been
anaesthetized. It wasn't working at all tonight. Wait for a
day or two. They will all come back in full force.*

*In fact they did not come back the next day, nor the
next, nor ever. The problems were there, but the worry had
disappeared. This was my first experience of the grace of the
Master. It is real; and its arrival is completely quiet and even
unrecognized for the moment. I have never worried since. I
hope it lasts all the next incarnations, too.*

5. THE NEW LIFE

O ne of Meher Baba's earliest and most frequently quoted discourses is entitled "The New Humanity."[1] The period of Baba's life that was the most minutely planned and carried out, and which involved the most important consequences for a large proportion of his followers, was certainly "The New Life." And yet it has been only fairly recently that the thought that these two subjects belonged intimately together has been raised.[2] There is one almost certain reason for this, while another is quite possible. The certain reason is that to this day the New Life period remains easily the most enigmatic and least understood in Baba's life. The possible further reason for the lack of association between the two similar phrases is that the parallel was so close that no one thought it necessary to point out the obvious.

Rather than indulge in further speculation on this curious fact, let us plunge now into the history of this all-important period in Baba's life. In January 1949 Baba began giving signs of a major shift in the manner of life he intended to lead in the future. These included warnings on severe cuts to be made in the financing of projects, as well as for the maintenance of those dependent on him. He also let it be known that the number of people who would be

---

[1] *Discourses*, pp. 3-9.
[2] D. E. Stevens, *Listen! The New Humanity* (St. Helier, Jersey: Companion Books, 1985), see especially p. 26.

allowed in the future to live close to him would be reduced drastically. The figure he quoted for the former was fifty percent, and for the latter, ninety percent. A really threatening reduction, particularly in terms of people.

It was also at this time that Baba gave Elizabeth Patterson and Norina Matchabelli the instructions and requirements they were to follow in their establishment of a center in the United States. They left at once for America, and after a considerable but fruitless search in various parts of the United States for a suitable site, suddenly there staring them in the face, they saw it in their own backyard. It was a large property owned by Elizabeth's father, who was in the real estate business in South Carolina, near Myrtle Beach. It was almost immediately seen to be ideal for their purpose. The results of their substantial efforts in building the center have already been described. The property continues to this day to attract thousands of people each year, both long-term devotees as well as many new persons. The latter are often attracted originally by stories they have heard, as well as simply through curiosity. All are enchanted by a composite of natural and man-made beauty, or should we say, woman-made, for it was truly Elizabeth and Norina who saw and planned the entirety.

Meanwhile in India, Baba set up meetings for the close followers to be held for several days starting on August 15 at 7:30 a.m. At the appointed time–in fact, fifteen minutes later than the designated time–several persons due to attend had not showed up. Nothing would upset Baba and send him into a mood more completely than late arrivals. (It was such a mishap that brought one of two tirades down on my head in later years.)

In fact, to be honest, when for example Baba said 7:00, almost always he was there by 6:45; whoever was not on hand at that time was chastised for arriving late. No matter that one might have arrived well before the appointed hour. The fact that one was not present and awaiting Baba's arrival was considered by Baba to be "late." Logically, it was unfair, but in the observance of submission to and love for the Master, it was the least one could do.

When the New Life meeting took up finally after some storming about late arrivals, several points were set out on the manner of organizing the meetings and the translation of the words into the necessary languages. Baba then began the substance of the session by outlining three points concerning his own personal arrangements:

"(1) I shall be absolutely helpless in the true and literal sense of the word on account of some personal disaster to me; before that happens after October 1st, I want to make what arrangements are possible for the mandali under the limited means at our disposal, because I shall then stop looking into the material affairs of anyone. (2) I shall allow only such persons to remain near me who are completely ready to carry out the conditions that will be laid down by me for that purpose. I shall be beyond the reach of all others. (3) Meherabad and Meherazad ashrams will be disbanded as I am going to wipe them off my map."

With benefit of hindsight, what, we might ask, happened in connection with these three declarations of Meher Baba? The personal disaster, if it is correct to interpret it as such, may be considered to be the tragic automobile accident of 1952 in America. There was a still later one, even more serious in its human balance, late in 1956 near Satara, India. On that occasion Eruch, while driving, suddenly lost control of the car, and it plunged into a nearby ditch after destroying a culvert en route. Dr. Nilu, another stalwart mandali, was thrown from the car by the force of the impact and killed instantly. Meher Baba suffered a lacerated tongue and, among other injuries, a broken hip joint. This latter was the more serious, as the joint proved to be beyond repair, and this immobilized him for much of the remainder of his life. More of all this later.

It is very tempting to suggest that Baba's raising the psychologically loaded subject of a disaster happening to him offered the potential for making drastic changes in arrangements for those who followed and, in many cases, were absolutely dependent on him. These alterations were in fact made, but Baba set up provisions nevertheless to take care of these people. Some of his ancient dependents and their progeny still rely on these arrangements, as well as subsequent ones set out in his Trust Deed in 1959. These provisions, incidentally, have final cut-off definitions. Baba did not make provisions enduring into eternity.

The second point made by Baba on this fateful morning, of providing for only a very few who would follow him into as yet still undefined adventures, was carried out. In fact, there were finally very few in number.

The third point, of wiping Meherabad and Meherazad off the map, went through some odd convolutions. Legal title to these properties was passed over to Nariman Dadachanji, Meherjee Karkaria and Sarosh Irani, three of Baba's long term disciples, and remained with them for many years. Almost everyone in residence at these two complexes was sent away, with the notable exception of Upper Meherabad, where the family of Kaikobad, and Mansari, remained–two more of the epic followers of Meher Baba. Mansari continued to live for the rest of her life (she died on January 12, 1997) at Upper Meherabad, near Baba's tomb, all the while following Baba's admonition not to cross over the railroad tracks at the bottom of the hill. She finally became the twin of Will Backett, bent to the horizontal, but still retaining a ravishing smile that took all in stride.

Continuing now with the manner of Baba's setting up of the New Life, as it is shortly to be called: as the day of conversations continued, Baba instructed that all proceeds from the sale of belongings and properties should be used to recompense existing obligations. As for spiritual benefits that might be expected from all of the past as well as the upheavals now envisaged, "No one will be left out spiritually, if I am spiritually perfect myself."[3] Here was certainly a test of one's faith.

The deadline to accomplish all these changes was set for October 15. Sarosh offered to take care of all the persons dependent on Baba who would not be setting out with him on the as yet undefined next phase. Baba smiled and reminded him that all the proceeds from the sales of properties and belongings were already earmarked for this purpose. As for those who would be accompanying Baba, they would be paupers and dependent on begging for their subsistence!

In brief, under the terms laid out by Baba, the men and women mandali were given the choice either of following Baba into the new adventure, or of going back into society and taking up jobs to support themselves and any persons dependent on them. If they elected to go with Baba, then they would have to meet certain conditions that Baba would shortly set out. For the women mandali, there was the additional provision that they could elect to leave everything in Baba's hands and follow whatever decision he might make for them.

On August 17 Baba specified that the decision of each man and woman, even if made for them in the case of the women as Baba had offered to do, must be affirmed by each person as being borne by them as their own sole responsibility. This was often to be a characteristic of the New Life, that one was on one's own, and there was no question of Meher Baba bearing the responsibility for this and that. They were on their own, even if they were to accompany Baba in the new venture.

On August 18 a remarkable event occurred. Baba arrived at Lower Meherabad at 6:50 a.m. and asked Donkin, Khaksaheb, Kaikobad and Kalemama to have at hand and to read out from the *Bible*, the *Quran*, the *Avesta* and the *Gita*. If they had not bathed

---

[3]Swami Satya Prakash Udaseen, *The New Life of Avatar Meher Baba and His Companions* (Hyderabad: The Meher Vihar Trust, 1967), Appendix I, p. ix.

that morning, they were to do so. Standing on the right of Baba, they started with Kaikobad, who performed the *Kusti* and read the customary prayer for five minutes. Donkin followed reading from the *Bible* with the description from St. Matthew of the crucifixion of Jesus the Christ. Khaksaheb did *namaaz* and silently accompanied with two *Raquat of Nafil.* Kalemama completed the occasion with seven *Shlokas* of the tenth *Adhyai* of the *Bhagavad-Gita.* After several more gestures by Baba and interpreted by Ghani, Baba had the following prayer read out as he dictated it on the alphabet board: "May God help Baba to definitely make this step, which he is taking to give up everything and to go away, irrevocable, so that from 16 October when he enters the new life, there will be no turning back."

The prayer was memorable first because, it was the first mention of "the new life," and also because it was the first time anyone had ever heard Baba invoke God's help. It was fairly common to see Baba in reverence during a prayer devoted to God, but to ask His help was unprecedented. How could this be reconciled within the fact of Oneness? Evidently there could be aspects of human life and its assumption by the Avatar which could cause him to enter fully into the dualistic aspect of physical life to the extent of asking as a human being for God's intercession. In any case, it was a unique and astonishing action on Baba's part.

Almost immediately Baba began to dwell on the fact that those who were finally to accompany him should under no circumstances expect to receive any kind of spiritual benefit from their participation. They were to consider themselves as if dead to the rest of the world, with no contact whatsoever with their old friends, family and associates. All this would be gone. Also, there was a strict injunction that emotions would have to be controlled completely. There was to be absolutely no expression of negative feelings or reactions. Baba would live among them as a brother, and yet they must continue to look upon him as the Master and to obey him. A very remarkable combination of contrasting requirements.

Yet it was to be this companionship with Baba which stood out completely, as Eruch and the women mandali later described the detailed events of their daily life with Baba during this unique period of more than two years. The sense of complete comradeship with the Incomparable dwarfed completely any sense of hardship or fatigue. Yet, just in the shadow, there was also the requirement for instant attention to any need or demand made by Baba. Nevertheless, hardships seemed to disappear from memory, and it was only the fact of the perfection of companionship which remained of this unique two years.

Again and again Baba laid out at the meetings in August the difficulties they would have to master during their stay with him in the New Life. He emphasized repeatedly that he would not help them in any sort of crisis or health problem. And all through this, they must remain unfailingly cheerful and not show the slightest mood of anger or sadness–a tremendous undertaking to agree to. It would be a person of supreme assurance and complete faith in the Master who could commit assuredly to such conditions. Yet, there were a fair number who were undaunted and so, volunteered to go.

Perhaps the most difficult condition of all to accept was that required of those who were to remain behind in the old life. They must abandon all hope of ever again seeing Meher Baba or any of those who would accompany him. It was in this sense that these latter were "dead" to the world.

All the various conditions discussed in the meeting were assembled in a document and a copy given to each person participating. Baba gave them four hours to make a decision on whether they chose to participate in this New Life adventure, and then they were to write an unequivocal "yes" or "no," sign the document and return it. Meanwhile, a "last oath" was given by Baba and read out:

"Before God, the Absolute, whom those who have realized

know as their own Self and whom believers believe to be All-pervading, All-knowing, All-powerful, All-loving and All-merciful–before this Infinite Existence, Baba, on behalf of himself and his followers, asks forgiveness for all mental, physical and moral weaknesses called sins, and for all lies and false dealings, and for all impure and selfish actions.

"Before this Infinite God who ever was, ever is, and ever will be, Baba decides today on the New Life that he and those who accompany him will enter from 16 October 1949, and lead on till the end. This New Life will be based absolutely on all that has been dictated by Baba in the circular of conditions; and Baba invokes God to make him stand by it as firmly and steadfastly as his companions in his New Life are required to do."[4]

It is interesting to compare the atmosphere of newness and adventure established by Baba in setting out on the New Life, with that which one finds in a paragraph of his discourse on "The New Humanity" given out years before:

"The New Humanity will be freed from a life of limitations, allowing unhampered scope for the creative life of the spirit; and it will break the attachment to external forms and learn to subordinate them to the claims of the spirit. The limited life of illusions and false values will then be replaced by unlimited life in the Truth; and the limitations, through which the separative self lives, will wither away at the touch of true understanding."[5]

The Last Oath taken by Baba for the New Life amounted to a very powerful and unequivocal statement to God. There can be no doubt of the serious base of what Baba is about to launch upon. And

---

[4] C. B. Purdom, *The God-Man* (London: George Allen & Unwin Ltd., 1964), p. 173.
[5] *Discourses*, p. 7.

also, note the word "companions" here. It will become a constant
theme for the New Life. It has become a constant theme for the New
Humanity. There is much already in the record to suggest that it is
to be a key underpinning to the life of mankind in the new manners
of living and searching for the Truth in the New Age.

Should one venture the prediction that companionship will also
become a principal support for human endeavor in practical affairs,
to give substance to dealings that have depended principally on legal
words and phrases that have not always been adequate to ensure the
final accomplishment of promises made?

Now back to the Meherabad meeting. Baba received the
responses of the persons present. After three hours they were all in
hand. Four women and sixteen men would go with Baba, fulfilling
all the conditions he had outlined. There were surprises, even to
Baba, like one of the very old and rugged disciples opting for the
"no," and a frail and relatively new adherent declaring "yes." Then
Baba advised them that he would be spending the time until October
15 winding up old projects, and that they should not expect him to
adhere to any particular schedule or itinerary. Those who had voted
"yes" were free to do as they wished until October 1, when they
should plan to be at Meherabad until the fifth, ready and with
everything they might need. Above all, they were to be prepared at
that time to turn their backs forever on all that they had lived with
in the past.

The only money to be taken on the journeys of the New Life
was a small provision, to be carried by Kaka, for fodder for the
animals expected later in the caravan. No human in the group was
to expect a single penny for his needs. The journey would begin by
going to Belgaum, a town well to the south of Poona in the direction
of Bangalore. Here Baba had decided they would set up a "training
camp" to accustom themselves to the conditions they would have to
meet in the New Life.

On October 15 Baba gave instructions for the following day to those coming with him. They were to wake up at 2:00 a.m., bathe and take tea only at 3:00, and then set out. Originally this was planned by foot, but in fact, much of the trip was made by bus and by train due to the weather, and perhaps because Baba felt it to be more practical. They were not all young.

A very poignant incident occurred at Belgaum, indicative of the life of absolute obedience that Baba was to insist upon thereafter. One of the New Life companions named Daulat Singh was a physician by profession who had lost all his possessions as well as his practice during the partition of India. Now embarked upon the New Life with Baba, he was very aware of the profound problems that the family he had left behind still faced, so his inner being was in turmoil, caught as he was between his devotion to the life of spirit and his worldly involvements. Moreover, his daughter was to be married on the very night that Baba, in his inimitable way, caught Daulat sobbing quietly, all alone, to his best knowledge unobserved by the rest. This was of course a breach of the spirit of a very important condition of the New Life. The result of all this was that Daulat asked Baba for a "two months leave of absence" from the New Life.

This put the cat amongst the pigeons, and the result was that Baba decided to send him back to his "old life." "I am sending you without any fault on your part, and without your having failed me in the least... If you obey and follow one hundred percent certain orders that I will give you, you will be sharing my New Life one hundred percent... The special orders for you are: Until you die, commit no lustful action, even with your wife; never lie, whatever the consequences; for one month every year, wear the kafni (long robe) that I will give you, and during this month live on food gotten by begging."

So Daulat Singh left Baba with heavy heart and rejoined his

family. The rest of the companions were barely able to hold back their tears, which would thereby have become a further breach of the conditions of the New Life. In turn, the conditions Baba had laid out for Daulat Singh proved so upsetting to his family that he finally left them and spent many months wandering and begging for his food. Finally, one day, as these things have a way of happening around the Avatar, Daulat was begging near the house in which Baba was staying for the moment in his New Life travels. Baba asked Eruch who that was outside. Eruch returned with the news that it was Daulat. A meeting with Baba followed at once during which Baba modified considerably the conditions of Daulat's life as laid out in Belgaum, all this in harmony with developments that had occurred meanwhile within the New Life itself. The final result was that Daulat returned to his family and remained devoted to Baba for the rest of his life.[6]

It was during this period in Belgaum that "The Song of the New Life" was composed. The first stanza was dictated to Dr. Ghani by Baba in Urdu, and the rest was composed by Dr. Ghani in Urdu on points stressed by Baba on the New Life. Final corrections on this were made by Baba. He then had Ghani translate it into English, and it was approved by Baba. The Urdu was transliterated into Hindi script, which was then published along with the English version, which follows as taken from the original printing.

---

[6] *Lord Meher*, pp. 3455–3457.

Song of the New Life

of

MEHER BABA AND HIS COMPANIONS

I

Listen to the silent words of Meher Baba;
The life story of all lovers (of God) is based on the
    practice of these words.
If you are serious about living this new life,
Then wholeheartedly renounce this ephemeral existence.

II

We have taken to this life, in which we rely only on God:
In this, our Will (to do or die) is strengthened by the
    oath taken:
We are merrily singing the song of hopelessness:
We are inviting all calamities and difficulties.

III

We neither wail over lost hopes, nor complain about
    (broken) promises;
We neither covet honour, nor shun disgrace;
Backbiting we know not, nor do we fear anyone;
This is now the colour of our New Life.

IV

No confusion in the mind, now, nor any ties left;
Pride, anger, lust and greed we know not.
We have no religions nor care for physical and mental fads.
The Sheikh and the Brahmin–typifying all castes and
    creeds–are now sailing in the same boat.

V

There is no small or great now, for us all;
The questions of disciple, Master or Godhood, no
 longer arise.
Brotherliness or fellow-feeling is the link that exists,
And this contributes to our present enjoyment
 of suffering.

VI

This world or the next, hell or heaven, we no
 longer bother about;
Shaktis and Siddhis, occultism and miracles, we no
 longer think of;
All these false impressions (thoughts) for us have been
 purged from the mind.
What has value and importance for us now, is to live
 in the active present.

VII

Dear ones, take seriously the words of Meher Baba
 when he says,
"Although now, I am on the same level with you all,
Yet all orders from me, good, bad, extraordinary,
You should all carry out immediately, leaving the
 result to God."

VIII

Even if the heavens fall,
Do not let go the hand of Truth.
Let despair and disappointment ravage and destroy the
 garden (of your life),
(You) beautify it once again, by the seedlings of
 contentment and self-sufficiency.

IX

Even if your heart is cut to bits, let there be a smile
    on your lips.
Here I divulge to you a point worth noting.
Hidden in your penniless hands, is a treasure untold,
Your beggarly life will be the envy of kings (of the world).

X

God exists indeed and true are the Prophets;
Every cycle has an Avatar and every moment has a Wali
For us however, it is only hopelessness and helplessness.
How else should I tell you what our New Life is![7]

While there are many statements in this "Song" with which
many students of the spiritual path would warmly agree, there are a
number of others which cause considerable perplexity, and even
consternation. As splendid a scholar and human being as Charles
Purdom, who wrote the first authoritative biography of Meher Baba,
The Perfect Master,[8] as well as the later detailed account *The God-
Man*, apparently could not believe that an error had not been made
in verse VIII. Consequently he rewrote the third line as "Let not
despair and disappointment...."[9] Purdom's version was accepted for
many years as the genuine one. It was only in the 1970s that
research on a new book brought to light the error that Purdom had
inadvertently introduced while thinking that he was correcting one.

It is evident from reading this revolutionary spiritual avowal in
"The Song" that Meher Baba was up to some very new things at that
time. But especially, one should note the occurrence of the word
"companions" again, and also the fact that Purdom's first book is
entitled *The Perfect Master*. On the other hand, his final account of

---

[7] *ibid.*, pp. 3469–3470.
[8] C. B. Purdom, *The Perfect Master* (London: Williams and Norgate, 1937).
[9] C. B. Purdom, *The God-Man*, pp. 178–179.

Baba's life written shortly before Baba dropped the body in 1969 bears the title *The God-Man* (Avatar).

It would have been of great interest to have asked Purdom whether he made this change because he concluded late in life that Baba had been the Avatar (God-Man) all along; but had Purdom only tumbled to this fact in his later years? Or whether, by chance, Purdom had regarded Baba as functioning in his earlier life as a Perfect Master, but in his later life as the Avatar? No doubt this would have been a very vigorous conversation. Purdom was a highly intelligent and a very brave man.

There are some very intriguing challenges posed in the "Song." The first line speaks of listening to "the silent words" of Meher Baba. This however is not a great puzzle. It is no difficult task for the pilgrim on the spiritual path to listen to silent words. If he has truly embarked on the Path, he has had to practice many times the exercise of stilling his busy mind and the cacophony of his impulses to allow the far more quiet voice of his heart express itself.

Then move on to "renounce this ephemeral existence." This call has also been written large in the mystic literature of both East and West for many centuries. Baba has pointed out that the true significance of Jesus' instruction to the disciples to "leave all and follow me" is really a very broad injunction to the inner man. Jesus' command was not centered on giving up the physical world, possessions and responsibilities. More important, and the heart of the command, was to cut the root force of the compulsions and desires of one's attachments. This is the truly important act.

If this can be done, it is of very little importance whether or not one cuts the physical ties as well. They may be kept or they may be discarded, depending upon the situation. The surprising fact is that in the vast number of actual cases arising during the ministration of Meher Baba, it usually meant a devotee's striving to remove the desires. Rarely was it extended as well to the physical domain.

"We have taken to this life, in which we rely only on God." This is a classic spiritual goal for the adept. The only thing unusual in this instance is that Baba insisted that it be real, that the companions should absolutely not rely on him. In their past experience, it had always been Baba who was the resource for the solution of their problems. Now he was to be that pillar no longer. Baba clearly meant it. And during the New Life, he showed constantly that this was a real principle by which they must live, and not a daydream.

One of the few exceptions to this command occurred during the first winter, when one of the old life disciples of Baba felt impelled to buy and transport carts of winter clothing and provisions, although such action was absolutely forbidden by the rules laid down by Baba before his departure. When winter was about to set in, however, the carts arrived by a miracle of geographic intuition. Baba raised no legal proceedings against the timid commander of the little caravan. Rules are rules, and normally their slightest infraction resulted in a thunderstorm. On another occasion, though, the rule might be broken, and it seemed as if the reason was understood by all.

The last two lines of verse II of the "Song" are among the most difficult. "We are merrily singing the song of hopelessness: We are inviting all calamities and difficulties." No doubt it is a Yankee inheritance in America based on strains of early Protestant rebellion which shun the word "hopelessness" as a moral bankruptcy. And as for *inviting* calamity, this is certainly the characteristic of the complete pessimist who has no faith either in life or in himself.

And why, one asks, should one even attempt to recover some value from these words as Baba has set them out in the "Song"? Certainly, one reason could be that after living in the shade of this man for many years, when he says something, even if it contradicts an ancient indoctrination, the devotee has learned to put the racing events of life momentarily into neutral and await further developments.

Several years ago a small group took on the project of reflecting deeply on "The Song of the New Life," and this problem of "hopelessness" was quickly determined to be one of the subjects most resistant to being cracked. It took quite an effort on the part of the group during several sessions, but finally the idea began to dawn that the word "hopeless" has to be considered in relation to its antonym, "hopeful."

Even this move does not seem to simplify nor clarify the problem very much. Yet, with a bit of intuition, one sees that hope is closely related to desires, which are sanskaras. It is, in fact, a very rare hope that does not have an immense amount of desire underlying it. It is very different to work for a goal because it is necessary, as contrasted with working for it because one desires it. Here is apparently the crux of the problem, as well as the kernel of the spiritual truth to be uncovered.

In the next line Baba may well be accused of overdoing it a bit in using the word "inviting" in relation to opening the door to calamities and difficulties. But the same London group's nimble minds inevitably turned up an obvious possibility. Usually we try in every manner to avoid and prevent calamity. Much of the current-day obsession with astrology is for just that purpose.

There is a very ancient part of the principle of karma that says that the past is engraved into the universal record, and that inevitably, a balancing action must be performed for each original happening. If this is indeed true, then what one regards as calamity may well finally be that necessary balancing complement. By extension, many other "balancing incidents" are the unexpected arrivals of good fortune. If the one is to be, then the counterpart will also inevitably occur. In such case, karma will have its way, and sooner or later, despite all of one's cleverness, one will have to face the negative in order to balance the already recorded positive, or the pain in order to balance what one day in the past one had inflicted on another. The story is very long and often very complex.

But what about "inviting"? This is what seems a bit too much.

Think about this possibility: if one faces up to the inevitable, and does not try to resist it, may it be that when it comes, one is psychologically better equipped to deal with it, and the results arrive and depart more easily? Psychologically this is largely true. Of course, one can think of some situations in life one would far prefer to postpone as long as possible, but this is because one is still very human. It is worth the try to see what happens when one does not resist, but tries simply and purely to do one's best at each turn of the screw. Is it possible that a big knot finally works out much faster and with less total pain in this manner? This seems to be the heart of what Meher Baba's "Song" is dealing with in this remarkable line.

Skipping over several very tantalizing phrases we arrive at the word "backbiting." Of all the things Baba brought up repeatedly, this and "not worrying" were undoubtedly two of his favorites. To dive at once to the roots of this key word, one should be advised that Baba repeated often that fundamental Reality is God, and one of the basic characteristics of God is indivisibility. And secondly, He is infinite, which automatically means that everything and everyone is really finally God also.

So, criticism? Now it is easy to understand why he warned against it constantly. First of all, to criticize someone else, one has to set oneself apart, thus emphasizing one's separation as well as one's difference from the other person. This results in denying two fundamental principles of Reality, and this is serious. One would be bad enough, but negating two surely has to bring serious consequences. In fact it does. Among other things, it ruins life. Instead of triumph, it produces a grim acid that eats determinedly at the base of happiness.

Verses V and VI are memorable, because if taken seriously, they toss into the wastebasket many of the things that one normally looks forward to in established religions. Certainly such words as Master, God-hood, hell, heaven and miracles are all written large into the fabric of conventional religions everywhere. Yet Baba is stating bluntly that these are all based on false impressions that have now been jettisoned. And why?

Before abandoning these two verses as a wayward whim on Meher Baba's part, note especially in V the comment that "brotherliness or fellow feeling is the link that exists...." Here are words that seem again and again to epitomize the essence of the New Life. It was in a statement made by Baba in 1932, quoted earlier, where the word "link" was used in a key statement referring to Baba's activity in the boys' school. It will be seen again, and even more strongly highlighted, in his "Last Message on the Alphabet Board" given out in the 1950s, well after the end of the New Life.

Should one be reminded now that Mohammed also used the term "companion" to designate those who had followed him from the earliest years, through all the crises of the establishment of God's message? Is there now coming into significant importance a deeper and even more vital role for this concept of the reality of inner connections between human beings and with the Avatar in the now just dawning era of the New Humanity?

Now we continue on to the troublesome verse VIII. Here is where Purdom felt justified in righting an "obvious mis-interpretation" of what Baba had said:

"Let despair and disappointment ravage and destroy the garden (of your life).
You beautify it once again, by the seedlings of contentment and self-sufficiency."

If you have built a dream castle of desire somewhere into your life, and suddenly it is attacked and threatened with destruction, *stop*! Stop a moment before you race to protect it. *Reflect. Withdraw.* Refuse for a moment to spring into action. Then turn inside. Ask yourself honestly, "What does this really mean to me? Is it necessary? Is it something I *have* to have? And if I have to have it, how did this come about? And *why* is it threatened just now with destruction? Is this evil? Can it be that this is inevitable?" This is the conversation within oneself which is implied by Baba's verse.

All these things may be true, and if they are true, then there is no real problem in re-establishing the garden again in the next moments after it has been destroyed. Perhaps its new beauty will outshine the old form and harmony that were lost.

As great a being as Meher Baba does not introduce a thought like this without there being a compelling reason for its being set out in words. And so, *reflect*. Ask a number of honest questions on origin and value. Above all, don't spring at once to the attack and try to protect the garden. Such internal discipline can help greatly on the path by which one returns to the Truth.

Verse X is a reaffirmation first of all of the reality of God and His representation in Creation. "Don't despair, ever. In some form I am always there." "But for you and me," Baba seems to continue his suggestion to us, "let us try to be of help on the road to the Truth by giving up the childish toys of wanting this and wanting that, even clothing them often in words that seek to give them virtue, whereas in fact they are weaknesses. We can dispense with them. It is not impossible, and after the first brave motion, it is not even painful."

Before leaving the "Song," let us recall the manner in which Baba discounts totally the terms disciple, master and Godhood. This seems truly incredible. It appears to fly in the face of all accepted concepts of what is spiritual reality and the relationships considered essential to win gradually to the realization of the Truth. But may these startling words be an anticipation of the future relationship between the ones who already know, and those who do not know but are searching honestly? It is amply apparent already that the convents and monasteries of the Occident are being transformed rapidly. It is not a simple question of degeneration and disappearance. On the contrary, one notes even more sincere seekers now than in the early years of the century. The seekers are present, and they are very diligent. At times, almost too much so.

In the Far East, the traditional home of the mystic circle with its guru-chela relationship, the old forms of the mystic circle would also seem to be under some pressure of transformation. At least, their transplants into the Occident are certainly going through a considerable change, or should one say "degeneration," as money enters increasingly into the picture.

During the New Life Baba insisted on a relationship of companionship. This was deliberate and appears to be important for the future. Here Baba does not seem to have been concentrating on breaking down sanskaric habit patterns, but deliberately setting up an archetypal form that he meant to endure for many centuries.

Baba also used on occasion the term "elder brother" in relation to himself. This too does not appear to have been by accident, nor does he seem on the other hand to have been establishing a sacrosanct area forbidden for use in the future. To the contrary, he appears to suggest that there is to be another spiritually important concept of relationship in addition to companionship, which is that occupied by the elder brother and the elder sister.

I respected my elder brother enormously. He was worthy of respect. I listened carefully to what he had to say. After I was about sixteen, when we had our final blow off of elder brother trying to organize younger brother's life, he never again made the mistake of trying to show me that he knew, and that I should simply follow his example. I think that is what Baba is suggesting to us here as he puts into the record of the New Life the term "elder brother." It is a type of relationship that is particularly adapted to the Occident, with our basic mistrust of imposed authority in which we have no voice in decisions.

As one reflects on the changing forms of both the manner and mechanisms employed now in the search for Truth, and how they may have been affected by the explosion of technology in this century, one inevitably concludes that it had to be the Avatar who planned the basic outlines of the technological revolution. Also, it has to be the Avatar who conceives how this new base for the mechanics of civilization can be trued with a method of searching for Truth in such a way that there will not be major friction between the two. This seems to be one of the major challenges to ongoing mysticism for some time in the future. This is certainly part of what the New Life as lived by Meher Baba and his close companions was about. In fact, during recent years the tender shoots of a new form of spiritual plant have begun to appear which promises to be capable of supporting and nourishing the search for the One into the indefinite future, while being in major part compatible with a life dependent on complex technology.

The "Song of the New Life" is a very powerful and challenging document, but it is time to move on into the substance of what Baba actually lived with the twenty persons who set out with him in October 1949. Throughout the New Life Baba insisted as a first principle that no one, wherever the group might go, should know his true identity, or even that he was a spiritual teacher. He was, if necessary, simply the "elder brother." As for sustenance, the essentials for each day was to be obtained by begging, and the master beggar was Eruch Jessawala.

The stay at Belgaum lasted only until November 12, but during that time the usual bouts of temper and misunderstandings cropped up. Eventually Baba asked each companion to come for the last time for a private interview, including Adi Irani, who had expressed himself as doubting just what Baba was up to. All came and reaffirmed their intent to continue, including Adi. The party left Belgaum by rail and, traveling through Poona, Bombay and

Moghalsarai, arrived early the morning of the 15th in Benares, where the begging for the necessaries began.

Baba's authority on all things and in relation to all beings in Creation now began to unfold, to the utter amazement of his Companions. For instance, Baba would send a couple of them to beg, of all things, for free train tickets for the entire group. Of these, four were to be in First Class. Those doing the begging were not allowed to accept money, but the benefactors themselves must purchase the tickets. As a further condition, the donor must not try to know the identity of the one for whom the tickets were being obtained, with Baba being referred to only as "our elder brother."

In another remarkable situation, the companions were required to beg for free accommodations "for a group of 20." The site should be a secluded property, with separate buildings to be available for men and women. Further, food for one month was to be provided at no charge, and again the condition was applied that the donor must never try to know the identity of nor try to see the "elder brother" in whose name these strange gifts were to be made.

All this actually came to pass in Benares.

Then, again, the planned stay was shortened, and they left on December 1 for Sarnath–closely associated with the life of Buddha.

In Sarnath the principal event was the saying of a prayer in a subterranean passage in some ruins, where Baba and all the mandali remained almost naked despite the bitter cold. The prayer was the following: "God, give me strength to follow the conditions hundred percent. God, help me to speak the truth and not to tell a lie under any circumstances. God, help me to control anger, and to keep away from lusty and greedy desires. God, help me to be just, fair, honest and kind towards my companions and towards those who come into contact with me."[10]

---

[10] Swami Satya Prakash Udaseen, *The New Life of Avatar Meher Baba and His Companions* (Hyderabad: The Meher Vihar Trust, 1967).

After several small stops in the near vicinity, they left Sarnath on January 1, 1950, for Dehra Dun, which was to become especially loved by Baba. (To this day, Dehra Dun is the home of a marvelous group of devotees who literally give off a fragrance of love.) In Dehra Dun there was a fundamental splitting of the group following Baba. Four chose to return to their homes and follow the conditions of the New Life there, while the remaining men except for Dr. Donkin, Gustadji and Kaka continued in essence the original program. Donkin intended to work as a doctor, and Gustadji, being too old and ill to continue, was to remain with Donkin but observing the rules of the New Life.

It was during this time that Baba stayed in Motichur not far from Dehra Dun and made several visits to Rishikesh, where he contacted and bowed down to many of the sadhus, saints and mahatmas living primitively in the surroundings. It was the occasion of the Kumbha Mehla, when the normal population is swelled by hundreds of thousands of pilgrims. On various occasions here Baba bowed down to hundreds, and finally thousands, of these devotees of the Spiritual Path.

Later, all of the companions left for the specific purpose of setting up a business in Delhi. In late May they were ordered back by Baba, and Donkin also gave up his medical practice. Again there was a great deal of discussion and changing of various of the rules for the New Life. Although no special mention was made of it, the term for those following Baba on the travels was changed from "companions" to "servant-companions." Something subtle had happened. In reading the detailed record of the events, it is not difficult to divine that Baba was not satisfied with the support he was being given. But there was never anything specific raised by Baba nor a crisis precipitated to pin things down.

It was a period of change, and great detail was gone into in working out specific rules of conduct. The entire record is available in *The New Life of Avatar Meher Baba and His Companions*, which was compiled from all available sources at the time.

Before continuing with details from the latter part of the wanderings of the group of companions with Baba in the new life, let us return to certain specifics of conduct laid out by Baba on March 3, 1950.

"Although the New Life has emerged from me, I am not at all bound by it. Plans I, II and III of the New Life with their four phases of labor, begging, gypsy and langoti life, will function as long as I am physically alive.[11] But this New Life is endless, and even after my physical death will be kept alive by those, who live the life of complete renunciation of falsehood, lies, hatred, anger, greed and lust; and who to accomplish all this, do no lustful actions, do no harm to anyone, do no backbiting, do not seek material possessions, or power, who accept no homage, neither covet honor nor shun disgrace, and fear no one and nothing; by those who rely wholly and solely on God, and who love God purely for the sake of loving, who believe in the lovers of God and in the reality of Manifestation, and yet do not expect any spiritual or material reward, who do not let go the hand of Truth, and who, without being upset by calamities, bravely and wholeheartedly face all hardships with 100% cheerfulness, and give no importance to caste, creed and religious ceremonies.

"This New Life will live by itself eternally, even if there is no one to live it."[12]

These terms laid out by Meher Baba are very difficult to contemplate even as ideals. To have Baba there in person

---

[11] Some years later as I was visiting Meherazad, one day Bhau stopped me and asked me to sit down. Mentioning his awareness of my fascination with the New Life, he offered to tell me of a key detail Baba had described later to him. It was that Baba and the mandali had lived through the begging, gypsy and langoti (the simple loin cloth) aspects of the New Life for all times, and it was now the daily labor component that would be the main characteristic of the New Life thenceforward.

[12] *The New Life of Avatar Meher Baba*, p. 66.

supervising intimately all actions every day and calling the penalties, had all the makings of an Olympic endurance contest in which only those of superhuman strength and resolve could cross the finish line. Add to this the background of no fixed place of abode, begging for the necessaries, being exposed to the elements, no contact with family or friends, no backlog of anything to guarantee against emergencies. Not easy. And so the endurance feat continued month after month, and all the while the site for living changed frequently. Constantly, Baba policed minutely the performance of the mandali in relation to the conditions agreed upon. On occasion he found fault with his own actions. In such case he would ask one of the mandali to slap him or hit him, and it had to be hard. It was not play-acting or make-believe fantasy. It was dead serious.

Years later, Eruch was prompted by some kind impulse to offer to recount a continuous history of the New Life, with Mehera, Mani and Meheru participating, and to allow this to be tape recorded.[13] For me this was a dream come true, as from my first contacts with Baba, the New Life drew me as a magnet. I felt instinctively that this was one of the great events in Baba's ministry.

As Eruch's story of the New Life drew to an end, he asked if there were questions or clarifications I wanted to ask. My spontaneous outburst was: How had it been possible to endure so much hardship and crisis for so long a period of time? Eruch looked at me in complete amazement.

"No, Don, then I have failed completely to give you the true feeling of being with Baba in the New Life. Hardships there were. It was not easy. But if you only knew the sensation of being in close companionship with the Avatar, you would know that all those things disappeared, and one was left with the sense of complete freedom and the wonder of just being with him. To imagine the

---

[13] Eruch, Mehera, Mani and Meheru, *Tales from the New Life* (Berkeley: The Beguine Library, Second Printing, 1979).

feeling of arising early in the morning, and to go out through the fields and to smell the smoke beginning to rise from the fires as the natives began cooking their breakfast. Because I was the one usually who had to do the begging. And to run through the fields so early in the morning with that scent in my nostrils and find the one hut that would have the freshly baked bread for the Avatar. I tell you, Don, there was never anything like it."

As I listened to Eruch and savored the sense of his remembered flight through the early morning mists and smoke, I too was caught up into a magic participation in the special love that one finds in the company of the One.

In *Tales from the New Life*, Eruch and the women mandali recount experiences of great human interest. One especially that Eruch recounted merits retelling here, being typical of the manner in which Baba continued even during the New Life to occupy himself with those who merited direct attention.

"I'll cite one or two examples of our search for truly needy ones.... It was because of that money Baba had collected when he stepped out of the New Life for one day that we could do this work—otherwise it would never have been done."

They were in Madras and Baba was thirsty. The best way to satisfy one's thirst was to drink fresh coconut milk. Eruch bought a coconut, and Baba drank the milk from it. During the negotiations, Baba overheard a story of a very wealthy man who had lost all his money. Baba appeared intrigued and asked Eruch to find out the name of the man and where he lived. It turned out that he now lived in a spot about 150 kilometers from where they were at the moment, but Baba insisted they go to the remote village. They arrived around dusk.

Eruch continues the story: "It was the Divali holiday, the Festival of Lights. As it was late I told Baba to rest on the station platform. I didn't like the idea of his going out in that town, so he rested with the other companions while I went alone and tried to locate the address."

After overcoming some small problems, Eruch continues the story. "It was a very poor locality, very poor indeed, but in spite of the poverty I saw in the street that there were lights lit for the Divali celebration. As it was the Festival of Lights, all were to have lights that night in their houses. Even a lamp is all right if one is very, very poor. But there was one house that had not even a single lamp placed outside, no light whatsoever. The child (from the village who was guiding him) pointed it out from a distance, saluted me and returned.

"I approached the door. It was open and through it I could see just a single room. I knocked at the door. A single oil lamp was burning dimly inside a room with no furniture whatsoever, but which contained a life-size statue of Lord Krishna. Before it was a young lady, worshipping Krishna.... I knocked at the door, and the young woman turned and looked at me. She came towards me and said, 'What do you want?' She spoke very good English. I said, 'I am sent by my elder brother. He is waiting at the station, and he would like to meet this gentleman. Is he here?' " Eruch said, giving the name.

"She said, 'Yes, he is here.' She invited me inside the room. I went in, and it was dark except for that tiny flickering lamp. I could barely see a man lying on the floor. On one side of the room I made out a lady, also sick." Eruch comforted her and explained that his elder brother was at the railway station, and had come from Bombay, as he had some work to do with the father. He asked to bring Baba within an hour's time. The young woman agreed and Eruch departed.

"I went straight to Baba and brought him back in a tonga. On our way I told Baba the whole story, and he really was very happy. Within an hour's time we were at the house." Eruch, resourceful as always, had all the paraphernalia Baba demanded for the occasion:

a bucket, water to wash the feet of the needy person, and a towel with which Baba would dry his feet. With all this in hand, they went inside the house. "Both parents were so sick that they couldn't acknowledge the visitor. Baba stooped down and gestured that I should start pouring water on one foot and then another... Then Baba sat down and washed his feet, after which we removed the basin and threw the water out... After the feet were dried by Baba, the towel was handed over to the lady, and Baba bent down further and put his forehead on the feet of the sick. Then he offered a large sum of money in an envelope to the man. He couldn't even move, so it was placed on his chest, under his hand.

"The daughter was told to take care of the sum that was placed there, and I said to her for Baba as was customary, 'Please accept this amount as a gift from God and oblige us...'

"We left the house, but before we could step outside the daughter started wailing and fell at the feet of Lord Krishna. In a very glowing voice she said, 'Oh, Lord, I never knew that you were so compassionate, so kind and merciful. No sooner do I implore you for help than within a few minutes you send the help.' "

One year after setting out on the New Life, on October 16, 1950, Meher Baba invited both the New Life and the Old Life disciples to a meeting at Mahabaleshwar. A total of about two hundred attended. Baba told them that he would make a collection during the meeting for his work among the masts and the poor. He also told them that his having stepped out of the New Life into the Old would last for only four hours. Then he asked God's forgiveness for not having been able to live the New Life as he had wanted. Following this, Baba gave the New Life companions the opportunity to opt out of their vow. Ten men elected to continue the New Life with Baba, the others choosing or being ordered by Baba for various reasons to go back into the Old Life.

On October 21 Baba again left for the continuation of the New

Life with Eruch, Gustadji, Baidul and Pendu. These four men were to be the ones to keep Baba company in the final part of the itinerary that succeeded the New Life and concluded these extraordinary wanderings of Meher Baba. At the end of this further journey Baba declared that the principal work to be achieved in the New Life had now been completed. Once more he called for a meeting in Hyderabad on the following June 21, 1951, for the Old Life and New Life disciples. On the 28 of June he gave out a declaration that he would take the step of Annihilation (of the mind) on the 16 of October, which apparently he expected to complete by the 16 of February of 1952. There are detailed circulars describing the annihilation of the mind that Baba intended to effect in this period. It is also called the Manonash period.

One should not jump to the conclusion that mental and intellectual processes were intended to be eliminated at that time. There is a great confusion between two "problems of the mind." It is true that Baba points out constantly that the mind cannot grasp God and spiritual truth. But he also clarifies in detail that the mental body is the seat of storage for the sanskaras and all the recordings of the activities of the individual drop-soul from the time of its imagined separation from the One. In this sense the "problem of the mind" is truly enormous. But usually when Baba is talking about the problem of the mind he is referring specifically to the blockage from Reality that the stored sanskaras bring about, even after consciousness is completely developed in the last animal incarnation.

On about December 24 Baba, among a number of other statements and actions, included the following words: "To try to understand with the mind that which the mind can never understand is futile; and to try to express by sounds or language and in form of words the transcendent state of the soul is even more futile. All that can be said, and has been said, and will be said, by those who live and experience the state, is that when the false self is lost, the Real Self is found; that the birth of the Real can follow only the death of the false; and that dying to ourselves–the true death which ends all dying–is the only way to perpetual life. This means that when the mind with its desires, cravings and longings is completely consumed by the fire of Divine Love, then the infinite, indestructible, indivisible, eternal Self is manifested. This is *manonash*, the annihilation of the false, limited, miserable, ignorant, destructible 'I,' to be replaced by the real 'I,' the eternal possessor of Infinite Knowledge, Love, Power, Peace, Bliss and Glory, in its unchangeable existence."[14]

At the time of this writing, I have not yet come across an explanation of what Baba was doing in this Manonash period that seems whole and satisfying. Later in this recounting of Baba's life we will consider at some length a very important statement he made about the gift to humanity in this avataric manifestation of broad powers of intuition. This has important implications in relation to the function of the mental and logical processes, but at the same time, Baba was very careful to clarify that mind and mental processes would not be wiped out, but only placed into a secondary role behind the intuitive faculties. Therefore one cannot jump to the conclusion that in the Manonash phase just following the main New Life period, Baba was truly annihilating mind. The mind does go on. It still plays an important role. However, as Baba's words forecast, one now sees a very much greater use of intuition than in the past. Where it will go from the present stage will be a fascinating development to follow in the next several centuries.

There is still one further hurdle to cross in the continental-divide chapter of Baba's life. It is the Fiery Free Life. He announced that going to the West in April, he would start the "Complicated Free Life" on March 21, this to be followed by the "Full Free Life" on July

[11] Swami Satya Prakash Udaseen, *The Life Circulars of Avatar Meher Baba* (Hyderabad: The Meher Vihar Trust, 1968).

10, and the "Fiery Free Life" on November 15. None of these latter phases was ever very clear to those not in the immediate company of Baba, and perhaps not to those near him either. In any case, these successive phases in 1952 were lost to sight by almost all in the excitement of Baba's first trip to the West in many years, and then in the heart-rending events surrounding the automobile accident during the summer. Everyone was concentrating so much on Baba's physical state, as well as that of other close ones, that such secondary matters as the destruction of the mind and various kinds of fiery and free life were noted and promptly forgotten by almost everyone. It is not evident to this day that especially the fiery free life has been seriously taken up and reconsidered by anyone. But have a care. I for one can testify that I have never yet known Baba to put something into motion which has not continued in some form, and then begun to reveal one day that it has a significant purpose.

When I asked Eruch one day what he made of the Manonash and Fiery Free Life Periods, he replied that Baba had said that in the Fiery Free phase he would set the hearts of his lovers on fire. Then Eruch added somewhat playfully, "And what could have been more insane and mindless than the start of the Manonash phase, in Hyderabad, when the car I was loading with the carved symbols of the great religions slipped its brakes and began careening down through the fields, with me unable to catch up with it. And then it stopped by itself in the middle of the field, and when I caught up, I found none of the precious sculptures had even been damaged."

6. PERFECTION

In previous chapters I referred to the New Life period of Meher Baba's sojourn on earth as the "continental divide" in his activities as a great spiritual figure. It is now the moment to take these words out into full daylight and examine carefully what might be meant by such a term.

Have you ever had to stay in a hospital in order to have constantly available the specialized treatment that your particular condition might need from one minute to the next? This is probably the situation closest to the function fulfilled by a Perfect Master. I believe he is the specialist in the spiritual world, charged among other things with the care of the top priority patient: the man or woman who is in the final stages of the search for the Truth, which is God.

Reading the foregoing paragraph, which is meant to give an important keynote to Perfection, you may well think that the writer has now gone beyond the bounds of both reason and legitimate speculation. Perhaps so. To establish the setting for what I am about to embark upon, let me describe for a moment a bit more of my own personal background. I think in important situations, each of us must rest within the natural boundaries of his or her formation. Mine was in the sciences, with a liberal admixture as well of the arts. But science predominated, and I will not try to put on clothing which is not my normal attire while writing on such an important subject as this chapter must handle. I think it is one of the most challenging complexes one can attempt to understand. While I do not have the qualifications of a Hafiz to spin appropriate phrases that befit a poem of great love, still, I will do my best to find adequate expression for this compelling subject.

Last evening I was sitting alone at the table in the kitchen enjoying some choice morsels of the black-foot Serrano ham Beatriz had brought back from Spain, when suddenly the final keys to a major insight into the different aspects of Perfection hit me. It was the puzzle of the often contrasting actions of the Perfect Master and the Avatar, and how such individuals differ in the techniques each uses within his respective responsibilities. The crux of the puzzle arises from the fact that both Avatar and Perfect Master are identical in final achievement, which is oneness within God, as well as in all of the qualifications and attributes available to them for their mission in Creation. This being the case, why should it be that often they do not use the same methods nor even have similar personal characteristics?

This is one of the most fascinating and also perplexing "contradictions" I have ever encountered, and it has puzzled me greatly for decades. To feel that suddenly, while doing something as mundane as eating black-foot ham, a key arrives–this is an important moment in one's life.

Let me put down as simply as I can what came to my mind. The base for everything I felt I saw was the statement by Meher Baba that from the first human incarnation, the one and only problem which still confronts the individual drop-soul is the dissipation of the sanskaras formed in the long development of individualized consciousness which has been completed before the first human incarnation. Having accepted that, then the next important consideration is whether the dispersal of the sanskaras is accomplished within the limitations of Creation, and subject to its laws and restrictions. If the role of the sanskaras is as Baba described it, and I now have no reservation on that score, and if their elimination does not involve miracles that evade the normal laws of functioning within Creation, which Meher Baba has also affirmed, then whoever is to handle these problems must work within the limitations of time and space.

The two great categories of doctor who tend to those human individuals who are in the final stages of involution are the Perfect Master and the Avatar. And they both work preponderantly within the limitations of time and space that were set down in the beginning of the creation of the universe.

The Perfect Master works within a very limited time-span—at most, of several decades. The Avatar works within an enormously longer time gambit, but he too must reckon finally with the limiting factor of time, and devise his techniques accordingly.

The Perfect Master is constrained to do his job relatively quickly, so he uses methods that demand minute by minute attention. Also, and very important, he must be near at hand for the stanching of the wounds that are almost inevitable in radical surgery. He has to be available to apply bandages to whatever wounds his treatment may have opened up. The Avatar, on the other hand, is often more concerned with techniques of spiritual medicine applicable to the mental body that are not as drastic in their effects, and more long-term in their application. Also, they are not likely to create wounds requiring immediate attention.

The relationship of the seeker to the Perfect Master has to have a very large component of deep trust and willingness to undergo immediate and acute pain. This is why I believe the Perfect Master makes little attempt to be appealing and bewitching. He is often even repugnant in his physical appearance. Witness the tales from the Orient of great masters who almost never bathed, dressed in rags or even in nothing. And yet, there are always many people who recognize instinctively that these are great doctors administering to the true travelers on the path to Truth. One could say very aptly that there is no time to waste in waltzes of courting and indecision. It has to be a relationship born of immediate recognition of paramount value. If not, there might not be the time to do the necessary.

Of the Perfect Masters of Meher Baba's day, the only one who would have been acceptable at a dinner party governed by protocol would have been Narayan Maharaj. He had all the necessary manners and clothing. The other Perfect Ones were either barely acceptable or even downright repulsive. Babajan dressed in barely civilized fashion, and there was a wild gleam in her eyes shining out from her photographs that would have put off the conventional individual. The spiritual path is not for the conformist. It is for the one who is desperate and has abandoned all falsity of approach. The exterior of the Perfect Master is almost sure to guarantee that someone does not slip in who will spend the next several years arguing with himself about inconsequentials.

For the Perfect Master there is as already noted a serious time constraint. In fact we have not yet broached just how grave this limitation is. It is very simple. It is that the Perfect Master in a very real sense is living on borrowed time. Once a human being achieves oneness with God, or God-realization as it is also known, he normally drops his body at once, or after a very brief time. There are, however, a certain percentage of perfected individuals who deliberately elect to remain for some years within Creation to help sincere seekers of the Truth. The length of time they remain is short at best, and in that interval they must do the necessary to bring a very limited number of individuals to that impossible chasm and help them leap across it to Oneness. Then, after that rather brief delay within

Creation, the Perfect Master drops his body definitively and is merged into eternity within God. He does not reincarnate. He does not continue to carry on terrestrial duties that he had started and not finished.

To speak, therefore, of being the reincarnation of such and such a Perfect Master is to speak in ignorance. The ancient traditions are clear and unanimous on this point. The only Perfect One who does reincarnate is the Avatar, and another human being never reincarnates as the Avatar. He is himself, and always the one and same self.

There is at present a great deal of romanticism on this score. In one instance many seekers speak of an advanced guru as being the reincarnation of a Master who is commonly known in India to have been a Perfect Master. It is sad that we should risk being misled by individuals who claim knowledge of and relationship with stages of spiritual development that they have not even dimly approached in their own right. One wonders inevitably about the nature of the master who allows such adventures on the part of his followers. But enough of that. A real Master can put up with some quite incredible performances for the sake of a sincere seeker.

As the Perfect Master knows the constraints of time within which he must operate, he wastes none of that precious commodity. The destruction of our beloved habit patterns can be very painful. We can hemorrhage badly in the event, and then the Perfect One must be on hand to place the bandage to stop the flow of blood. You and I do not know the science of all this, and we should not pretend to. Also, we should not criticize. Our function is to wish the voyager well and try to help if we can, even for one moment. It might be that our own gift of grace will be received one day as a consequence of having given this small helping hand.

All that I have read and heard from those who lived the often dramatic and painful events of life with Meher Baba in his early life bears all the earmarks of someone mounting serious attacks against the sanskaric patterns of those around him, and being immediately on hand to bandage over the serious wounds if they developed. Often this emergency aid was nothing more than a marvelous sense of humor. I have seen how it works. But why Meher Baba took on himself this rather lengthy responsibility to function as a Perfect One in residence I do not know. I am not aware of a similar period in the lives of Mohammed or Jesus Christ, but this may be because of lack of resources or clarity on my part.

It may be quite simply that during the early twentieth century the needs of humanity during the switch-over of the ages was so great that Baba had to do double duty. I also wonder if it may not have been the time to bring up a living situation that would call to our attention the relationship as well as the contrasts in functioning of the Perfect Master and the Avatar. To observe both examples in the life of one and the same individual was almost bound to strike a number of people as singular and important.

If the Perfect Master is the doctor on duty to handle important priority emergencies, and to be on-the-spot available to administer first-aid, then how does the Avatar function in contrast?

Before addressing this highly interesting question, let us pause for one more look at the historical Meher Baba and the consistencey or inconsistency of his actions before and after the "continental divide" we have chosen to highlight. Also, let us be completely honest. There **are** stories of Baba giving very rough treatment to close mandali even after the New Life. The question of technique **did** remain fluid, but then there is no doubt in my mind that the New Life marked an important watershed in Baba's ministry.

It is right here that I have been sitting and puzzling for some years. From my first meeting with Meher Baba, it was evident that he was not following the same procedures with me that he had followed, from all that I knew, with many

others in the past. I counted as personal friends a number of
those closest to Baba during the period of 1920 to 1952, the
year I met him face to face. There were many opportunities
for them to relate stories to me of their relationship with Baba
in those early days. In fact, to them, those days had not
terminated. For some reason they continued to expect the
same type of severe handling they had received over so many
years. And yet, in all the times I was in India with Baba and
various of those close to him, I never witnessed the sort of
harsh and arbitrary corrections that had abounded in earlier
days. Did Baba just hide them from me? I do not think so, as
these friends from the earlier days never seemed to have the
slightest hesitation to tell me any episode that had happened
with the Master.

And myself? What exactly was my record of correction
and harsh imposition of obedience with Baba?

In all the conversations we had over some 16 years, plus
seven years of correspondence before the first meeting, there
were exactly two suggestions that Baba made to me, and one
promise he asked me to make to him. The promise, which was
the closest he came to a command, was that if a certain
relationship should finally begin to undermine my health, I
would cut it off.

In fact, the same statistic applies to my relationship with
my Sufi Murshida, Rabia Martin. She never demanded
anything of me, nor laid down any ruling, either arbitrary or
rational. She outlined always the course of wise action for a
searcher on the Path, but the one really critical matter that
came up was the two weeks she gave us to decide if we would
follow her under Meher Baba's spiritual guidance.

One obvious question must be raised. Was I for some
reason such a favorite of the Murshida and the Avatar that
they could never bring themselves to lay down the law to me?

I had to ask myself that very question, seriously, and my answer finally was a curious one. I concluded that they had shown me favoritism in several instances, but what I interpreted as favoritism, I suspected, was simply that for some reason I was an early guinea pig for changes that were being made in the mechanism for the search for Truth in the new Avataric Age.

But let us go back now to the methods used by the Avatar for eliminating sanskaras. After long observation it appears quite evident to me that his method is often to arrange our daily lives in a fashion that brings up clearly and poignantly the sanskara that is to be put on the chopping block. The course of events in the universe is infinitely variable in its potential. The one thing that is not variable is the actual structure of individual karma. That is as fixed by natural law as the effects of gravity. Even the Avatar does not wave the wand and disperse or basically modify it.[1] His job for the ones he selects to be directly responsible for in a given lifetime often consists in arranging their lives so that the necessary sanskaric patterns are revealed clearly to the conscious mind. Then the individual can enlist all his forces and his trust in and great love for the Avatar to deal with the sanskara.

Many people tend to regard the events of daily life as being the outcome of the Avatar constructing and controlling their lives. This I am convinced is a serious misreading of what is going on. He is not here to redo and to change. He is here to facilitate the unwinding and unknotting of the snarls that have been produced during the development of the consciousness of each drop-soul. None of this has he fabricated, nor does he fabricate the circumstances within which we perceive the problems that must be resolved. His action is one of arranging meaningful scenarios within which we can clearly

---

[1] *God Speaks,* p. 269: "The *Avatar* never takes on the *karma* of individuals...."

perceive the nature of the problems that exist within ourselves. All this is entirely within and in harmony with the workings of karmic law.

Although we touched on it earlier, I would like to go back now to inspect together again the exact path that is taken in the formation of each iota of consciousness.

Consciousness is produced by two or more separate (seemingly) centers, or contrasting facets, coming into close relationship with each other. It is like two human beings looking at each other and commenting on the length of each other's nose. A tiny surge of nose-consciousness is produced. But at the same instant, there is a record made as it were in the sensitive being of God within the substance of God's imagined Creation, and this record has two singular properties. It has a tendency to repeat itself in similar circumstances in the future—a primitive habit, in other words. And in our example it also causes the tiny iota of consciousness just produced to focus on noses as *the reality*.

Strange, no? If we can trust the mystic, noses do not finally exist other than in a dream, and the only thing that really exists is indivisible, infinite God. But the record of the event just enacted, tragically enough, causes the tiny iota of consciousness to concentrate its attention on the event of seeing noses. This then becomes *the reality*.

When consciousness is eventually developed to the degree in which it is possible for it to reflect and finally comprehend even the bare fact of Godhood, that is, from the first human incarnation, then the long process of disidentification from regarding itself as **being** a nose, along with billions of other external incidents, begins to occur. To give this some reality, an example I can cite that has real meaning for me is the experience of what happens in a real human relationship. You have friends. You love certain people. You have complex experiences and often angry ones, and they all seem external. Then, one day, one of those persons is no longer out there.

He or she is inside. The individual's presence and worth has become something internal. How did it happen? Without my being aware of it, certainly. There is no logic. Something wears thin, and the without becomes the within. One has the suspicion even in the first instance that perhaps what is now clearly within one's own being was always there, and that it was just a misconception that the external was the important reality. It always really was within one's own being.

When a fundamental habit is up for surgery, unconsciously we muster all our resources to protect it. On occasion it even becomes in our minds a matter of life and death. We will do mortal battle rather than change or give it up.

It is only in our time, as we have said, that the nature of sanskaras and their key importance in the ongoing of the individual has been clarified by Meher Baba. This is of the greatest help in giving us a clearer idea of what we are up against in our quest for meaning and fruition in life. It is also basic to our understanding of the actions in Meher Baba's life, and in giving us insight into the fundamental difference between the mode characteristic of the Perfect Master in his fulfillment of his work in Creation, and that more generally used by the Avatar.

The Avatar does not work within the same time constraint as the Perfect Master. The methods of the Avatar are spread out over a greater length of time and probably in consequence are less in need of his constant physical presence to administer first aid. If the Avatar, particularly in the age we are now entering, uses situations in daily life to precipitate one's confrontation with important sanskaras, then the individual will certainly be found normally to exercise a self-adjusting balance in which he gets on with what he can stand, and rejects that with which he cannot cope for the moment.

Of course, this could be self-defeating and result in endless rejection of what one does not want (directed by the pertinent sanskaras, of course). But this is only a logical possibility and is not

in practice the controlling factor. One does not enter the spiritual
path until one has experienced some sort of very great deception in
following one's own desires and impulses. Often the disenchantment
has to take a brutal turn before the individual wakes up to the fact
that he is the one who has been kidding himself. Then the dawning
of honesty arrives, and the real potential for progress is at hand. The
waggling finger of honesty within oneself is worth ten thousand
admonishments by someone on the outside.

I think I am a typical example of someone Meher Baba handled
during the Avataric period of his life. I can certainly see the results
of over forty years of trying to follow as best as I can the challenges
I felt he posed both when he was physically present, as well as what
I feel now intuitively to have continued to be placed through
challenges in my daily life. There is a great deal of motion, and what
I see, although by no means completed, represents progress that I
would never have thought possible in one lifetime. I have described
this in detail elsewhere and will not go into the rather lengthy record
again.[2]

Certainly, the methods Meher Baba used with me are vastly
different from many of those recounted by my friends in endless
stories through the decades about their experiences with Baba. Also,
I personally have seen almost no signs of rough methods in my visits
in India, many of which were characterized by a very simple daily
life, not by vast public gatherings, and therefore should have been
far more open to the expression of harsh treatment. True, I know
any number of persons devoted to Baba who came to know him after
he left physical form, and who claim with the greatest distress that
Baba has been putting them through sheer hell for years. This
implies that Baba created that hell, and this I just do not believe. I
feel we create our own hell, and if this is what the Avatar must
incorporate in "scenarioing" our daily lives, then hell will result. He

---

[2] Don E. Stevens, *Some Results* (St. Helier, Jersey: Companion Books, 1995).

does not change the form of our karma. That we created ourselves, and he deals with what he sees already within us. No magic wands.

Before drawing to a close this comparison of the methods associated with the Perfect Master and those of the Avatar, one further obvious difference remains. This is the question of relative numbers. The Perfect Master appears to take on a direct and central role in the lives of relatively few seekers, and these apparently are individuals who are already approaching the end of the long path back to Oneness. The Avatar, on the other hand, exists for all Creation. Baba used to love to point out that when he gave a shove to Creation, it was felt at all levels, even to the hordes of ants that inhabit the earth.

It becomes evident that the precepts, the rules, the suggestions laid out by this omni-responsible Avatar, are much more general in both their nature as well as their application than those applied by the Perfect Master. Much of the change in observed manner of treatment of individuals is immediately seen as related to this vast increase in scope of responsibility.

This discussion of the basic differences between the methods of the Perfect Master and the Avatar I felt was both necessary to try to understand the dichotomy in Meher Baba's life, as well as to lay out a principle in mystic development that is almost certainly fundamental. Now let us return to the final portions of Meher Baba's physical presence on earth.

7. THE AVATAR

There is an ancient tradition that each time the Christ/Avatar comes on earth, he makes a gift to humanity of some great principle which previously had not been fully accessible. The gift of deep love is said to have been the gift that Jesus the Christ gave to humanity. This does not mean, we are told, that great human love did not exist before the days of Jesus. Rather, that its depth, force and general availability to humanity was enormously increased by him. Whereas before, it might be said that only the heroes were able truly to love, from the time of Jesus, in contrast, the simple man of no great inner development was also able to scale great heights of love.

This tradition is intriguing, and Meher Baba said that during his lifetime his gift to humanity would be a greatly increased capacity for intuition. He hastened to add that by no means should this be interpreted to mean that intellect and logic would be discarded. Simply, rather, that the primary means used in daily life in weighing, judging and deciding on courses of action, would become that based on the intuitive processes. Mental activity would still be there and still used, but as a secondary tool.

Even in this lifetime a remarkable change in this regard can be noted. Also, there is now a strong wave of trust in intuition and a correlative mistrust of head processes. Sometimes this preference seems rather overdone, but there is no question that intuition is

Meher Baba giving darshan in India, 1950s.

"in" and head is increasingly "out."

The general availability of intuition to humanity is so important that one may well suggest that for the first time in human history this increased capacity for intuition combined with the force of love so abundantly released by the Avatar may give humanity the opportunity to make and maintain, even when the Avatar is not in physical form, a direct personal relationship with him. If this is true, then there is room to change drastically the forms of search for Truth by the ready aspirant.

It would be too simple if this were all predicated and supported on just one change in human nature, regardless of its importance. There is another essential ingredient, however, which Meher Baba had suggested way back in 1931 when he said that his purpose in the school project was to establish "links." On October 7, 1954, not very long after the closing of the New Life phase lived by Baba with his companions (and finally designated as servant-companions), Meher Baba gave out the "Last Message on the Alphabet Board." Listen to what he had to say:

"There is no reason at all for any of you to worry. Baba was, Baba is, and Baba will also be eternally existent. Severance of external relations does not mean the termination of internal links. It was only for establishing the internal connections that the external contacts have been maintained until now. The time has now come for being bound in the chain of internal connections. Hence, external contact is no longer necessary. It is possible to establish the internal link by obeying Baba's orders. I give you all my blessings for strengthening these internal links.

"I am always with you and I am not away from you. I was, I am, and will remain eternally with you, and it is for promoting this realization that I have severed external contact. This will enable all persons to realize Truth by being bound to each other with internal links. Oh, my lovers! I love you all. It is only because of my love for my creation that I have descended on earth. Let not your hearts be torn asunder by my declaration concerning the dropping of my body. On the contrary, accept my Divine will cheerfully. You can never escape from me, even if you try to escape from me. It is not possible to get rid of me. Therefore have courage and be brave.

"If you thus lose your heart, how will it be possible for you to fulfill the great task which I have entrusted to you? Be brave and spread my message of love far and wide, to all quarters, in order to fulfill my Divine will. Let the words 'Baba, Baba,' come forth from every nook and corner of the world and from the mouth of every child, and let their ignorance be reduced to ashes by the burning flame of my love.

"Come together in order to fulfill my will by taking your stand on Truth, Love and Honesty, and be worthy of participating. I give you all my blessings for spreading my message of Love."

It is still early to hazard judgment, but evidence is accumulating that "inner links" forged by love is an essential handmaiden to intuition in its role in the search for Truth. It is the mortar that real companionship produces, and this in turn allows the companion to offer effectively the often necessary "truing" of the product of intuition. Oddly enough, this appears in the future to be the modern democratic counterpart of the role so long played by the Eastern guru in the mystic discipline. How it will eventually function depends on a delicate evolutionary process, which Meher Baba appears clearly to have foreshadowed.

After his return from America and Europe in late 1952, Meher Baba began increasingly to retire into periods of seclusion. Even those very close to him were frequently unable to contact him over long periods of time. This was very disconcerting to persons who had become very much habituated to running quite frequently to Baba to discuss various family and business problems. But even when one could get to Baba in this new phase of his life, often he would give no personal advice. The old custom of going minutely into actions and decisions was quite changed. Increasingly the dictum was, "Do your best and leave the results to Baba."

Now, on various occasions, Baba commented that a certain course of action or a crisis that he had to undergo might entail his physical death. In the past, he had also made such statements, but as his age increased and very noticeable infirmities became evident, this began to be worrisome, and it was in this context that Baba formed his words for the "Last Message on the Alphabet Board." Moreover, many who had been young when they first started to follow Baba were now showing signs of age also. There is nothing that sharpens the realization of mortality more than to see the evidence in one's own self.

This was the period when my own direct contact with Meher Baba started and blossomed. The experience of meeting him physically in New York for the first time was followed at once by much correspondence related both to the editing of *God Speaks*, which he entrusted to Murshida Duce and myself, as well as to many aspects of Sufi affairs, which spanned the continent. Murshida Duce lived in New York City where her husband was stationed in the oil industry, while the bulk of property and financial affairs of the Sufis was centered in San Francisco where Murshida Martin had lived all her life.

There was a third important subject which rapidly came to the fore and demanded considerable interchange between India and America. Meher Baba had intimated even in Murshida Martin's lifetime that he would reorient the Sufi Movement under her. Among the Sufis one was well aware of the ancient tradition that this was exactly what the Prophet Mohammed had done for the Sufis in his day, and so it came as no surprise that this should happen again in Meher Baba's lifetime. Baba noted that while Sufism was only one of five important mystic schools, still, he went on to say, its principles were especially adapted to the needs of the current era of civilization. This automatically suggested a tie to an ancient tradition among Sufis that within the currents and tests of daily life lay one of the most important sources for the lessons to be learned in the spiritual life. Was this perhaps now to become of great importance to all of humanity in the New Age?

There are two centrally important subjects to look at in this next phase of Baba's life. The first is the possibility, as already suggested, that the New Life marked a major division point in his life, the first part often having been stamped by actions and projects typical of a Perfect Master, the later part preponderantly by that of the Avatar. The second central subject for consideration is the nature of whatever provisions he may have made for the search for Truth in the new age now dawning.

The first resource to examine is the written record left by Meher Baba himself. Of the multitude of published works concerning Baba, those directly authored by Baba himself are few but distinctive. The first and most detailed in relationship to daily life is the *Discourses*. These were presented and collected in the 1930s at the time that a great many Westerners were living close to Baba in India. Although these discourses were spelled out on the alphabet board, they were written down and edited at once, and Baba himself referred to them frequently in his later life. There is no question that they represent the authentic pronouncements of Baba, and that they were checked on many occasions by Baba in later years.

The second and even more directly authored work is *God Speaks*. I personally witnessed Baba's comment, repeated at least two or three times in my presence, that he had entrusted to Ghani the writing of a major work. At Ghani's death, Baba had one of the mandali bring out the material that Ghani had been compiling presumably under Baba's instructions. On inspection, though, what had been written bore very little resemblance to the material Baba said he had given Ghani. In transferring the manuscript of the final *God Speaks* to Murshida Duce and myself, Baba included the writings of Ghani, suggesting that we might wish to save and publish part of it. He left that entirely to our discretion. The decision to save in its entirety the work of Dr. Ghani and to publish it in *God Speaks* was made by Murshida Duce.

Baba and Eruch described to me in detail the manner in which *God Speaks* finally came into being. Baba would during the daytime give Eruch detailed information, on which Eruch took copious notes, which he would then transcribe during the night. The next morning he read out the full rendition of points given by Baba the previous day, and Baba listened and corrected any inaccuracies. There can be no doubt that *God Speaks* is direct and carefully corrected material from Baba himself.

When I visited Baba in 1955 for "The Four Language Groups" meetings described immediately below, Baba invited me on the final day to come to the top of the old water storage tank building which had been adapted into two large dormitory rooms. Baba was sitting on a chair and next to him was Eruch. On Baba's knees was a collection of papers. After several interchanges Baba motioned to the papers on his lap. He said that they contained different addresses he had given out at public meetings over the years which were largely unpublished material but similar to the *Discourses*. He asked if I would be interested in arranging and editing them into a logical order and make a small book from them. Then he added, if by any chance it would be of interest to include also my impressions of the meetings that I had just attended, he would make available to me the transcripts taken during the meetings by two secretaries.

This was a tremendous assignment, and my real qualm was whether I was up to it. I said this to Baba. He replied that he would help me. What else could I ask? I accepted the assignment. It was made clear to me at the time that all of the addresses that Baba had on his knee had been dictated by himself and then corrected in the same meticulous manner that had characterized the writing of *God Speaks*. In the book I assembled, entitled *Listen, Humanity*, the portion from the papers on Baba's knees is integrally Part II.

There have been comments from even very highly respected followers of Baba that, in fact, we do not have Baba's direct words, and that these at best had usually been taken down as notes and later amplified from memory by the original note takers. This is not an accurate description of the material in *God Speaks*, or Part II of *Listen, Humanity*, or in the transcript portion of Part I of *Listen, Humanity*. These are direct from Baba and checked carefully by Baba. I feel that the *Discourses* are also beyond reproach as authentic and direct material.

There are more direct resources, which are the two little books *Beams*[1] and *Life at its Best*.[2] The former, especially, was the product of questions Murshida Duce and I put to Baba during the editing of *God Speaks*. It was his direct replies to us, and the material was so fascinating that we asked if they could be published also. His affirmative reply adds another resource of material that we know beyond doubt is directly from Baba and checked by him for accuracy. For the remainder of his physical life Meher Baba did not give out further major works.

When I had said good-bye to Baba in New York in August of 1952, I did not know when or whether I would ever see him again. In 1954 he invited as mentioned above a small group of men to come to India during some public meetings he planned to hold. I was included in the list of those to come, but it was at this time that the urinary infection finally came to a head, and was at long last

---

[1] Meher Baba, *Beams from Meher Baba* (Connecticut Printers: Sufism Reoriented, 1968).
[2] Meher Baba, *Life At Its Best* (Peter Pauper Press: Sufism Reoriented, 1957).

correctly diagnosed and treated. In any event, a stay in the hospital and subsequent convalescence ruled out my going with the group to India. The next year, 1955, Baba set up the internal India gatherings which he called "The Four Language Groups," to which Baba invited me and Francis Brabazon, as the only Westerners, to come. Perhaps the whole sequence was staged by Baba at the controls. I do not know, but if I had had my choice, I would have chosen the second meeting. The events in 1954 were however a marvelous experience and are fully described in the book *Three Incredible Weeks with Meher Baba.*[3]

On the occasion of the language groups sahavas I was so busy observing Baba's contact with a group composed totally of Indian devotees that I had little time to speculate on what was going on inside myself. Several incidents still stand out in my memory, however. The first to manifest itself was the manner in which Gustadji became my guardian parent for the occasion and constantly shoved me up into the front row or even next to Baba's feet. Gustadji, you remember, had been a disciple first of Sai Baba, who passed him on to Upasni Maharaj, who in turn told him it was now time to follow the one who had the power to move the heavens with his little finger: Meher Baba. Gustadji remained the rest of his life a devoted and favored follower of Baba.

A second memory-fixing event was the colorful arrival one afternoon of Godavri Mai, the devotee and successor of Upasni Maharaj at the Sakori ashram. Her smile and devotion to Baba were pictures to remember for a lifetime.

The third painting hung in the gallery of memories was to see Baba surrounded by the very simple and human crowd of men who were devoted to him. There was nothing in the least theatrical in their actions, nor in Baba's towards them. The total simplicity and sincerity was remarkable. Rarely was there any demonstration of

[3] Malcolm Schloss & Charles Purdom, *Three Incredible Weeks with Meher Baba* (Myrtle Beach: Sheriar Press, 1975).

unusual emotion. Perhaps the one great exception was when Baba had called on the one small boy in the crowd, the son of a very early devotee, to express his feelings. He recalled Baba's earlier trips to Dehra Dun, where he lived, and the great joy of all at seeing Baba each time. Then he remembered that they had not seen Baba in Dehra Dun for some time, however, and this perhaps reminded him that with the ravages of time and accidents, they might not see him there again. He did not say this, but his thoughts were projected onto a screen of common understanding, and there were very few who did not weep with the small boy in his thoughts and fears.

During June of 1956 at Meherazad, while resting and recuperating from intense work in seclusion at Satara, Baba sent out another of his various Life Circulars, No. 26, wherein once again he forewarned his lovers of a great personal disaster in the near future. Later, in July 1956, he made the second of the three final voyages to the West, continuing to California and then on to Australia. His visit to Meher Mount near Los Angeles, where Jean Adriel (Schloss) had helped dedicate a property for his future use, was outstanding in its stew of rich human emotions and constant humor. Here was one of the few occasions when I heard Baba deliberately take upon himself the changing of the karma of the present lifetime for a devotee. A young girl was lamenting the lack of children in her marriage. Baba looked long at her and said, "Because of your love for me, I will grant you two in this lifetime. You were not supposed by your karma to have children in this life, but your love for me is such that I will give you two." She did have the two.

After Baba's return to India from Australia and the newly founded Avatar's Abode, he set out on a variety of meetings and travels. On one occasion in December 1956 he travelled by auto from Poona to Satara, where he had often stayed in previous years during the very hot pre-monsoon season. Nearing Satara, Eruch, who was driving, suddenly found the car out of control, and they plunged into a shallow ditch with such force that the passengers were thrown in all directions. Dr. Nilu was killed instantly, Pendu had internal injuries from which he never really recovered, and Baba had lacerations and a broken hip. It was the latter that was really grave, as the joint was destroyed with no hope of it being healed in a fashion to allow normal walking in the future.

Despite the serious handicap of the smashed hip that resulted from the accident, Baba organized a great sahavas meeting in Meherabad in February 1958 and three months later was again in America. In a dramatic change of plans, he announced that he would not continue on to Australia as originally planned, and then shortly after, again changed courses and reinstituted the Australia visit, but on a shorter schedule than originally announced. A month's planned sojourn was reduced to a fortnight's whirlwind round-the-world itinerary.

It was during the late 1950s and early 1960s that Baba entered the drug scene, especially in America. This he did through his close relationship with three university students from Boston who had become devoted to him. These were Rick Chapman, Alan Cohen and Robert Dreyfuss. At that time Timothy Leary and Richard Alpert from Harvard University had collected a large following of young people interested in the effects of the drug LSD. Rapidly it had become a sub-cult closely associated with the entire field of the search for inner experiences and on into the early phases of mysticism.

On one public occasion a photo of Baba was projected onto the screen, and shortly several people became interested in who he was and what he stood for. In those very experimental days it did not take long to follow up on whatever sources seemed to offer some new avenue of approach, and soon several of these young searchers had made contact with Baba by letter. There was very little time wasted in establishing exactly where Baba stood on the subject. He pointed out very clearly that any drug-induced experience barely scratched the surface of the real inner resources and at the same time risked irremediable damage to the psychic system of the individual. If there was any value at all in LSD-induced experiences, Meher Baba said, it was in introducing the person to the possibility of further realms of experience which could never be approached by LSD or any other drug.

Baba gave the three students the task to get out in front of university audiences and tell the young people what the true story was. This they did, with astonishing impact. Appearing before hundreds of meetings of university students, they soon had a considerable counter-wave of distrust of drug-inspired search activated. Baba went so far as to say that if this preoccupation with drugs was not curbed, especially in America, there was the risk that an entire generation of young people would be permanently undermined in their lives and quest for Truth.

It is not possible to quantify the final impact of the three Boston students on the LSD wave of the 60s, but it is interesting to note that the tidal wave of interest in experimentation with LSD began to subside from that time. A small pamphlet entitled *God In a Pill?*[1] laid out in blunt language the case against this type of search through chemical means. Also, Baba specifically included marijuana as to be avoided. He declared that drugs were harmful physically, mentally and spiritually.

One final paragraph must be added to this recounting. I had been responsible for collecting the material for this small pamphlet and at that time also had a number of ex-drug users in a small study group with which I met. They had pretty well indoctrinated me in a popular dictum that marijuana was no more dangerous than the American cocktail so popular at the time. When the pamphlet was ready for press, I had not included marijuana "Martini" therefore in

---

[1] Meher Baba, *God In A Pill?* (San Francisco: Sufism Reoriented, 1966).

the list of drugs Baba specifically condemned by name. But one member of the group insisted I should check Baba on the point, and promptly Baba wrote back that by all means marijuana should be on the list of substances to be completely avoided.[5]

Much of the rest of Baba's life was characterized by intense physical suffering. First it was the smashed hip joint, until one day he disappeared from Guru Prasad in Poona, to be found later walking calmly back up the driveway to the house, unassisted. For months before he had been carried most of the time in a chair with extended handles. When asked what had happened, he said very simply, "I was sitting on the porch, when suddenly I reflected, how undignified it would be for the Avatar to spend the rest of his life as a cripple." So he walked, and subsequent x-rays showed that the hip joint had re-established itself to the degree necessary to sustain weight and modest walking.

Despite the pain and physical weaknesses that accumulated, Baba in 1962 announced plans for what he called "The East-West Gathering." Here he planned to invite key devotees from Europe, America, Australia and the Far East to be together for one week in his company. In fact, the meeting was held at the beginning of November 1962, but for four days rather than a week. All of this time, and on one day far into the evening, Baba was constantly before and with a great crowd of people. One hundred and thirty-seven came from Europe, America and Australia, and about three thousand from India and Pakistan. There were messages from Baba, entertainment by different groups and persons, as well as the reading out of prayers. It was completely kaleidoscopic and, despite the numbers, extraordinarily heart-warming.

On one occasion I got tired of sitting in one of the front rows, where Baba had specified the Westerners were to sit, and I wandered

---

[5] *Listen! The New Humanity*, pp. 81–90.

back under the awning erected to cut the direct sunlight. Finally, perhaps halfway back, I spied a convenient empty seat and settled down, looking at the people who surrounded me. Suddenly something made me look up, and I saw that Baba was making some sort of a gesture to someone in the audience. I looked around to see who was waving back at Baba. No one. Then I looked again. Baba was looking right at me, a considerable distance, and again he waved. Then I tumbled that this was for me.

An Easterner among the many hundreds sitting under the same awning had an almost identical experience. He was sitting for two days on a certain seat among the last rows allotted to his group. The next day he had a thought, wondering whether Baba had ever noted him sitting way out there, and then decided to change his seat. A few minutes into the program for the day, Baba sent someone over to ask why he had changed his seat that day.

A relationship with Baba was always intensely personal. You felt that you were the center of the universe. In fact you were. Baba never put on. You were unique, and there was never anything to suggest that you were other than the most important thing before Baba. This was not good avataric relations. It was Reality.

On the final evening of the East-West gathering the gates of the residence where it was held were thrown open, and Meher Baba continued until well into the night to give his blessing to the thousands who came.

The hip problem was hardly more than mitigated when a neck pain began to be really debilitating. It gradually grew so serious that the most celebrated nerve specialist of the region was finally prevailed upon to travel from Bombay to Ahmednagar to inspect the difficulty. Not long after Baba and Dr. Ram Ginde, the specialist, first met, Baba arranged for me to become involved enough in the Ginde family affairs to meet first the doctor and his wife, and eventually a son, Suhas. Dr. Ginde explained to me the neck problem and his diagnosis of the cause. There had been a wearing of the vertebrae in the neck portion to the point that the passage for the spinal cord had been seriously narrowed. This produced pressure directly on the spinal cord and hence the agonizing pains that Baba experienced.

Ginde was very precise in his own attribution of the cause for this wear. By the time I knew Ginde, he had already succumbed to Baba's charm and become a complete devotee. As such, he knew in intimate detail the entire life history of Baba, and in this he pinned on Baba's long-standing custom of washing the feet of the poor and bowing down to them. Often this entailed up to a thousand persons in one single program. Ginde declared flatly that it was this unusual and continual motion over many years that had finally worn the vertebrae to their present state. What to do? Nothing. That was the trouble. Baba suffered acute pains in the neck for the rest of his life. In addition, he gradually developed further physical disabilities, among these the building up of blood uric acid content even beyond the levels that normally cause the patient to go into a coma. Baba did not, but no doubt this was one of the major problems at his physical death.

A large part of the final years of Meher Baba's frequent seclusions were spent, according to him, in attending to what he called his "universal work." Many remarked on the amount of time that Baba spent in this manner. Eruch, the one regarded often as being Baba's closest male disciple, offered a guess by saying that at the end of an Avataric period, the Avatar must spend a fair amount of time balancing out the various accounts in Creation. At the end of an Avataric age, which was now the case, and the Kalyuga age being now terminated, there were the additional accounts of the entire age to be balanced. Even given the attributes of the Avatar, this was no mean job, and so a great deal of time had to be passed in scrutinizing and making the necessary adjustments to allow the start of the next age to go ahead on a clean base. This conjecture makes sense.

On occasion, speaking of his Universal Work, Baba would announce that a particular phase of this had been completed 100% to his satisfaction. Rarely, he would bring up the possibility of his breaking his silence, but now almost always in connection with his Avataric manifestation, when the Avatar gives all of Creation a push forward, and also when his status and responsibility as Avatar becomes much more widely known.

I feel personally that the act of manifestation occurred somewhere in the mid-1960s. It was then that I noted an extraordinary increase in the rate of search for the Truth and progress in the lives of those diligently searching. It was almost as if all of living creatures had taken on a new acuity of being. I could not believe, for instance, what was happening to dogs and cats that crossed my path in this period. They were vastly different from the animals I had known as a child. And the faculty of intuition was undoubtedly there. I believe we are living in the full flood-tide of the manifestation and love of the Avatar.

What I observed and experienced during my own presence with Baba cannot be denied. So, without hesitation, I will plunge into the personal account of being with Baba on repeated occasions during the 1950s and 1960s.

Let me start off by describing a typical day with Baba in the period 1952 to 1968, which is when I had almost unlimited access to him. I would be staying at Meherazad, perhaps in the blue bus. I would wake up in the morning without being called and wash, shave and go to the bathroom. Sometimes, if I were very lucky, Naja would have prepared a herb omelet for me. The meal was simple, and I ate it alone. A little later, I would join Eruch for a short walk out beyond the front gate of the property and up the road leading towards the dam in the direction of Pimpalgaon. Then we would turn back to the compound where the men had their quarters. Baba had spent the night in the two-story building beyond the men's section, surrounded by a lovely garden planted and largely tended by Mehera.

Somewhere around nine-thirty we were all assembled in mandali hall, a small room built into the long shed-like structure where most of the men mandali had their rooms. Then Baba would arrive. We all rose. Baba went to his chair in the corner between the two windows opening towards the fields of Pimpalgaon.

More often than not when I was there, the first order of business was an inevitable sequence of questions: "Don, how did you sleep last night?" "How was your digestion?" "Did you go to the toilet, and did you have a good movement?" If it was the first day after my arrival, the answer to the last was almost always, "No." Then Baba would make a sign to someone, who would know exactly what that was all about, and two or three minutes later a glass of an orange drink would be brought to me. I detested and still detest carbonated beverages, as I cannot burp, and so the gas and I play hide and seek for an hour or so.

I do not know to this day what the magic was with Baba's supply of orange, but always in ten or fifteen minutes, I would have to go to the toilet, and Baba without asking would obviously be satisfied. And I would too, because otherwise the morning was very uncomfortable, sitting crouched against the wall. In later years I was granted the privilege of sitting on a stool, but at that time I sat on the floor as everyone but Baba did.

This morning questioning concerning the most basic of the bodily functions was not at all unusual for Baba. The proper care of the body so that it would serve its purpose as a vehicle was a basic matter of concern for him, and he frequently included the subject at the very beginning of a conversation, especially if he had not seen the person for quite a long time. I have seen Baba on several occasions interrupt a line of devotees waiting for his embrace, often after many months, to look especially closely at a young man distinguished by his emaciation. Although this was not unusual among young Indians, Baba had a way of spotting an old friend and seeing that all was not completely right.

"You look pulled down," Baba would gesture. "No, not especially, Baba," the reply would almost always come back. Baba would insist, and frequently the ensuing story was the same. The person being questioned was doing hard manual labor, but at the same time was observing a strict vegetarian diet. Baba would always show surprise at this news. After some further exchange, while all the line waited patiently, Baba would tell the young man that he could not expect to do hard manual labor and still carry out a vegetarian diet. Then he would prescribe the inclusion of some meat, while pointing out that it was important to do what was necessary for the body in order that it might continue to function as the instrument in the search for Truth. What good the search if one neglected the vehicle, and finally one day it ceased prematurely to work? I have even known Baba to prescribe one, almost-raw beefsteak a day to one of the most devout persons I have ever known. And she did it. I am sure she lived for at least twenty years more this way than if she had neglected her tendency to anemia.

Perhaps one thinks that living in the presence of a great Master is necessarily filled with inspiring dissertations on the nature of God and the practices necessary to win through to His presence. This may be true in some or even many instances, but it was not the usual diet with Baba. On occasion he would bring up a fascinating point in the spiritual realm, but it was not the usual topic. There was the mail, and stories about what had happened to different people, and projects since the last time one had been together. In my case, there were from time to time clarifications of points that had arisen in the various editings that always seemed to be en route. These observations by Baba related to the literary projects proved often to fit in beautifully with subjects that came up later in various Baba groups, but there was no systematic course of study set out by Baba.

Quite often there were amusing diversions such as playing the game of seven tiles, or occasionally also a special game of cards in which Baba seemed to have the automatic right to change the rules at his whim. (He mostly won. Then the head of the losing team and often all its members had to rub their noses on the floor, at which Baba always rocked with silent laughter. Baba would point out to them what good fortune they had to do this before the Avatar.) Baba had a fantastic sense of humor, and whenever things got tense, which they did on occasion, almost always Baba found an amusing point which relieved the tension. But not always.

There was the occasion when Baba was finishing a long seclusion, and the qawalli singers from the Ahmednagar group were to come out the following morning at ten o'clock to sing for Baba, to end officially the seclusion. Eruch and I, as was our custom, decided to take our morning after-breakfast jaunt towards the dam, but not without Eruch's intuition having registered the fact that this happening could well provide the means for an episode with Baba. Anyway, Eruch decided we had plenty of time, so off we went. Almost arrived at the corner near the dam, a truck approached. Standing in the back of the truck was the group of qawalli singers.

"Oh, oh, we've had it," Eruch said. I looked at my watch, and it was not even 9:40 yet. I called this to Eruch's attention, and that we would have returned in good time to meet the 10 o'clock deadline. Eruch looked unconvinced but said nothing. We walked back leisurely and arrived at 9:50.

There was Baba, surrounded by the Ahmednagar group. He did not seem to be paying much attention to them. I had a presentiment of disaster. It struck! Baba gesticulated furiously at Eruch, and from Eruch's reply I judged Baba wanted to know where we had been. I tried to disappear behind Eruch, but Baba singled me out. He gestured again equally ferociously at me, and Eruch obligingly translated for me. "You have spoiled my day!"

You may think that this is the time to point out to Baba that it is still well before the agreed hour and that you are present. But have you ever had the full blast of the anger of a great spiritual Master? It is not the time for logic. You also know that any excuses are equally out of the question. I took the full explosion, said nothing and completely crumbled apart inside myself. I have never experienced such a feeling of total devastation. Regardless of whatever logic to the contrary, to have spoiled the Avatar's first day after a long seclusion has to be about the greatest sin one can commit. I knew not how I could breathe in the next moment.

Baba turned on me. He looked deeply into my eyes for some seconds. Then abruptly he snapped his fingers and gesticulated, "Let's enjoy ourselves now."

My inner being re-established itself instantly, and I felt more joyous than I had been in many long months. The pleasure of the beloved is beyond logic. It is, and if it is not, then all the world is unraveled. When I saw the happiness in Baba's eyes, I was happy again.

I do not know what Baba was attacking in those few brief moments. I can only say that I have never known such a concentration of emotion in such a short time, nor a sense of such complete disintegration. And then, contrarily, such a total re-establishment of inner being, beyond the levels of even the highest of happiness in usual living. It was a tremendous experience, and a demonstration of the force which a great spiritual master can concentrate into a moment of non-time.

Does all this indicate simply that a Master, at least Meher Baba in this case, has a complete supply of human emotions and failings? Baba explains that the Avatar and the Perfect Master also after achieving realization take on certain sanskaras that are "non-binding" in order to have a human personality to which we can relate. Eruch explained this once to me as being absolutely necessary. Without this "human" side to which we can naturally relate, we would be so caught up in the unusual and the divine aspects of the Perfect One that we would not be able to live through the natural actions which are necessary to move our own inner knots along the way to dissolution.

The simple stories of life with Baba are replete with how he would stir up an argument among the mandali around him, and when it was at its height, suddenly pick out a humorous aspect, and in a moment all the tension would disappear. I have seen a close friend use quite naturally the same method. In a business conference, when everyone is completely upset by the attitudes of others, he will suddenly interject a droll comment that cracks everyone up. Then in the next moment there is almost always found a solution to the impasse of only seconds before.

I am struck repeatedly by this. Is it a formula of Reality which has as its product the return of the focus of consciousness to the fact that nothing we deal with in physical life is real nor really important? Perhaps humor has the magic to re-establish the unconscious knowledge of this fact, and sanity can quickly find a position acceptable to all. The trick is to have the ability to step outside the rage in the air and see the point of humor. This is difficult, even almost impossible. We are too busy with our own rage and the massive logic of our own point of view.

How can I describe the manner Baba could look into my eyes for just a few seconds, to establish that he had done something necessary inside me? Then in the next instant his mood would change totally with sunshine and the softness of spring everywhere. But not just in him. It changed instantly in me as well. But I never risked being less than ten minutes early for appointments with Baba after that. It worked well.

On occasion there would be a visitor who in some way had pierced the safety net that protected Baba from intrusions during his seclusion. Most of the time the unexpected arrival would be an old devotee overcome by some family crisis, frequently of health. I have already described the typical situation and Baba's response. But on one occasion the unexpected visitor turned out to be a hitchhiker from America. It all started during an intensive discussion of some topic in mandali hall. Suddenly I noted Baba pausing in his gestures. Then he looked at Eruch with the obvious question written on his face, "What is going on outside?" Eruch disappeared.

On his return Eruch spoke to Baba in Gujerati, which was a nice way of advising me to keep out of the subject at least for now. Baba looked even more concerned, even angry, and even I could see that he was motioning for the person to be sent on his way. Baba repeated the gesture "away" for good measure. I was certain I knew what was going on even without benefit of Gujerati.

Baba turned towards me and Eruch translated his hand gestures. "There is an American boy outside that Adi sent, despite Adi knowing that I am still in seclusion and that there are strict orders that no one is to disturb me. I am telling Eruch to send the boy away."

Baba's words cut into my heart like a sword, and involuntarily I said to myself before I could control my thoughts, "Baba, you are a bastard!"

Immediately Baba turned his gaze back to me. "Don, what are you thinking?"

Dear God, what do you do then? I was torn in several directions all at the same moment. Where my words then came from, or how I could justify them under the circumstances, I do not know. They came out anyhow: "Baba, I was thinking, 'Why me?' "

In fact, this was really the crux of the situation, and in fact already, on several occasions, I had had to look at myself and ask, Don, what right do you have to be here in Baba's presence when others are denied it? Each time the thought had come to me I hastily pushed it back from consciousness. This time I had to leave it in

Baba's hands. But now the further words, related to this problem, came out involuntarily. "What right do I have to be sitting here at your feet?"

Baba looked at me for another long five seconds, snapped his fingers and gesticulated quickly again at Eruch. In seconds the young American was sitting in front of Baba. He had hitchhiked and worked his way on freighters all the way from Miami to see Baba. Now by an unexpected act of grace and a messy confusion in Don's conscience he was sitting at the Master's feet.

Seven tiles was another of Baba's favorites to break the work routine. It consisted in stacking seven broken tiles and dividing the men present into two teams, one which pitches at the tiles and the other which tries to catch the ball before it bounces a second time. If achieved, this puts the "in" team "out." It is a unique and quite exciting game. One of the cook boys was the prize pitcher, and Eruch the prize catcher. Guests such as myself, and on one memorable occasion, Dr. Deshmukh, were included in positions of honor.

I was middling, but Dr. Deshmukh would never qualify for the Indian Olympic team. For him, Baba halved the distance to the pile of tiles. Deshmukh took aim and threw again. It was worse than the first try. Again half the distance. No good. Baba had Deshmukh stand literally right over the tiles, and again he missed. By this time Baba and all the teams were rolling on the grass. I wonder how much Deshmukh put on to give Baba a good laugh. He could be as droll as Baba in his very sober-sided, professorial way. He was a professor of philosophy in the university in Nagpur.

As the clock up on the wall opposite Baba began moving towards 5:00 p.m., we could not keep our eyes off it, as somewhere about now Baba would announce his intention of leaving for the day. Finally the announcement would come, and always there were efforts to try to find reasons for Baba to stay longer. Normally Baba would give in for a short extension, but by 5:30 it was almost always time for him to start moving towards the double door facing Mehera's garden and the house where he spent the night, as did several of the women mandali also.

I remember so many times through the years when we would all stand on either side of Baba as he faced the garden, frequently with Francis Brabazon supporting him by one arm, and then he would have Eruch read out "The Master's Prayer," composed by Baba:

O Parvardigar, the Preserver and Protector of all!

You are without Beginning, and without End;

Non-dual, beyond comparison; and none can measure you.

You are without colour, without expression, without form, and without attributes.

You are unlimited and unfathomable, beyond imagination and conception; eternal and imperishable.

You are indivisible; and none can see you but with eyes divine.

You always were, you always are, and you always will be;

You are everywhere, you are in everything; and you are also beyond everywhere and beyond everything.

You are in the firmament and in the depths; you are manifest and unmanifest, on all planes, and beyond all planes.

You are in the three worlds, and also beyond the three worlds.

You are imperceptible and independent.

You are the Creator, the Lord of Lords, the Knower of all minds and hearts; you are omnipotent and omnipresent.

You are Knowledge Infinite, Power Infinite, and Bliss Infinite.

You are the ocean of Knowledge, All-Knowing, Infinitely-Knowing; the Knower of the past, the present and the future; and you are Knowledge itself.

You are all-merciful and eternally benevolent.

You are the Soul of souls, the One with infinite attributes.

You are the trinity of Truth, Knowledge and Bliss,

You are the Source of Truth, the Ocean of Love.

You are the Ancient One, the Highest of the High; you are Prabhu and Parameshwar; you are the Beyond-God, and the Beyond-Beyond-God also; you are Parabrahma; Allah; Elahi; Yazdan; Ahuramazda; and God the Beloved.

You are named Ezad, the Only One worthy of worship.

In addition to "The Master's Prayer," Baba composed one other which he always regarded as equally important, "The Prayer of Repentance," which is given in Purdom's *The God Man* and many other sources.

On one occasion as Eruch was reading out the two prayers at Baba's command, Baba asked him to go faster. Then faster. And faster again, until Eruch was reading as fast as an express train. He burst out laughing. Baba immediately reprimanded him, explaining the importance of Baba's participation and the assurance to humanity of the benefits of these prayers.

Baba, during the reading out of the Master's Prayer, would stand with his two hands palm to palm before his chest, with his eyes closed, and one had the sense of his being in communication with himself as the One. It was always a very moving time. Then Baba would move abruptly and make for the porch of the house, still on the arm of Francis in most cases. Once he asked me to take his arm. At the steps one of the women was there to take him on inside the house for the night. On this occasion, as I turned to go back, I heard his clap and turned at once to see that he wanted me to return for an embrace. I felt the warmth of his arms about me, and then it was evident that I should leave. I started back. But the mandali in front of me called out that Baba wanted me to return again. I walked back, and he folded me again tenderly in an embrace and kissed me on the side of the cheek. I turned once more and made my way almost in tears to mandali hall. It was the last time I saw the form of Meher Baba inhabited by his soul.

Here we must mention once more the suffering of these last years of Baba's life in physical form. During the final days, at the slightest movement great jerks would rack his physical frame, which he would describe as his "crucifixion." On one such occasion, he asked Eruch to tell him a funny story. As it happens, Eruch's mind refused to concentrate on such an occasion, and all he could think of was a story given in the newspaper about a yogi with a large following. Beset by the cares and responsibilities of his disciples, one day he announced that he would be going away for a short time, but "I will be back," he assured his followers. In fact, he never returned. Eruch had forgotten that this was not a funny story, but too late. It was told, and Baba made no comment. In one of his final spasms, Baba managed with great effort to show by signs to Eruch, "But I will come back." Eruch had no idea what Baba was talking about. And then one day, after Baba's leaving the body, Eruch remembered his joke. It was Baba's last message to him and to the physical world.

One day in 1967 we had had news that Baba was planning again for another great darshan for his followers in the West, having just given several important meetings for those in India. We did not know how his health would allow this, nor did his close mandali, but Baba insisted he would do it. Then one day I had a very early morning telephone call. And this led to the establishment of the second pillar of my life, and it too was given me by Meher Baba.

I was living in London in early 1969 on indefinite assignment there by the international petroleum company for which I worked during most of my professional career. The head office being on the West Coast of the United States and my position having some relative importance, it was not uncommon for the phone to ring well past midnight London time. As I picked up the phone it was often my president's secretary who would apologetically explain that my superior had had a sudden problem he wanted to talk over with me.

On this particular occasion in the black of night in late January 1969 I had the instant conviction as I awakened that the ringing phone was once more my impulsive superior. As I picked up the receiver I prepared to let fly a really lethal broadside. But instead of his cheery voice saying, "Oh, did I wake you up?" I could only hear a noise that sounded like someone choking.

Alarmed by such an obvious sound of distress I asked, "Who is this? Is something wrong?"

Again the choking and gasping, prolonged; but not even a word. Again I questioned, quickly, forcefully. Finally I made out indistinctly the words, "He's gone. He's left."

"Who's gone? What happened? Who is this?"

"It's Delia.[6] He's gone. I just had a phone call from Adi Jr.[7]"

"Who's gone? What is it?"

"It's Baba. He dropped the body early this morning."

I was thunderstruck. Meher Baba, whom I had known and loved for 24 years, had died. Granted, for quite some time we had been warned repeatedly that his health was very fragile. But it was Meher Baba himself who had kept us all on our toes for months now planning the great meeting with him in India for the springtime. It simply could not be! And yet it had to be, as Adi would certainly be one of the first to have such news. I exchanged a few other comments with Delia and then hung up the phone.

I looked at my watch. It was just after 5:00. I turned out the light and sat upright in my bed trying to think what to do. It was obvious: get to India at once and hope to see the

---

[6] Delia DeLeon, one of the earliest of the Westerners to join Meher Baba in the early 1930s on several occasions in India and Europe.

[7] The youngest brother of Meher Baba, then living in London.

beloved form once more.

It was Saturday morning. In those days also, Americans had to have a visa for entry into India before an airline would allow one to set foot on their plane. I had been through the procedure repeatedly and knew it by heart. One had to apply at the India High Commissioner's office in Aldwych and wait for one or two days even for an expedited reply. Enough! Although it was the weekend, perhaps luck would be with me.

Timing my arrival at the High Commissioner's office on the stroke of nine, I pressed the bell at the side of the closed door. Again. Again. Finally there were slow footsteps inside and a brown face appeared as the door cracked open. I explained my problem. With great kindness, which is normal for these people, the man explained that he was an attendant in the building staff, present only to ensure safety. He went on to specify that even the duty officer was away for the weekend–unavailable–no telephone contact at all.

I was sick at heart. I walked slowly up Haymarket and turned instinctively into the office where our company made its travel arrangements. I knew Rod, the head of the travel section, very well, having been constantly on his doorstep for a year.

Rod told me what I already knew. But he did have a suggestion. "Go to Air India on Bond Street," he advised. "They should be open by now. They may have some emergency procedure I don't know about. And, Don, good luck."

I took a cab to the Air India door. In a sleepy fashion the office was unfolding its pleats for a lazy Saturday morning. As I entered the office at the corner of the building a slim, stately young woman dressed in a sari came through a door from a back room just opposite me. "Can I be of help to you?" she asked. I admitted she could, and she led me to a desk at the

*side of the room. As I sat down I noticed a small nameplate:
"Miss Irani."*

*Although the name Irani is almost as common as Smith
among the Parsis, still, in India with all its teeming millions,
there are less than a tenth of a million of them in total. To
walk in off the street in London and find someone in Air
India with Meher Baba's family name Irani was therefore
quite a shock. I took heart at once, as instinctively I sensed
unusual motion behind the scenes. My pulse quickened as I
sat opposite Miss Irani.*

*Briefly and in a business-like manner I explained my
problem. She laid out the relevant rules, already well known
to me, but did add that the Port Commander at Bombay's
Santa Cruz Airport had discretionary authority in an
emergency to accept a passenger without a visa. Perhaps he
would use this power in the present situation.*

*"Where will you be going from Bombay for the burial of
your friend?" Miss Irani asked.*

*"First to Poona, and then directly on to a small city
nearby called Ahmednagar, where he lived much of his life."*

*"Interesting. I grew up in Poona. What was the name of
your friend? I might have known him or some of his family."*

*"By coincidence, his family name is the same as yours:
Irani. But after his boyhood he was never called by his given
name. His friends gave him sort of an affectionate nickname–
Meher Baba–which they have used for the rest of his life."*

*"That's extraordinary! My uncle was his schoolmate in
Poona and his close friend all his life. He's dead now, but I
remember his devotion to Meher Baba. Of course I will help
you. We must get you there in time."*

*Underneath, my sense of mathematical chance was
dizzied by the improbable succession of events. But
mathematics was drowned at once in the joy of a real*

possibility of doing the impossible–getting to Ahmednagar in time.

Between us we drafted a rather lengthy Telex of appeal to the Santa Cruz Airport Commander. Miss Irani promised it would be sent at once urgent priority, and that with luck, in two hours' time at 12:30, we should have a reply. The Air India flight, the only one available to me, was scheduled to leave at 3:00. If all went exactly right I should just make it. She would be off duty after 12:00, but she would brief her replacement, and I could start calling him at 12:30.

With the required name and telephone number in my wallet and a ticket for Bombay and an "open" coupon to Poona in my jacket, I caught a taxi home. After tossing a few instinctive necessities into a light bag I took another taxi to Heathrow, arriving shortly before 12:30. With my eye on my watch, at precisely the minute agreed I called my contact.

"Sorry, Mr. Stevens, no reply in yet. But we still have time. Call me again at 1:00."

Heart in mouth, a cavity in my stomach, hand shaking as I tried to dial, I called again at 1:00.

"It just came in, Mr. Stevens. Santa Cruz has issued an emergency order accepting your arrival without visa. I am sending a Telex to the captain of our plane at Heathrow instructing him to accept you on this basis. Good luck and bon voyage, sir. I hope you get to your friend in time."

I was shaking all over as I placed the receiver back on the hook. My eyes filled with tears, and I had trouble controlling my emotions of relief and joy. To this day, as I write about it, I am bathed in the same sense of infinite compassion which encompassed me on that day, and quietly the tears come again.

Suddenly exhausted, I went up to the mezzanine café and sipped without thought on a cup of the hot water my

*English friends offer as coffee. Still dazed, I went back down
to the Air India check-in counter and explained who I was.
The girl said at once that the authorization Telex had been
received from the Bond Street office only moments before and
that everything was prepared for me.*

*Through passport control, brief moments in the waiting
lounge, onto the plane and to my assigned seat. I did not even
know when the plane took off. I had fallen into an
untroubled sleep.*

*Some time later I came to and found myself in a half-
empty plane skimming through sparkling blue sky above
dense clouds. As I focused, it seemed to be the signal for the
loudspeaker system to come alive. A pleasant voice began to
speak.*

*"Sorry for the delay, ladies and gentlemen, in welcoming
you aboard and giving you a few details on our flight plan
today. This is Captain Irani, your pilot. There was so much
overcast at Heathrow and on the continent as we took off,
and we're pretty busy here in the cockpit under those
conditions, that I delayed talking to you until we'd gotten
above the weather. We are now overflying Geneva, and from
here our flight ...."*

*But there I lost him. Once more I was caught up in a
great wave of bemusement. Another Irani! Two people in Air
India critical to my mission, and both named Irani!*

*Then the sly humor underlying it all quickly hit me. I
burst out laughing, but suddenly controlled myself as I saw
inquisitive stares turned towards me.*

*"It's OK, Baba," I shouted inside myself. "I get the
message. Even methodical, plodding Stevens understands
what you are trying to get over to him."*

*And then I thought, how extraordinary, how typical of
Meher Baba. Within 24 hours of leaving his physical body he*

dreams up a characteristically humorous but indelibly clear
message. Its content is unmistakable: He is still as actively
present and concerned with his literal-minded Western oil
friend as when he was here in physical form. In fact, in an
unexpected manner, I must admit that he is even more
immediately present now than before, because he is no longer
absent even for a moment.

I relaxed completely. Every once in awhile I gave an
inward chortle as I thought of the typical manner and with a
slightly zany sense of humor that Baba had used to get his
message over. The flight became a delight, for I understood
already as if with a lifetime of experience that I had not been
cut off from my companion and Master, but gained him
knowingly forever. The sense of complete oneness with him I
had experienced at our first meeting in New York in August of
1952 was now established in even a further, unexpected
manner.

One must hand it to the Perfect Ones, they never leave a
stone unturned. I was about to learn a bit more of this
thoroughness in the present instance.

As I awoke in the wee morning hours, we were deplaning
passengers and refueling in Delhi. No one had disturbed me.
A sweeper boy whisking bits of rubbish down the aisle looked
over at me. Seeing my eyes gradually prying open he reached
somewhere beside him and tossed the Delhi edition of the
"Indian Express" over to me. (How did he get an early
morning edition?) I looked disinterestedly at the first page. A
one-paragraph article caught my eye. Sarosh Irani, disciple of
the spiritual Master, Meher Baba, had made the decision to
postpone interment of the deceased Meher Baba until Sunday
to allow his devotees throughout India to reach his tomb.
Incredible! What luck!

Again a doze, and then we were coming in to Bombay's

Santa Cruz Airport. I was recognized and passed at once through passport control and customs. "Good luck, Mr. Stevens." On to Indian Airlines counter. Early flight to Poona just loading and a few vacancies left. Then I was standing in one of two check-in lines. Each person had to give his or her name to compare with the flight manifest, the scribbling on one's ticket being so illegible that even the airline employee did not hazard trying to read it.

As my turn came and I was about to give my name, I halted for a moment and listened to the young man in the line at my side. Right on cue: "Mr. Irani."

"Don't rub it in, Baba; even slow, literal Don understands now what you are up to."

A faultless flight to Poona; an empty cab at the airport; a driver who demanded not more than twice the normal fare to drive me to Ahmednagar and up Meherabad Hill to Baba's tomb, prepared years before. Very quiet, but there was unusual tenting and electric wires strung about where none had ever been before. No doubt to take care of the public, even at night.

Suddenly I saw a familiar face coming around the corner of one of the smaller buildings. Eruch!

"Good lord, Don, how did you get here?"

"Too long a story for just now. But am I in time to see Baba?"

"Time? Yes, you're in time. Sarosh has decided to postpone putting the lid on for another 24 hours, there are so many people phoning and sending telegrams from everywhere."

We walked slowly to the familiar tomb. There he lay exactly as I knew him, as if in a rare moment of sleep. A fly droned down. Eruch flicked it away with a whisk. I had come in time, by his own magnificent grace.

*Still not the end. A Perfect One always sees another detail
to be filled in that I would never have dreamed of. Some
minutes later as I sat leaning against one of the tent poles, eyes
closed, I sensed someone at my side. I opened my eyes and
looked up. There was a tall, elderly, gentle-faced man I did not
know.*

*"You probably don't remember me." I agreed that I did
not. "Baba introduced us years ago when I was visiting here
and you drove up for just one hour in a taxi from Bombay
before returning to Tokyo." I remembered the situation but
still not the man. "Where did you come from, San Francisco?"
I told him that it was now London. "What airline did you
come on, Air India?" I assented. "Then you must have had
my son as your pilot–Captain Irani.[8] He was scheduled for the
flight from London yesterday."*

*There is no way to describe the grace and exquisite
thoughtfulness of a Perfect Being. It surrounds one with a
total, encompassing knowledge of love and security. To find
this reconfirmed so completely and with such humor in its
elegant expression was entirely unexpected. I knew, and I was
deeply touched.*

There is one last little story to add, which occurred several
weeks after the placing of the cover over the physical body of Meher
Baba in the tomb on Meherabad Hill. Baba's promised Great
Darshan for the springtime of 1969 did take place at Guruprasad in
Poona, and also at his homes in Meharazad and Meherabad.
Different groups from all over the world came to pay their respects
and to receive the spiritual blessing and love from the Master, which

---

[8] Some months later I found through an Indian friend that at that time there was one office
staff member in Air India with the family name Irani, and one pilot. I had been given both
of them on the same day.

filled the space and the hearts to overflowing.

As events began to quiet down at the end of the time, one day Eruch was seated with a group, among which there was a man he had not seen before. As the interchange carried along in the informal fashion so often associated with being with Baba on such an occasion, this man raised his hand and then asked if he might say something. Eruch at once said yes and then wondered what he might be letting himself and the rest of the group in for.

His fears were promptly confirmed, as the individual started by admitting at once that he had been a great critic of Baba through the years. The cause of his negative attitude, he clarified, was Baba's continuing announcements to the public that he would break his silence at a specific time and place, and then did not do so. Moreover, he commented that Baba never even bothered to acknowledge the change of plans nor the reason. And above all, the man added, this seemed to make no difference to Baba's followers. They even grew in numbers.

For this reason, he continued, he had criticized Baba for years, until now. And now, he wanted to speak out about the conclusion he had reached after all this time. This was that only God could do such a thing repeatedly and have the number of those who loved him increase regularly and constantly. Therefore, he, after all these years, wanted to say simply that now he took Baba to be God indeed.[0]

---

[0] Baba often made the comment that, "You are equally God also. The only difference between us is that I know this to be true now, but you do not know it yet."

8. HIGHLIGHTS

I n his later life, Meher Baba said repeatedly that he is the Highest of the High, The Ancient One, the Avatar of the Age.

In the earlier years of his life he functioned almost certainly with his devotees using frequently the techniques one associates classically with the Perfect Master. In his later years the pattern he predominantly manifested corresponds to the role one attributes to the Avatar. This is perhaps the first instance of the One taking on both the role of a Perfect Master as well as that of the Avatar in the same incarnation and body. Why this was necessary is very much open to conjecture. There appears to be no evident reason for this singular combination. The two roles fell into two separate and distinct portions of his life. Scholars of mystic literature may well be interested to look carefully for evidence as to whether the Avatar might have fulfilled these dual roles in other lifetimes.

The techniques used by the Perfect Master and the Avatar have marked differences due to the different constraints under which they operate, primarily the very shortened time span of activity of the Perfect Master. On the other hand, the Avatar too fulfills his duties in creation within the limitations of time and space, but the Avatar's span of responsibility extends much longer, into a length of hundreds of years, and so his techniques used for achieving the desired spiritual results are frequently very different from those of the Perfect Master.

Meher Baba stated that his Avataric gift to humanity was that of greatly enhanced access to the faculty of intuition. This opens up immediately the possibility of increased contact between the aspirant and the Avatar even when the Avatar is not in the physical body. The implications of this in regard to characteristics of the spiritual path followed by the aspirant are momentous for the future.

A key period of Meher Baba's life was named the New Life. There is a great deal of evidence suggesting that this was a dividing line between his Perfect Master phase and his functioning as the Avatar. It is also very likely in this period that, assisted by those remaining with him on his travels, he laid out the basic forms especially for spiritual search in the next avataric period.

During the New Life, the terms "companion" and "elder brother" were used repeatedly and significantly. Also, shortly after the New Life, Meher Baba in his "Last Message on the Alphabet Board" emphasized repeatedly the key phrase "inner links," which he had introduced into the record as far back as 1931. It appears from what one can observe that this is also a vital key to the mechanism for the search for the Truth in the next era.

Meher Baba evidenced almost an allergy to the working of miracles. He emphasized that they were no indication at all of spiritual status. He also cautioned that the aspirant who gives them great attention incurs considerable risk of being sidetracked from the true search for spiritual enlightenment.

Meher Baba also repeated many times that he did not interfere with the course of the individual's karma. On the other hand, he was observed apparently to do exactly that on rare occasion, attributing his action to the love of the individual asking his intercession. I would like to suggest that, under the circumstances in which I observed what appeared to be a breaking of his own rule, the karma of the individual was perhaps simply postponed, and not canceled nor basically modified. In any case, I know of only two such instances which appeared to involve the changing of this lifetime's karma, the one to which Baba admitted in 1956 in California, and the other in the case of a fatally ill small boy. The entire family, which was devoted totally and classically to Baba, prayed constantly to him to take this burden from the child. The miracle happened. But I suspect that either this or another balancing out will occur in a subsequent lifetime, undoubtedly when Baba will not be subjected to such intensive and selfless love.

Should one speak, therefore, of the modification of the timing of karma in these rare instances, rather than changing the karma itself? He said many times that he was the slave of the love of his lovers. I believe it, but only rarely to the point of interfering in the functioning and almost certainly never to the point of breaking his own laws.

Once more, the Avatar has taken on himself a great burden of suffering for all of mankind. It was sad to see. I recall to this day the action of Dr. Ginde when I visited his home in Bombay after attending the entombment of Meher Baba. He saw me in his living room and at once prostrated himself flat on the floor, his forehead touching my feet. I was stunned. He whispered from the prone, "No, Don, I see on your shoes the dust that has come from the tomb of the Avatar." He had lived intimately the final suffering of the one who does not fail each time he is with us to take on a part of our own suffering.

Now I realize it is time to put my own self on record in this

complex issue of Meher Baba's Avatarhood. I described in the
beginning that it had been one of two completely indigestible
situations when Murshida Martin first introduced her mureeds to
the subject of Meher Baba. And so, you have the right to ask, what
happened after that?

When I first met Baba face to face in New York in August 1952,
any and all questions of Avatarhood completely disappeared. I have
to be honest, the subject had neither interest nor importance for me.
This may seem an incredible lack of following through on my part of
high priority issues. Perhaps it was. I do not say the contrary, just
that it was a fact that the stature and qualities of Meher Baba that
were overwhelmingly present at that first occasion relegated any
question of his hierarchical status to a secondary position. I had too
many matters of far more immediate concern to me to digest and
also to face up to, because it was evident from the start that Baba
represented equally a challenge and a total assurance such as I had
never encountered before. This became immediately apparent in my
life with a dizzying speed. Above all, it was no time to occupy my
store of time and energy with questions for which I had by no means
the experience nor the capacities to handle them.

For better or for worse then, the matter stayed in the realm of
the irrelevant for years except on the rare occasion when some
individual relatively new to the subject of Baba raised the question
of his Avatarhood with me. My answers were never satisfactory to the
inquirer, but I could not speak on a subject both irrelevant to me as
well as intellectually unresolved. It was not to remain so indefinitely,
however. Finally, when *Listen, Humanity* was to go into a new
edition through a new publisher, I was asked to write a new
"Introduction," bringing matters up to date. This was especially
important due to the death meanwhile of Baba.

As I wrote, I realized that I would have to make some comment
on public reaction to the subject of Avatarhood. I looked inside my
mind and saw at once that it was where it had been since August

1952. Then I went deeper. I opened the door to the home of the inner man, and promptly the answer was there waiting. He had quietly made his assessment and conclusion while I was busy with other things. "Of course he is the Avatar. No one could possibly have done the things that you yourself have witnessed through the years in his company, nor in the manner in which they were accomplished other than the Avatar himself."

The conclusion of the inner man was definitive. As soon as I was aware of it, I recognized that this I too now knew consciously, and there was no question of the base on which the evaluation had been made.

PART II

9. THE WHIM

I t all starts with the Whim.[1]

In the preceding part we have touched on Meher Baba's starting point in considering the nature of Reality, that this is God, infinite and indivisible and, in His original state, completely unconscious. However, in this original completely unconscious state, God embodied the innate characteristic of the possibility to wish to know His divinity consciously. In addition, a brief description was given of the beginning of Creation, the beginning of which was precipitated by the surge of this potential that rested latent within unconscious God, to wish to know consciously His state of divinity.

Still further, some consideration was given to the important extension Baba has made to the subject known classically as sanskaras, this being so closely tied into some of the important facts of the history of Baba's life with his close followers.

Although the material already presented to this point on Reality, the origins of Creation and the nature of sanskaras, may have seemed complex, we are now at the stage where these subjects must be laid out in considerably greater detail. While the words used are ancient, the concepts Baba ties to them are relatively new and therefore not easy to grasp. But their importance for understanding

---

[1] *God Speaks*, p. 10.

what Baba has offered concerning the meaning and mechanics of Creation requires their further elaboration.

To clean the slate for what follows, consider that the words "time," "space" and "desire" are in the end almost certainly meaningless, in fact non-existent within a state of infinite unity. Even to say that such fundamental terms may finally be without enduring substance can come as a shock and be found almost impossible not to reject out of hand. Yet, a few moments of reflection will suggest that all of these concepts exist only where there is division, separation, contrast. If the very original as well as the continuing state of God is one of infinite and absolutely unity, without separation even in imagination, then the "enduring" existence of space and time have to be called into serious doubt. In fact, Baba does insist, repeatedly, that these concepts must be discarded as meaningless in the understanding of the final functioning of human consciousness within the realm of Reality.

Equally important from the human standpoint is the fact that in Reality there is no such thing as desire, or even the relatively feeble "wish." Meher Baba's choice of the term "whim" as the origin of Creation is therefore a very careful selection; usage of this word is fraught with meaning for the entire spread of his description of the universe, its characteristics and its final reason for being. A *whim*, as the word is used in the present day, has little or no connotation of emotion. If anything, its closest cousin is a sense of humor. It is not a meaningless observation to reflect that a keen sense of humor is often an important characteristic of a highly developed spiritual figure. Meher Baba's own words bear out this sense:

"The infinitude of the God-Is state made God absolutely independent.... To exercise a whim is always the mark of an independent nature, because it is whimsicality that always colours the independent nature.... Whim after all is a whim; and, by its very nature, it is such that 'why–wherefore–when' can find no place in its nature."

All this discussion of the words "whim," "desire," "wish," "sanskaras" may strike one as an academic toying with words. It is just the opposite. It is the necessary preparation for attempting an understanding of the all-important statement by Meher Baba that, from the very first human incarnation, the one central problem facing each human entity is that of elimination of the habit patterns (sanskaras, impressions) stored up during the long course of the evolution of consciousness. These habit patterns are the cause of desire and inevitably also of man's misconception, as described in Chapter I, that a vast segment of "reality" revolves around the nature and the end goals of these desires. Since they are almost universally rooted in the outside world, then reality for each human being tends to begin and end in the material world which surrounds him. Granted, a few special human beings do value inner principles and attainments, even to the detriment of the external; but statistically, this is a vanishingly small proportion of humanity. For the vast majority the focus of consciousness is directed almost universally onto the physical surroundings.

To pose the problem that faces each human being in his quest for Truth and Reality in its simplest and most blunt terms, it is to shift the focus of attention from external to internal values. For thousands of incarnations the center of Reality has been ingrained into us as being external. For even a beginning of progress to be made, the suspicion must dawn on the individual that the seat of Reality is internal. After that almost impossible flip in viewpoint, then the job of deconditioning oneself from the product of those thousands of incarnations of wrongly assessed reality has to be undertaken. (It is not too early to suggest right here that this is really hard work, as the enormous burden of millions of acts of misidentification will require an incredible number of diametrically opposed actions to begin to equilibrate the account. This is our heritage of ancient, individual evolution. Certainly a reason here for quite a few rebalancing deeds, one begins to realize.)

All this accumulation of "false reality" has been made unthinkingly. It is in fact the product of an automatic basis of judgment and memory. Any internal facts, such as emotions produced in the developing external situation, have almost always been considered as products of the "real out there," and therefore as secondary in priority and with a lesser content of practical reality. One recalls society's almost universal adoption of the rule of action that one must try to avoid unwanted complications in important living situations through the intrusion of emotional factors which can color one's judgment. In brief, the "in here" is not only of lesser importance than the "out there," but is often considered to be definitely detrimental to the exercise of balanced decision and "getting on with the job."

Now, having stated the nature of the fundamental problem, one may suggest for the present an important working principle that will be encountered repeatedly in our further consideration of the implications of what Meher Baba has embodied in his words. This is that there appears to be a firm work rule embedded in the game of spiritual advance that insists that there be some sort of division of labor between the aspirant and the spiritual Master who helps him along the way. Neither does the whole task by himself, but even the formula for the proportioning of the shares seems to vary formidably from situation to situation. We will revert to this complex partitioning later.

Meanwhile, we return to the Whim which was the start. Even the word "start" is now charged with significance. It was truly the start, because all time began with the manifesting of the Whim. Here it was that contrast and the simplest form of separation began, the necessary base on which time can exist.

Meher Baba is very clear that the surging of the Whim constituted a disturbance in the infinite and undivided nature of the original unconscious God. He likens it to the effect produced by a little boy passing a still pond, who has the impulse to toss a stone into the water. The previously unrippled surface is immediately disturbed and small wavelets form. Fascinated, the boy tosses in a second, a third and still other stones. The result is a great complex of intersecting waves and complex patterns formed on the surface of the originally still surface of the pond.

Although charming, the example of the little boy throwing stones into the water bears little further resemblance to the vast complexity of the Creation that springs from the Whim or original urge of God to know His own divinity consciously. However, it does give the picture of wave motion which is the underlying principle of all material creation. Even the most complex forms and phenomena resolve to at times enormously intricate combinations of different types of wave motion. As discussed earlier, this fulfills also the fundamental requirement for the generation[2] of the most rudimentary as well as the most sophisticated levels of consciousness. This requisite is that there be contrast, separation, even opposition, to act as the two poles of the battery, as Jung aptly described. The universe and the possibility of God knowing His own Divinity consciously are therefore established in one and the same moment: that of the birth of the disturbance produced by the Whim itself.

The foregoing perhaps seems too simple to be true, yet there it is in its stark and magnificent simplicity. One often observes that just such simplicity seems characteristic of all that flows directly from God. When we as humans, in a different context of multiplicity become involved, complexity and obscurity too often enter the door. This is certainly the case as soon as we try to understand how and where a human being fits into what has just now been created. When

---

[2] "Generation" is in fact inaccurate in the sense that consciousness already was present in latent form in the infinitude of unconscious God. Therefore, all of the complex interaction in Creation, from which consciousness emerges, does not really create or generate consciousness, merely bringing the original latency into a manifested form. However, for our purposes we will often use the terms "generate" and "produce," for example, in connection with the action of Creation on God's latent infinite consciousness, although the implication of the production of something new is false.

in all probability a mystic suggests to us for the first time that all life and all Creation are no more than a dream within the final infinite and undivided reality of God, then the conscious work begins, and perhaps that work never does end within the infinitude of the dream of Creation.

To return to the complex wave forms created by the surging of the Whim, one should understand at once that the fundamental nature of the Whim is to arrive somehow at the goal of God's realization consciously of His own divinity. Until that goal is reached, the Whim is unfulfilled. Obviously the first act of the crest of a tiny wave regarding the trough of the same wave is unlikely to produce an iota of consciousness sufficiently complex to reflect within its own being the infinitude of God. But at least it is a beginning.

Before going on to the next phase of this fascinating process of creating Creation and a level of consciousness capable of reflecting the infinitude of God, it would be well to pause and consider for a few moments the nature of consciousness.

What is consiousness? How does it work? Where is it stored when it is created? How is it related to awareness–another term that seem dangerously close?

These are all pertinent questions which need some attention, even if finally we are unable to resolve them. But in such case, at least one is aware of the unknowns of the voyage.

So, first, what is consciousness?

Here I would like to offer a page from my own personal experience. In an odd series of developments when I was first initiated onto the mystic path, I found myself trying to find a way to control excessive anger when it occurred on occasion in daily life. In my observations and experimentation, I found gradually that I could separate consciousness from anger for a fraction of a second if I caught it at the very beginning of the event. From there it followed fairly naturally that I should try to prolong the period of suspension

of anger from consciousness. This led inevitably to knowing
consciousness all by itself, without source or object. In my own
naive way, I called this my "neutral plateau." And what is it? It
just is. It exists, once generated, independently from all sources and
all objectives. It is, nothing more.

    I am well aware that other techniques for arriving at just pure
consciousness exist. Many objectives can be approached by a variety
of avenues. Regardless of the means by which one achieves a
state of unadulterated pure consciousness, it exists completely
independent of both the generating complex as well as the object
on which it may be focused.

    Meher Baba indicates that consciousness and the individual drop-soul survive all events, accidents and processes related to Creation. Evidently they are the two indestructible realities that emerge from Creation and all the actions that occur within its realm. The drop-soul, Baba explains, is the result of the surging of the Whim, which creates a froth of bubbles which are all of the same nature and being as God. But the separation into a separate bubble exists only in imagination or the dream, as in Reality, God is indivisible.

    Even the so-called consciousness formed in the process of the interaction of separatenesses within Creation was already latent within the original unconscious being of God before the Whim surged. But once having been developed from latency into a manifest function, it continues in that state until the dream is terminated, for it never really was. Hence, in fact there only exists the One Reality and the latency within that One infinite Reality. Consciousness is of this latter category, and it is for its development from the latency into the Reality that all of Creation is brought into being by God's Whim.

    Where is consciousness stored? Since it is inseparable from the oneness of God, it is stored everywhere within God. In our dream of separateness, it is associated[3] with each drop-soul, which carries out its responsibility to develop the specialized functions of consciousness from the time of its formation within the vortex of the Whim. This also means inevitably that consciousness, regardless of where it is generated, is finally accessible by all the other drop-souls in Creation.

"Awareness"–a very ambiguous term which has many of the connotations of the word consciousness itself. Consciousness exists independently of all things. It was brought from latency into active manifestation through things, but its existence is completely independent of them. It may be focused on those things during the time it remains within the confines as it were of Creation, and it is in this act that awareness springs into being.[4] Just as a searchlight exists even when the rays of light are cast off into space, so consciousness exists independent of any materiality. But once focused on some thing, it illuminates that thing and awareness is the result. But the "thing" illuminated is not necessary for the being of consciousness. The act of illumination only produces the physical evidence of the existence of consciousness.

The "tragedy" involved in the creation of consciousness, to use the viewpoint of the human being who is stuck with the problem and as yet without the understanding of the entire picture that could make it appear reasonable, is that consciousness as it is developed identifies with the scene of action and not with the Reality that is hidden within the action of the dream.

---

[3] "Associated" is the manner in which Meher Baba speaks of the relationship of consciousness with the individual drop-soul. This is in contrast to the sanskaras, which Baba describes as being stored in the mental body of the individual human being.

[4] The act of focusing consciousness may be more or less sophisticated, depending on the developed talents of the individual. Thus in early life, awareness may be relatively simple, becoming more complex in later life as the accumulated talents involved in this focusing are gradually increased. This easily leads to the confusion of regarding consciousness as being "developed" during the course of one's life. In fact Meher Baba says flatly that this is not true, that the level of consciousness reaches its maximum in the last animal incarnation, and does not normally increase nor decrease thereafter.

Meher Baba describes in a most simple and beautiful manner the basic activity within Creation: this is the development of consciousness within the duality and contrast that typifies Creation, and the identification of that consciousness with the finite rather than the Infinite, which is its true goal:

"The phenomenal world of finite objects is utterly illusory and false. It has three states: the *gross*, the *subtle*, and the *mental*. Although all three of these states of the world are false, they represent different *degrees* of falseness. Thus the gross world is farthest from Truth (God), the subtle world is nearer Truth, and the mental world is nearest to Truth. All three states of the world owe their existence to cosmic Illusion, which the soul has to transcend before it realizes the Truth.

"The sole purpose of creation is for the soul to enjoy the infinite state of the Oversoul *consciously*. Although the soul eternally exists in and with the Oversoul in an inviolable unity, it cannot be conscious of this unity independently of creation, which is within the limitations of time. It must therefore evolve consciousness before it can realize its true status and nature as being identical with the infinite Oversoul, which is one without a second. The evolution of consciousness requires the duality of subject and object—the center of consciousness and the environment (that is, the world of forms).

"How does the soul get caught up in Illusion? How did the formless, infinite, and eternal Soul come to experience itself as having form and as being finite and destructible? How did *Purusha*, or the supreme Spirit, come to think of itself as *prakriti*, or the world of nature? In other words, what is the cause of the cosmic Illusion in which the individualized soul finds itself? To realize the true status of the Oversoul—which is one, indivisible, real and infinite—the soul needs consciousness. The soul does get consciousness; however this consciousness is not of God but of the universe, not of the Oversoul but of its shadow, not of the One but of many, not of the Infinite but of the finite, not of the Eternal but of the transitory. Thus the soul, instead of realizing the Oversoul, gets involved in cosmic Illusion; and hence, though really infinite, it comes to experience itself as finite. In other words, when the soul develops consciousness, it does not become conscious of its own true nature but of the phenomenal world, which is its own shadow."[5]

While consciousness is brought into active being within the duality of Creation, another product also results, the sanskaras already discussed in simple form. This will shortly demand a separate and detailed consideration, as here is the Janus produced within the drama of Creation. The nature of sanskaras, their role in the development of physical form, and their final dissolution into the nothingness from which they came is so important and all-pervading that it will be developed in the next chapter, which is devoted entirely to the subject. Meanwhile, it is necessary for the moment to understand that they are the product in the surging of the Whim which both underlies and finally sustains form as it becomes increasingly complex, but also diverts consciousness from Reality. Further, the sanskaras are the driving force underlying the evolution of form. This is an astonishing clarification made by Meher Baba, and certainly it will be the source of debate as extended and lively as that which greeted Darwin's original description of his Theory of Evolution.

Essentially, then, in the first instant of the manifestation of the Whim, there are created the three major building blocks of Creation: matter, consciousness and sanskara (the recorded impression of the "event"). Ultimately, matter disappears; consciousness, which was originally latent in the original state of God, has become manifest and remains; and curiously enough, the

---

[5] *Discourses,* p. 223.

impression also remains in a subtle manner as the "individualized" aspect of the "infinitely individualized consciousness" of God. This is perhaps unexpected, but is too firmly anchored into the record to be doubted. Finally, one must conclude that all the infinitude of drop-souls that sweep through creation were latent in the original state of God, and hence the immortality of each individual was inherent in the original nature of God. More of this later.

Going back to the series of events occurring in what is now Creation, which is the product of the Whim of God to know His divinity consciously, there are certain basic developments and products which are fundamental to all of the later subjects which characterize our complex universe. Perhaps the first to be described is the spectrum of "disturbance" produced by the surging of the Whim. There is no reason to suppose that something as fundamental as the first creation of disturbance within the infinite indivisible nature of God should be limited to one type or even a limited series of characteristic wave motions. In fact, our knowledge of Creation as we already see it from a scientific standpoint is one of an enormous spectrum of different types of waves extending over extraordinarily wide ranges. This we know from physically verifiable evidence.

Meher Baba in simple fashion states that the disturbance which is Creation extends in fact well beyond the bounds which we have explored scientifically to date. As do other great spiritual authorities throughout the centuries, he speaks in the foregoing quotation of two additional domains of existence beyond the physically verifiable: the "subtle" and the "mental" spheres. From all evidence and within the implications of what Baba describes as being the fundamental source of Creation, these two additional spheres should not be thought of as separate or removed. Rather, this concept of "spheres" seems to be only a convenient manner of grouping together bands of wave phenomena when going from the longest wavelengths to the shortest.

As the Whim moves to express the potential to manifest

consciousness already latent within God, a curious phenomenon accompanies this action. It is the formation in imagination, or within a "dream" as it is often put, of limited portions of God Himself which appear for the present to be separated and to begin to lead an independent existence. These, as noted above, Baba terms "drop-souls," and immediately on their formation they associate with both the material disturbance created by the movement of the Whim, as well as with the minute iotas of consciousness that begin to be produced within the creation of contrast.

In a private conversation during the editing of *God Speaks*, Meher Baba clarified that in fact this association stretches back in the evolution of form into sub-sub-gaseous states, before continuing on into the gaseous, and thence as he describes in *God Speaks*, to the stone, metal, vegetable, worm, fish, bird, animal and finally man states. He said that he would add the sub-sub-gaseous states in the future to the list of forms through which the association of the drop-soul with matter passes. At the same time he emphasized again the importance of understanding that consciousness is fully developed in the last animal form and does not increase in the human stages.

It is interesting that Meher Baba describes these transitions from stone through human forms as the "seven major leaps" through which the evolving form passes.[6] This is the same number of planes through which the individual has been considered to progress during his involution back to his original state as God, but in the end with complete consciousness of that Godhood. It is very easy to see why so many persons become fascinated with the coincidences, or more, that exist in the realm of numbers.

It is helpful to place this progression through the planes in relation to the system of spheres that corresponds to the higher spectra of wave form that Baba calls the subtle and the mental. He explains first of all though that this progression through the planes

---

[6] *God Speaks*, p. 30.

does not begin as soon as the drop-soul arrives at the human stage. The barrier of sanskaric inheritance is so formidable, with its identification of reality as being external, that Baba states quite bluntly that it takes quite some thousands of reincarnations for that monolithic identification even to begin to fissure. When this does start to happen, and the individual drop-soul identifies consciously with an honest search for a more enduring and better-based system of value, then he is said to go on the Path. This is a psychological state of some importance, and it too will be discussed at length below.

Here, finally, the individual has made a decision of great importance concerning value and the investment of himself in the future. There is never any real turning back after this, as the perception of value in life has been so fundamentally reoriented that all of the old attractions that might cause a reversal of value have been gone through and seen to be faulted. The conviction is not philosophical. It comes through actual personal experience and so is not susceptible to argument nor to the temptation of experiencing yet another attractive passage of fleeting enchantment.

Once this decision has been made concerning true value and where investment of one's time and energy are to be made in the future, then, according to Meher Baba and a great majority of spiritual masters, the individual has won the right to help from those who have gone before him. There is a very ancient tradition of the existence of a spiritual hierarchy which bears a continuing responsibility to assist certain meritorious souls along the way to realization of the Truth, which is God. Just where and how this spiritual hierarchy functions is described in different manners by different authorities. Meher Baba gives no blueprint for its workings. He does define clearly the nature and responsibilities of the Avatar, whom he describes as being the first human being to complete the full trip of evolution and involution.[7] He is at the same

---

[7] *Discourses*, p. 268.

time the son of God and the one who in permanence must return into Creation periodically to give humanity a push forward when it has come again to identify so completely with materiality that spiritual progress has almost stopped.

In addition to the Avatar or Christ, there are, according to Baba, always present and functioning on earth five Perfect Masters–those who have recently completed the long and arduous climb back from complete identification with the physical realm to the realization of one's own Godhood. These constitute the core of the functioning spiritual hierarchy, to which Baba adds certain angels, agents and probably advanced spiritual aspirants. But where these last may fit in is not clear from Baba's discussions of the mechanics of spiritual unfoldment. Other spiritual disciplines go into the subject of angels and spiritual agents in some detail. My personal impression is that much of the material cited falls into the realm of conjecture and not necessarily fact. In any case, while we mention that Meher Baba has described these entities and ascribed roles to them, nevertheless for our purposes we leave this realm to the qualified specialist.

Normal physical life and consciousness centered in the physical world are all grounded in the physical sphere according to Baba. Even entering onto the Path is not necessarily accompanied by any major change in this arena of experience and judgment of reality. Persons may have on occasion unusual experiences or coincidences in their lives, and even may master in a mechanical fashion certain laws which pertain to the higher spheres. However, neither these occasional experiences nor their mechanical mastery imply a higher state of spiritual unfoldment. Unfortunately, once alerted to the probable existence of such higher spheres, the aspirant is often so ambitious that he attaches great spiritual significance to incidents that are primarily introductory "seedings" intended to awaken. Also, such incidents provide a certain sense of being supported by reliable friends who are constantly at hand.

One is, as it were, on the threshold. Then one begins to have experiences that are the product of the sensing mechanisms of both the physical as well as the subtle body.[8] These experiences may be unusual sounds, sights and smells. Here is where one may experience the "music of the spheres," about which many have written and exclaimed. The most magnificent symphony of our classic literature runs pale before the beauty of this higher form of music. At this point one begins to function on the borderline between the physical and the subtle spheres.

This border is also often referred to as the "astral" world. In fact it is not a separate world, but a sheath as Baba describes it between the two which has certain properties of each. It is chiefly of importance in that it is here that the individual arrives after dropping his physical body, when he is said to have died. In fact, all that happens in death is that the old physical body, which is subject to the same wear and tear as an automobile or a set of clothing, is discarded and the drop-soul, still identified with its subtle and mental bodies, retires for a period of stock-taking of the events of the previous lifetime. Here it is also that at times the individual arrives during sleep, when the physical body and its processes are in abeyance.

Heaven and hell also have their relative existences in the astral. Meher Baba explains that they are not actual locations, but rather composite emotional states that are experienced, dependent upon the major experiences of the just-past lifetime. If the preponderance of those experiences were those of inflicting hell, then one experiences even more vividly the hell of what had been lived. In the case of a preponderance of loving and benevolent sentiments, then one experiences a heaven state. In any case, the life just lived is reviewed in detail, and the essence is stocked in the mental body to become, as Baba puts it, a part of the intuitive wisdom of future lives. This is indeed an incentive to live one's life productively, as the

---

[8] *God Speaks*, pp. 44–58.

essence will stand one in good stead into the far-removed future of further lifetimes.

Having outlined such an attractive beginning to the spiritual path, which includes support by a spiritual hierarchy, one must stop however and take fully into account something that Meher Baba describes as "being led under the veil." Once an aspirant has formed a strong and dependable relationship with the spiritual Master, and especially if this Master is a Perfected One—that is, God Realized, then the occurrence of fascinating and even miraculous incidents is rare to non-existent.[9]

This can be disconcerting, as we are so conditioned to judging spiritual attainment by the frequency of occurrence of miraculous events that we are tempted to feel that we have fallen off the spiritual circuit when they do not occur. Meher Baba is very clear in explaining why a great Master avoids them. It is simply that such an experience in itself is not an indication of spiritual progress, nor does it necessarily contribute to advancement. It is most often given to confirm the aspirant on his way, and to give him the necessary resolve to meet and overcome some of the more demanding events which inevitably are encountered along the Path.

Unfortunately, the pilgrim frequently takes the unusual event to be an extraordinary indication of spiritual importance and immediately tends to develop a desire for more. This is a detraction rather than an assist on the Path, and so the Master must sidetrack and administer antidotes to this desire.

Even so, after many years of regarding how a great master handles this complexity, I might suggest that, with a remarkable sense of humor the master can give both the sense of his constant, continuing presence, as well as cut through the cathedral effect we build at once into that presence. True, there is a very warm sense of being cared for, while at the same time there is a delicate smile at

---

[9] *Discourses*, pp. 155–156.

the manner in which it has been effected.

The first, second and third planes are all contained within the subtle sphere. While the first two are concerned principally with unusual experiences of the senses, the third gets more serious from the standpoint of what the aspirant can now effect within his environment. Here the resources are those of power, both those related to the physical sphere, as well as the unlimited power resources of the subtle plane. One is able to perform miracles of astonishing magnitude, but one is not yet developed morally to the point of knowing when and how to use such power. It is the beginning of a period of enormous danger. Hence the individual led under the veil by a Perfect One may seem, as he is indeed, a very lucky person to be able to avoid pitfalls that can result in real tragedy.

Just as the first plane within Creation was a border between the physical and the subtle, so the fourth plane in turn is the border between the subtle and the mental. Here the individual has at his beck and call infinite energy, and the making and destruction of worlds and universes is within his capabilities. The problem is that the moral base of judgment is still not developed to the point of discriminating between the healthy and the undesirable. It is a great temptation to such an individual to use these powers for all types of self-aggrandizement, controlling others, even wreaking one's revenge.

This is the time when the presence of the Perfect Masters in Creation is necessary, largely to prevent the type of catastrophe that such a fourth plane master can precipitate. The Perfect Master is one with God, and therefore knows all that passes within Creation and therefore can control the fourth plane master if he verges on effecting a major catastrophe to Creation.

Nevertheless there are several types of monstrously unwise actions that the Perfect Ones do not guard against. These can result in the fourth plane master crashing down and regressing all the way back to the stone stage of consciousness. Baba gave examples of such catastrophic action as the killing for lust and using the powers to satisfy one's craving for fame. Why the Perfect Masters prevent physical catastrophes to Creation but not the more personal cravings on the fourth plane has not been explained. Perhaps this passes into the domain of personal choice and testing which seems a constant occurrence on the spiritual Path.

Once the fourth plane is passed, the aspirant arrives at the fifth, which is that of the saints and is fully in the mental or third sphere. Here there is no longer a temptation to use the universal powers for personal reasons. The moral base of action prevails, and the soul is protected from any further possibility of a great fall. Even so, there is still another fact in this area that is often distressing to the Western mentality. This is that the saint may be either a warm and loving individual, or a fiery and chastising person. Both are equally recognized as being truly saints. The nature of God is all-inclusive, and Godliness is not necessarily at all the discarding of all that we regard as being negative and the conservation of all we feel to be pure and loving. Rather, it is the equilibrating of the opposites and surpassing them.

Saints are frequently utilized by the Perfect Ones in helping the ongoing of other human beings in their quest for God. This would lead one to believe that they are often or even always included in the spiritual hierarchy which performs duties in the spiritual quest.

Still in the mental sphere, the sixth plane is characterized by the aspirant seeing God in all that surrounds him. God is literally everywhere. All who come in contact with a sixth plane saint benefit by that contact. Hence the tradition in the Far East of trying to be in the company of a very advanced soul, even though that person may live in filth and act in a manner incomprehensible to the logical mind. His spiritual greatness is sensed rather than proven.

Here it should be remarked that the usage of the term "mental" for the third sphere has little to do with logic and reason, or even with being reasonable. In fact, individuals resident on this plane are more often than not quite unreasonable in their actions. They see through to the heart of matters, and their actions are designed to act on those heart matters. This they do by a sort of balancing out of forces that are not at all apparent to the logical mind bound up in daily physical events.

One needs to recall that it is in the mental body of each individual that is found the storage mechanism for the memories of all incidents that have ever happened in the long history of evolution of each individual. Such "permanent" storage is possible because the "stuff" of the mental body is far finer than that of the physical body, and therefore not susceptible to the wear which is characteristic of physical objects. For this reason the mental body goes on as if forever while different physical bodies are adopted, worn out, discarded and the process repeated many, many times. The subtle body that exists in the second or subtle sphere has a comparable longevity. For this reason it is true that "as one sows, so shall one reap," as the permanent storage record exists within oneself.

Then, somewhere, sometime, in some manner, events occur which precipitate the sixth plane Master into the seventh, which is that of God-Realization. Meher Baba often repeats that this leap is greater than the total of all the previous leaps from one plane to another. In fact, he says the difference is infinite, and that it can only be accomplished through the intercession of a Perfect One, in other words an individual who has already made the jump.

As a matter of interest in this regard, when on his visit to America in 1956 Meher Baba advised a small group one day that the West has now arrived generally at the spiritual level necessary to sustain the development of Perfect Masters, and that they would be increasingly found in Western countries from this time.

The one final elucidation offered in this area is the fact that the majority of individuals who achieve Realization drop their bodies almost at once. However, there are exceptions by individuals who have chosen freely to remain in Creation for some time afterwards to help others along the path. The statistic is that there are always 56 of these in the world at all times, and of this number, seven have gone on to become reintegrated into consciousness of the physical world about them. Of these, five function as the Perfect Masters in charge of overseeing Creation and also guarding against the type of accident that for instance a fourth plane master might precipitate. The five Perfect Masters oversee the plans for Creation set out by the Christ Avatar, and when they precipitate his advent each seven hundred to fourteen hundred years, they retire at once from their duties, and the Avatar assumes the complete direction of Creation during his life in the physical body.

Thus goes the story of the Whim and its far-reaching consequences. In fact, all of Creation is the outcome of the surging of the whim of God to know His divinity consciously.

10. SANSKARAS

The surging of the Whim has three important and immediate results. The first is the birth of the basis for material substance, the second is the beginning of the production of the most simple and minute iota of consciousness, and the third is the recording of the event that produced this first iota of consciousness. This last is what Meher Baba defines as a sanskara (impression, habit).

The exact nature and manner of its recording he does not describe.

These are the three pillars which underlie Creation–all materiality, including the entire universe; the infinitude of events occurring between apparently dissociated or contrasting elements, which is the basis of the infinitely individualized consciousness of God that results; and the extraordinarily complex recording and storage process of the "knots of psychic energy," as Meher Baba terms them, which are produced as a result of each occurrence of interaction within duality. These are the sanskaras (impressions, habits) which in turn result in the complex series of adventures each droplet of being within Creation must undergo in the unwinding and dispersing of those recordings (sanskaras) of individual events which have been mistaken as being Reality. When this is accomplished, then consciousness accomplishes that for which the entire scheme was set en route, for the One to know Itself consciously as divine God.

It is this concept of what is a sanskara, and above all its role during the initial development and the later freeing (perfecting) of that fully developed consciousness, to which this chapter is devoted. In its detail it is a unique contribution by Meher Baba to man's intellectual comprehension of God and the role man plays in the seemingly endless complexity of Creation.

Did you ever sit down and suddenly realize that there was absolutely no base for your insistence on doing something in a particular manner? Many years ago, while living in San Francisco and shortly after having read Baba's Discourses on sanskaras, I was walking down from Nob Hill to my office on Bush Street. As I walked, I suddenly realized that I was taking the same way that I took every day. And I wondered for the first time if there was any reason to take that particular route. I even speculated that it might be interesting to try a different combination of streets. But to my amazement, as I did this, I found that I was invaded by a vague, uneasy resistance to the idea. I didn't want to change. I even thought it might be harder, or that, inexplicably, I might get lost. Crazy, after having lived in or near the heart of the city for decades. And yet this was my reaction. Does this give you a beginning appreciation of what a habit pattern is, a sanskara, as Baba prefers to term it? Or sometimes he calls it a knot of psychic energy deposited in the mental body of the human being. We will return to this when we progress to the section dealing with the major outlines of Baba's description of mankind and the Creation in which he lives.

"Selfless service and meditation are both spontaneous when they are inspired by love. Love is therefore rightly regarded as being the most important avenue leading to the realization of the Highest. In love the soul is completely absorbed in the Beloved and is

therefore detached from the actions of the body and mind. This puts
an end to the formation of new sanskaras and also results in the
undoing of old sanskaras by giving to life an entirely new direction.
Nowhere does self-forgetfulness come so naturally and completely as
in the intensity of love. Hence it has been given the foremost place
among the methods that secure release of consciousness from the
bondage of sanskaras."[1]

The fundamental trait of the sanskara to express itself in action
at a later moment, and to do this in the same manner as that by which
it was formed, has been mentioned before. Also, the manner in which
the focus of the formed iota of consciousness rests on the physical
environment in which it was manifested was pointed out as being a
crucial and stubbornly persistent bias. This results later in the history
of each drop-entity by its having to pursue a long route of unlearning
before the consciousness it has developed can be brought finally to a
new focus, which is then on the only Reality–God.

The mechanism described by Meher Baba as being required
for the expression of the accumulated sanskaras is simple in its
beginning form. This is only that the physical form with which the
sanskara, as well as the iota of consciousness, is associated must
be of sufficient complexity to allow adequate expression of the
sanskara.

This is not a surprising condition, as present-day complex
technological civilization is replete with examples of various types of
recorded information which require a specialized form of "reader" or
projector to express the recorded information in an adequate manner.
Musical recordings and photographic images are examples of this.

The physical form required by the sanskara for its expression
is comparable to the record player or the magnetoscope attached to
the television set. When technology (the sanskara, in the case of

---

[1] *Discourses*, p. 54.

Creation) moves ahead, then a more complex "player" is needed to transmit the recorded information.

This, according to Meher Baba, is precisely what happens in the basic three-part system of simple physical entity (starting as he said with sub-sub-gaseous forms), iota of consciousness, and recorded impression or sanskara of the original action. It is, Baba says, the degree of complexity of the sanskara itself, which causes the surrounding physical continuum to associate in forming a physical body sufficiently complex to express the resident sanskara.

Just how all this happens, Baba does not explain at this point. But he does say pointedly that it is this characteristic of the sanskara which is the moving force of evolution.

Those who spent long years with Meher Baba use a key phrase which he engraved into their memories to describe the manner in which a sanskara expresses itself through a physical happening. "Spending up" is the phrase which Baba used repeatedly to describe this key process. There is a complex meaning attached to these deceptively simple words. They imply that something has been collected, stored, and is ready to push its way into active manifestation. When it does so, the force or energy or pressure is "spent" for the moment, which in some way is implied in the word "up."

The catch in all this is that the very action in which the original sanskara is "spent," in turn becomes the relevant new action which is then recorded and must later be "spent up" in turn. So, a virtually endless succession of events, recordings and pressures-to-be-expressed is created. At the same time that the storage tank, as it were, of sanskaric energy is being drawn down by expression or "spending up" in the physical environment, a new quantity of similar or even more complex sanskaras is being stocked, in turn leading to further "spending up," and so on.

This is the essence of what Meher Baba describes as being the manner in which sanskaras function in Creation. The last batch of sanskaras just produced is slightly more complex than the preceding, and therefore requires a slightly more complex physical medium for its expression. Thus evolution of form becomes necessary and does occur in a completely natural and inevitable manner. It is as if the sanskaras were essentially magnetic and attracted to themselves the physical components required for their adequate expression.

This is a substantially different mechanism from that posed for Darwinian evolution, which remarks simply the presence of naturally occurring variant physical forms. These are then subject to choice by natural selection of those which prove to be more adapted to the rigors of the surrounding environment, and through the mechanical selection that ensues, evolution of form occurs.

For Meher Baba, the entire system of Creation is purposive from its inception in expressing the potential within God to know His divinity consciously. This is set in motion through the Whim, and it is the Whim that underlies all of Creation and is its final moving force. Darwinian selection of the fittest is inherent in the principles that Baba gives, but Baba goes beyond this in explaining the manner in which sanskaras underlie the form and characteristics of the physical body. Further extensions will be apparent in the following discussion of the nature of sanskaras.

Meher Baba describes throughout his works the important facts underlying Creation and the cause which manifest consciousness and underlie the process of evolution of physical form. Nowhere is this more clearly expressed than in a few brief paragraphs in the *Discourses*, which follow:

"The driving force of evolution consists in the momentum consciousness receives owing to the conservation of the impressions (sanskaras) left by diverse desires or conditions. Thus the sanskaras cultivated in a particular form have to be worked out and fulfilled through the medium of a higher form and a correspondingly more developed consciousness of the gross world. The soul, therefore, has to assume higher and higher forms (like metal, vegetable, worm, fish, bird and animal) until at last it assumes a human form, in which it has fully developed consciousness–in all the aspects of knowing, feeling, and willing–of the gross world.

"The manner in which sanskaras result in the evolution of consciousness, and the corresponding forms, has a useful analogue in ordinary experience. If a man has the desire to act the part of a king on the stage, he can only experience it by actually putting on the garb of a king and going on the stage. This is true of aspirations and desires; they can only be worked out and fulfilled by bringing about an actual change in the entire situation, as well as the medium, through which the situation may be adequately experienced. The parallel is very helpful in understanding the driving force of evolution, which is not mechanical but purposive.

"The sanskaras are not only responsible for the evolution of the form (body) and the kind of consciousness connected with it, but they are also responsible for the riveting of consciousness to the phenomenal world. They make emancipation of consciousness (that is, the withdrawal of consciousness from the phenomenal world to the soul itself) impossible at the subhuman stage and difficult at the human level. Since consciousness clings to the previous sanskaras and experience of the phenomenal world is conditioned by the use of an adequate form (body) as a medium, the soul at every stage of evolution comes to identify itself with the form. Thus the soul, which in reality is infinite and formless, experiences itself as finite and thinks of itself as being stone, metal, vegetable, worm, fish, bird, or animal, according to the degree of the development of consciousness. Finally, while experiencing the gross world through the human form, the soul thinks that it is a human being."[2]

While the sanskaras have established their importance in the

---

[2] *ibid.*, pp. 224–225.

fact of being the detailed motor for evolution, the areas in which they exercise considerable influence on key aspects of both form and action within Creation have by no means been exhausted in this one consideration. They are also in a sense the arbiter between God and man. This may seem a dramatic statement, and in fact it is not a property that the sanskaras have taken on in a willful manner. Their intrusive role is simply due to the fact that the sanskaras have become the focus of consciousness instead of that focus being directed to the Reality (God) that lies immediately behind the dream of duality.

It is as if one worked as a slave for centuries to achieve a certain presumed goal, only to find at the end that the objective one held all during that time was not real. Gradually the slave begins to understand that the true objective of his long labors had been hidden all the time by an object lying just in front of it. What an incredible error, but there has never been anything in the contract between God and the multiplicity of Creation that guarantees a quick and faultless arrival at the final goal. Rather, each step appears to include a multiplicity of flexibilities of choice, error, achievement, misidentifications and even occasional return almost to the beginning. It is hard work, but is any great goal free of this base of risk and required effort in achieving the important final value?

Meher Baba returns frequently in his works to the fact that the realization of one's own identity with God does not occur until the very last of the sanskaras has been eliminated. Granted, there is ample indication that long before this final decisive removal of the screen, one may have encouraging, even inspiring glimpses of the ultimate Reality. However, there is no room in the unchangeable perfection of God for the slightest residue of this or that, of otherness, of desire for that which is elsewhere. The very last of the sanskaras and their heritage of need for this and that must disappear completely before the screen is removed, and That which always was, is once again established as the Real.

To achieve this final dissolution of the sanskaras, an extraordinary process of dissipation of forces, of uprooting, of control and non-expression, of intercession of already Perfected Ones must intervene. The minute detailing and attention to all this is described repeatedly by Baba. The complexity of the route traveled should not come as a surprise to a scientist, who is familiar with the intricate balances that operate everywhere in nature. But even this is not preparation enough to anticipate the final equilibrating that is necessary for each human being to undergo before the end of the dream is achieved.

Many individuals have sufficient experience in introspecting into their lives to be aware of the complexity and diversity of the events that fill every moment. There is not only the mundane daily routine of earning a living, keeping the house clean, eating and sleeping and keeping the body in order. There is also the infinitely greater complexity of the emotional life one leads with all its unbalanced accounts accruing from an incredible number of human situations, all of which have an impossible tendency to get more complicated, and even frequently to run out of control.

Well and good, one might say, but a lot of all that is just in our own imagination and has little of final reality in its make-up. But in the infinitely sensitive system of God's presence within Creation, all this intangible human involvement and its cross-currents of emotions also has its importance and its balancing needs. Recall, that each happening in Creation is recorded. And even if it is a bare whim or passing jealousy, this too is faultlessly recorded and one day must also have a balancing-out of its final account. This is why it is so important to keep one's thoughts on a strict leash. They have their reality and importance, and therefore their necessity of a final reckoning, too. They do not just disappear forever, once they are thought. Their residues remain. And importantly, they remain with us, stored in our own attic of the mental body.

Almost totally disregarded as well is the energy aspect of our thoughts and emotions. Although they may seem effortless, the energy meter turns merrily around at each passage of a thought, and often that wheel spins with spectacular speed when we are captured by a traumatic recollection of past events or fears for the future. All of this expenditure is being made from a finite storage within ourselves. Often, when our recollections are long and complex, we are exhausted at the end. They are far from simple and without cost to our system.

Should one make the observation now that all of Creation came from a zero, and each part of Creation that returns to its Source must also come to that ultimate energy zero before its return?

Science suspects more and more the fact of the ultimate zero, and the ultimate balance this implies. Human beings are just such an ultimate equating and balancing entity. Each drop-soul in its origin was materially a zero, being no more nor less in reality than a drop-soul of undivided and infinite God. Its final return to God will have to observe this same principle. The equating out of all the pluses and minuses of myriads of lifetimes, not just in human form, but extending all the way back to the stone and sub-gaseous forms, all of which the individual must undergo to achieve the final, necessary balance point, is a mathematical necessity that boggles the capability of the universal mathematician who contemplates it. In fact, Meher Baba tells us, only one already perfected and equipped with the extraordinary qualities of infinitude can really help in a sure and efficient manner.

This is why Baba repeats constantly that real progress on the spiritual Path is secured only by placing oneself in the hands of a Perfect One. And this can happen only if one has had the good luck to work hard in the conviction that there must be an answer, and that one's own attitude and comportment in some manner lead to access to such a One.

In fact, Baba tells us, this is true. One's inner qualities and attitude, coupled with the actions one carries out, often over lifetimes, earn the grace of the attention of such a being. In this system, the fact of a spiritual hierarchy with duties related to the deserving, becomes a key element in achieving the final goal. It is not a superstitious dream of the naïve. It is a reality of the highest importance.

Before going on to a careful consideration of the manners in which one may help the process of dispersing the sanskaras, there remains one very important role played by the sanskara to be described. While not spelled out, the part it fulfills is implicit in all that Meher Baba describes so minutely in his unique exposition of the origin and eventual demise of the sanskara. Put simply, it is the unappreciated control mechanism which allows the increasingly complex physical apparatus necessary for achieving constantly higher levels of consiousness to be achieved through increasingly complex physical interactions. It is the very habit nature of a sanskara that is stored and which goes into operation to ensure the increasingly complex functioning of the physical complex that allows the physical organism to "live." Without this retained habit functioning being retained through increasingly complex evoluting forms, the highly complex life processes gradually achieved would have no means of being maintained. Certainly the conscious capabilities available to direct this vital base of form would be totally insufficient.

To clarify this further important function of sanskaras,
I will diversify by going back into a fascinating series of
personal experiences which occurred while spending the first
real hospital stay of my life. But first, a further word on
where Baba and Darwin diverge in their descriptions of the
progress of life forms. While the term "evolution" for both
Meher Baba and Darwin involves increasing complexity of the
medium concerned, "involution" does not figure in Darwin's
terminology, nor, as used by Meher Baba, does it imply in the

*least a retrograde movement. Rather, Baba uses it exclusively
to characterize the gradual freeing of the developed
consciousness from the restraints imposed upon it by the
sanskaric habit patterns developed through the long course of
the development of consciousness. Herein lies the root cause of
a profound confusion concerning the basic nature and
function of sanskaras in the scheme of the evolution of
consciousness. I confess at once to have been one of the most
naive in this respect. But to undertstand more clearly the basis
for the misconception, let us go back to one of the most
frequently stated observations made by Meher Baba himself
concerning the role of sanskaras in each human being.*

*During his lifetime Meher Baba frequently pointed out
on all manner of occasion that in the last animal form
consciousness was "fully developed," and that thereafter the
one remaining and key problem facing the human being was
that of annihilating in one manner and another the combined
load of sanskaras formed and stored in the mental body
throughout the long course of the development of
consciousness. While at no time giving the slightest cast of
negativity to the role of sanskaras throughout evolution (of
both consciousness and form), no doubt many readers of
Meher Baba's philosophy have unconsciously made the same
error I did, of casting the sanskaras in the villain's role. If
these, and they alone, are the barrier separating each
individual human being from the cardinal goal of God
Realization, then certainly they are a unique and devastating
force impeding arrival at the final end of human endeavor.*

*Perhaps many others have also experienced my own
fairly frequent observation even in early years of seeing that
my own habits, and my insistence on having them fulfilled,
was one of the greatest sources of my own woes. Long before I
knew that Meher Baba existed along with the entire concept*

of sanskaras, I had deeply formed this attitude of regarding my own habits as a profound obstruction to positive motion in my own personal life. When I first became familiar with the presence of a Meher Baba in the world, and shortly thereafter his emphasis on the importance of habit patterns in our quest for spiritual motion, I had already deeply ingrained in me a basic disgust with my own habits. Then, seeing what an impediment they were to the final tough steps to Illumination, I quickly fell into the habit of terming them "the refuse accumulated in the coming to consciousness." And sometimes my terminology was far more expressive.

It was not until quite late in life that I had the first hints in my own living experience that I had been hasty and far off the proper appreciation of sanskaras. It all began when I was in the hospital recovering from the removal of the prostate that the first hint arrived. It was a classic of the manner in which a real master sets about correcting an important misconception. (While a Perfect Master would have to be still present in the physical body, the Avatar is not impeded by such a limitation.) I was loaded with tubes and bottles which seriously hampered everything I wanted and needed to do. This reached a crisis stage when, on the second morning after the operation, the nurses announced that, while they had bathed me in bed the first morning, this time I was to do the operation by myself. I was astonished and frankly hurt.

Lamely I asked where I was supposed to do all this, and how. They responded, in the bathroom, and that they would help me to move the bottle and tube decorations with me. Nuts! But I got there, and finally decided as they withdrew to sit on the edge of the tub and use a washrag to sponge myself off. It worked, more or less, but when I got to drying myself I found I had to concentrate hard not to rub vigorously with the reflex actions I normally used at that point. And even then, I found shortly that I had neglected to dry quite a few spots, and so had to do a second and even third inspection.

This went on for several days until all the tubes and bottles were taken out and dispensed with. Then came the day when I could take for the first time an unhindered shower, and the exultation was incredible. But the drying off! It was a disaster. I couldn't get my old reflex system to take over. My conscious actions of several days duration, necessitated by having to avoid tearing out tubes and breaking bottles, had put it into a state of blockage. I did a terrible job. And you know? Not even today, many months later, have I recovered my old ease and efficiency of drying after a shower.

That astonished me, and for the first time, gave me a hint that our habit patterns are not just a negative hang-over from more productive matters, such as developing consciousness. It was not necessarily an obstructive by-product. Perhaps it might even have served some purpose in the scheme of creation.

It took Meher Baba a year and a half of successive personal experiences in my own daily life to build upon that first suspicion of positiveness. And then, one day as I was thinking again of the three basic and instant products of the surging of the Whim: matter, consciousness, and a record of the interplay of the action just occurred, which was the sanskara or habit pattern, I saw the inevitable answer. Habit patterns, or actions that insist on repeating themselves, start out as extremely simple actions, but they grow in complexity, and they are inherited and maintained as evolution discards one physical form after another, until they underlie and support the enormously complex combinations of basic physical functioning which are necessary to support the physically complex organism that is required to experience the

*level of consciousness that, finally, is capable on reflection of
knowing itself as God.*

*Incredible, but there it is in all its stark simplicity. The
fact simply put is that the only way the complex organism
finally necessary to develop the upper levels of consciousness
can be kept functioning is to have developed a base of
unconscious habit of extraordinary complexity. Consciousness
itself could never give out all the decisions and directions
necessary to keep the blood and the digestion and the cellular
metabolism all functioning on which that complex organism
depends, and so it is based fundamentally on a great and
complex inherited system of interwoven habits. Habit,
sanskaras, therefore, are just as integral and necessary in the
scheme of Creation as is the contrast that produces
consciousness, and that is basic to the wave motion which is
elemental for form. These are the three fundamentals of
Creation, and all three are absolutely necessary for the Whim
of God to know His own divinity consciously to be produced.*

If sanskaras are so important in the search for Truth, which is
God, then what is the manner in which they are equated and
neutralized?

Meher Baba's first comment on this is so discouraging that one
is inclined to take off to the nearest mountain and pass the rest
of eternity relaxing on its forested slopes. He says that the
mathematical fact is that each compartment of our life has its own
specific nature, and therefore the balancing of sanskaras that is
necessary is one of balancing compartment by compartment. This
means that sanskaras relating to gluttony have to be balanced out in
experiences related to gluttony. Sanskaras related to selfishness have
to be balanced out in experiences related to selfishness, and so on,
and on, and on. This is what one's sense of realism would have
predicted, and Baba confirms that it really is exactly so.

Then Baba inserts a promise of grace. This is that when one has merited finally the help of a Perfected One, that One has the capability of interchanging for us between even our specialized accounts. The miracle then is that if there is a positive surplus in the gluttony account (no doubt because of a lifetime passed in abstention from eating rich foods) and a deficit in the avariciousness account, the Perfect One is able to make a deft transfer between these and thus profit from the excess account by placing part of it in the deficit account. It takes little imagination to see the accounting simplification that results. Even so, there is always the principle quietly understood that the Perfect One does not just fabricate the excess on his own by some sort of miracle of compassion. The reality, which is not underlined for our conscious recognition, is that something has to be earned.

The Perfect One apparently can help enormously, not only in these transfers from plus to deficit accounts, but also in clarifying to us in one manner or another what are the real issues we must face. A further and equally important contribution made by a Perfect One is that he gives the aspirant the knowledge of the presence of one who knows and understands. This has an incredible faculty of easing the pain and uncertainty attendant on the entire taxing process.

So, finally, after an enormous expenditure of time and effort that is required even with the help of the x-ray eyes of the Perfect One, the sanskaric accounts are balanced. Then the final act is the intercession of this same Perfect One, or even another, and the final chasm is passed over. One realizes oneself for what one was and has been all the time, infinite indivisible God.[3]

This is not the end though to the important contributions as well as barriers made by the sanskaras in our makeup. A third is the nature of our personality, and even our appearance. Meher Baba describes this in the following manner:

---

[3] *ibid.*, pp. 57–60, discuss the role of the Perfect Master in wiping out the sanskaras.

"The plane on which one can possess physical consciousness is the gross world. The planes on which one can possess consciousness of desires are in the subtle world, and the planes on which the soul can have mental consciousness are in the mental world. The source of desire is to be found in the mind, which is on the mental planes. Here the seed of desire is attached to the mind; the desire exists here in a latent form, in the same way as the tree is latent in the seed. The mental body, which is the seat of the mind, is often called *karan sharir*, or the causal body, because it stores within itself the seeds or the causes of all desires. The mind retains all impressions and dispositions in a latent form. The limited "I," or ego, is composed of these sanskaras. However, the actual manifestation of sanskaras in consciousness, as expressed through different mental processes, takes place in the subtle body.

"The soul, which in reality is one and undifferentiated, is apparently individualized through the limitations of the mental body, which is the seat of the ego-mind. The ego-mind is formed by the accumulated impressions of past experiences and actions. And it is this ego-mind that constitutes the kernel of the existence of the reincarnating individual. The ego-mind, as a reservoir of latent impressions, is the state of the mental body. The ego-mind, becoming spirit and experiencing activated and manifested impressions, is the state of the subtle body. The ego-mind, as descended in the gross sphere for creative action, is the state of a physical incarnation. Thus the ego-mind, which is seated in the mental body, is the entity that contains all the phases of continued existence as a separate individual.

"The ego-mind, seated in the mental body, takes lower bodies according to the impressions stored in it. These impressions determine whether individuals will die young or old; whether they will experience health or illness or both; whether they will be beautiful or ugly; whether they will suffer from physical handicaps, like blindness, or will enjoy general efficiency of the body; whether they will have a sharp or a dull intellect; whether they will be pure or impure of heart, fickle or steadfast in will; and whether they will be immersed in the pursuit of material gains or will seek the inner light of the spirit."[4]

While considering for the moment the major aspects of the results of sanskaras' determining influence on the individual's actions and appearance, it is perhaps best to consider now the nature of one of the most deeply rooted and troublesome of all the complexes in this domain. It is that which we term quite simply selfishness, as expressed through lust, greed and anger. Lust of course has to do with the instinct for reproduction. This is so basic to Creation throughout the long course of evolution of form, that it has resulted in the formation of knots of habit patterns and desires of enormous complexity and force. As a consequence it, along with gluttony and anger, are among the most troublesome areas to be dealt with on the Path to the One.

Perhaps it would have been better to include this portion of review of Baba's works in the chapter on Love. However, as love is so powerful in its positive and redeeming characteristics, I frankly did not have the heart to introduce such a thorny question there. Instead, it seems to go well under sanskaras, which is well suited both in subject matter and in some of its nettlesome qualities to contain this, the often disastrously explosive knot of the ego that each of us deals with on a daily basis. I will not go into Meher Baba's brief but pointed comments that he makes especially in his chapters on Sex and Marriage in the *Discourses*,[5] but include here a short commentary written by one of those immeasurably privileged individuals[6] who has passed virtually all of his life in the close proximity of Meher Baba. In it he captures vividly the spiritual

---

[4] *ibid.*, pp. 328–329.

[5] *ibid.*, pp. 99–110.

[6] Private papers, Meherwan Jessawala.

problem that selfishness, lust, greed and anger pose in both practical daily life, and especially on the spiritual Path as one starts seriously to discern and follow it.

"The strife, turmoil and resentment which today predominate in the life of man could all be traced to one trait in him—selfishness —which has reached devastating proportions. It seems to have transgressed all known bounds of decency and morality in human relationship, endeavoring to eat into the very vitals of his own nature, and driving him to the limits of his endurance, and on to utter desperation. Not only does it cause him untold suffering and frustration, but engulfs him and all his surroundings in misery. The more he tries to escape its clutches, the tighter its grip gets, egging him on to unimaginable depths of exploitation, not only of all in his proximity, but also of himself.

"This inevitably leads man to search for avenues which could save him from inevitable disaster. Meher Baba analyses the problem by taking it to its very origin in the following words: 'Selfishness comes into existence owing to the tendency of desires to find fulfillment in action and experience. It is born of fundamental ignorance about one's own true nature.... The entire life of the personal ego is continually in the grip of wanting, that is, an attempt to seek fulfillment of desires through things that change and vanish.... The chief forms in which the frustrated ego finds expression are lust, greed and anger.... Man experiences disappointment through lust, greed and anger; and the frustrated ego, in its turn, seeks further gratification through lust, greed and anger. Consciousness is thus caught up in a vicious circle of endless disappointment.' "

In his works on sanskaras, Meher Baba often uses the word "impressions" as an equivalent term. One should also understand that in the expression of the sanskaras, they are awakened as it were in their stored state in the mental body, move to the subtle body where they become manifest in the form of desires, and in turn frequently are translated into physical effort in the physical body. It is above all in their subtle form as desires that we become most aware of them. In fact, often a desire is so automatic and "natural" to us in its expression that we are not even aware of the fact that the original source is a stored habit pattern. It is for this reason that sanskaras are frequently so insidious in their expression. Their presence is so habitual and natural that we accept them as necessary and right. It does not even occur to the person that they might be very special to oneself while another person may well have a totally contrary habit pattern with its own characteristics of "inevitable" and automatic "rightness."

The influence of habit patterns or sanskaras on personal appearance is often noted, but its source had remained obscure until Meher Baba's epic treatment of the subject. Many note the acquisition of certain facial characteristics such as cruelty and kindness, warmth of spirit, coldness of character. This is due very simply to the accumulation and expression of these habit patterns over the years. It is not necessarily a usage of one's intuition to read the character of the person. It is evident in their facial traits.

One also notes frequently the manner in which a couple living together over many years begin to resemble one another. This is only true, however, when the pair share similar judgements and emotions. Then they produce similar actions and emotional reactions, that in turn form the base of the stored sanskaras. If two persons living together hate each other and arrive at opposite conclusions, then their facial characteristics gradually contrast remarkably.

Given the extraordinary complexity and the sheer bulk in numbers of personal sanskaras, it would be a miracle if one were able to make any substantial progress in their dissipation in an entire lifetime. Again, the manner in which Creation is organized is relevant to this fact as well. Meher Baba points out that at the time the drop-soul is about to reincarnate into a physical form, apparently it takes on for concerted work during the ensuing lifetime a certain "wedge" of the sanskaric "pie." Meher Baba says on this subject:

"Ordinarily, life in the physical body is terminated only when the sanskaras released for expression in that incarnation are all worked out." He continues by discussing the special case of premature ending of a lifetime through accident or suicide, with the complications this brings. Returning then to the original subject, he concludes, "In normal cases, death occurs when all the sanskaras seeking fructification are worked out. When the soul drops its physical body it is completely severed from all connections with the gross world, though the ego and the mind are retained with all the impressions accumulated in the earthly career. Unlike the exceptional cases of spirits still obsessed with the gross world, ordinary souls try to reconcile themselves to the severance from the gross world and conform to the limitations of changed conditions. They sink into a state of subjectivity in which a new process begins of mentally reviewing the experiences of the earthly career by reviving the sanskaras connected with them. Thus death inaugurates a period of comparative rest consisting in a temporary withdrawal from the gross sphere of action. It is the beginning of an interval between the last incarnation and the next."[7]

One of the implications of Meher Baba's comments on the selection of certain areas of sanskaras for work during a given lifetime is that these may then become relatively lightened in their expression during further lifetimes. The same may not be at all true for other sanskaras in other domains in the individual's makeup.

---

[7] *Discourses*; pp. 304–305.

This may well result then in a person who is relatively "enlightened" in one area of his or her nature, while in another the individual may be quite primitive. In fact, this can be disconcertingly apparent in one's life with real human beings. It often comes as a shock to live with someone rather intimately over many years, and come to depend unconsciously on encountering in that person a consistently balanced and predictable manner of dealing with problems. Then one day, unexpectedly, a situation arises in which the friend reacts with a fury that is unaccountable and disproportionate.

Of course, one is shocked by such unaccustomed behavior. And worse still, it is entirely likely to continue whenever this domain is touched, and may even extend into other previously undisturbed areas of life. One speaks of "an unexpected reversal of character," but it is more likely to be due to the fact that an area of activity with its original sanskaric content still intact has been touched for the first time in the relationship. One can reason and argue and blame, but usually to no avail. The sweet reasonableness that may characterize the friend's attitude in other domains fails completely to transfer into this particular arena.

How are sanskaras removed? How does the aspirant start the process, and how can he know where he is in such a complex field where the subjective is so likely to falsify completely one's ability to judge honestly what is good and what is bad?

A psychologist might suggest several techniques for uprooting a habit pattern. No doubt the first would be to refuse to put it into action whenever the occasion for action arose. By non-fulfillment, eventually one would hope that the pattern would be exhausted and disappear. Another method might be to find or establish a very strong outside influence which impeded the habitual action. This would inevitably have dangers, though, as the spiritual master who had prescribed this procedure might well be the object of sharp resentment on the part of the aspirant.

Still another approach could be some kind of indoctrination which suggested the undesirable end results of the habit. No doubt this would have some beneficial effect on the aspirant, but anyone who has smoked or drunk alcohol will know at once the pitfalls that beset a course of logic in trying to destroy a habit.

More puzzling still, what does one do when contemplating habits that are admittedly habits, but which are universally regarded as beneficial? Like brushing one's teeth, or helping old ladies across streets? Baba early on in his philosophical expositions on this subject sets out almost at once that habits may be either of iron chains or golden chains. Both, he points out, end up in the same result of binding.

It takes no great deal of imagination to conclude that if habits have to be broken, then if a willing and able person is available, the best solution is to put the responsibility into that person's hands. Almost certainly he can be more objective and insistent than one can possibly be oneself. This is precisely what a spiritual master is. And I can confirm from my own experience, that on occasion, a bit of violence or anger can accomplish miracles in upsetting a habit pattern. A spiritual master has to be prepared to do this. But he must have another arrow in his quiver as well: a truly deep relationship with the one being blocked. Otherwise, blunt rebellion followed by departure is almost bound to occur.

In brief, if habits are the principal roadblock to final enlightenment, then the best method is to have complete confidence in someone outside oneself to oversee the job, and hopefully, that that person be equipped with the divine ability to know one's deepest inner workings. Deliberately, he must win one's confidence, and above all, one's love and trust. Then the work can really begin. In this context, a liberal admixture of anger and even physical violence comes into focus. It is seen to have possible meaning, even great importance, in getting on efficiently with the job.

Meher Baba deals extensively with the formation and the elimination of sanskaras in the *Discourses,* but while this is his classic exposition of the subject, he also includes further important material in *God Speaks* and *Listen, Humanity,* as well as in a not too well-known work entitled *Sparks.*[8] This last was collected by the original editor of the *Discourses,* Dr. C. D. Deshmukh, one of Baba's closest followers for many years and also a distinguished professor in the University of Nagpur. We will follow first the methods for elimination of the sanskaras that Baba lays out in the *Discourses,* and then consider the somewhat contrasting points he raises in *Listen, Humanity* and *Sparks.*

In the section of the *Discourses* which Meher Baba entitles "The Removal of Sanskaras, Part I, The Cessation, the Wearing Out, and the Unwinding of Sanskaras," he lists five principles that may be used in this all-important activity:

"1. The cessation of creating new sanskaras.

This consists in putting an end to the ever renewing activity of creating fresh sanskaras. If the formation of sanskaras is compared to the winding of a string around a stick, this step amounts to the cessation of the further winding of the string.

"2. The wearing out of old sanskaras.

If sanskaras are withheld from expressing themselves in action and experience, they are gradually worn out. In the analogy of the string, this process is comparable to the wearing out of the string at the place where it is.

"3. The unwinding of past sanskaras.

This process consists in annulling past sanskaras by mentally reversing the process that leads to their formation.

---

[8] Meher Baba, *Sparks* (Myrtle Beach: Sheriar Press, 1971).

Continuing our analogy, it is like unwinding the string.

"4. The dispersion and exhaustion of some sanskaras.

If the mental energy[9] that is locked up in sanskaras is sublimated and diverted into other channels, they are dispersed and exhausted and tend to disappear.

"5. The wiping out of sanskaras.

This consists in completely annihilating the sanskaras. In the analogy of the string, it is comparable to cutting the string with a pair of scissors. The final wiping out of sanskaras can be effected only by the grace of a Perfect Master.

"It should be carefully noted that many of the concrete methods of undoing sanskaras are found to be effective in more than one way, and the five ways mentioned above are not meant to classify these methods into sharply distinguished types. They represent rather the different principles characterizing the spiritual processes that take place while sanskaras are being removed."[10]

Baba then proposes in this same section to consider the first three methods of eliminating sanskaras, and as his first concrete suggestion on how to go about this he raises the subject of "renunciation." Immediately one sees that what Baba is aiming at is an inner frame of mind that is far from easy to achieve. He notes almost in passing that renunciation usually starts by the renouncing of outer objects and relationships. However, at once he calls attention to the fact that this type of renunciation does not go very far towards the objective of stopping new sanskaras from forming, if the outer renunciation is not decisively followed by inner renunciation.

Anyone who has tried to give up something in his personal life knows exactly what Baba is talking about, as one can renounce

---

[9] Meher Baba speaks constantly of the energy content of a sanskara. In another passage he notes that a sanskara is solidified might. *Discourses*, p. 38.

[10] *Discourses*, p. 41.

eating chocolate cake and stand some chance of making the decision stick. But what is far tougher to accomplish is to stop the daydreaming about eating a piece of the chocolate cake. Unless this latter is accomplished, the renunciation may be very brief in duration. This is perhaps too mundane an example, but one sees the principle which Baba is trying to establish for us.

Take another case, which may be uncomfortably close to the sort of thing that arises in real spiritual life. Suppose one is a musician, and is also trying to progress on the spiritual path, when the idea crosses one's mind to renounce dependence in one's professional life on praise from the audience and the press. Have you ever tried getting up before an audience to deliver an address or concert, and while doing so, to divorce yourself from the audience's reaction? This is extremely difficult to achieve, and yet this is precisely what Meher Baba is telling us must be accomplished when he states that external renunciation is of no use in dealing with sanskaras if our inner self is still holding onto the results.

Perhaps, if one is lucky and persistent, after several years of inner battle, and probably after a lot of public presentations went really sour, one may get to the point of enjoying the act of offering, and what the audience accords in response slowly becomes secondary. But even that is not easy. Renunciation is a challenge that may not result in any apparent progress in a whole lifetime of hard effort. Perhaps the ego is just too big, and it may stubbornly insist on some return, or even a lot of it.

Meher Baba is far from finished with his suggestions for the stopping of new sanskaras through renunciation. He gives two very important further examples of what one may try to do, in the area of solitude and fasting. Both of these, he points out, have very great spiritual significance within themselves, and so merit persistent effort. However, again, he suggests immediately that, as an example, fasting can become a way of vaunting one's spiritual efforts, in which case one might just as well not fast. Or if fasting is done just to get the body into a beautiful state so it can be admired, here again fasting is of no use. The real fasting is internal. Baba only briefly mentions this, and leaves the exploration to us.

I must add my own observation to this, that when fasting interferes with the aspirant's ability to carry on the necessities of life, such as undermining his health, Baba is the first person to insist that the results do not merit the damage being done. He has often said in my presence that a physical discipline that threatens to undermine the bodily functions must be set aside. For, of what use to try to speed up the spiritual process, if finally one dies of the results and then has no physical body to carry on the processes of experience so necessary for any chance of progress?

In this same formidable discussion of methods and their limitations, Baba pins also on penance as a wonderful method of unwinding sanskaras. After suggesting how we carry out penance and even reinforce through it our sense of deep regret for what we have done, he brings up once more the temptation for a misuse of the method that we are only too likely to fall into. This is the old principle of, if a little bit is a good thing, then why not a lot more of it? Baba lays down the rule: recall *once* whatever it is that you feel you must repent and try not to do again. Reinforce the feeling of regret. Live it through again, slowly, in detail, and then close it all off and never go back to it. Resist the temptation to return another day and to repent again.

It is easy to see intuitively what Baba is suggesting we avoid. It is self-destruction and self-negation. This is not healthy. Better, if necessary, to find oneself one day repeating the act that had to be repented. Then repent again, and try to mean it a bit harder this time. And then? Close it off as on the previous occasion, and don't go back to it. Trust that this time the barrier to this sort of action has been built high enough in the act of repentance so that it will not be repeated.

Another technique Baba recommends is the nonfulfillment of desires. Just say "no" to yourself when the possibility comes up. This is hard, but possible. In this particular section on the principle of negation, Baba also introduces the expression "spontaneous cogitation." He says that as one says "no" to oneself, there is plenty of opportunity for this spontaneous cogitation. Is it too much to suggest that here Baba is introducing us in an understated manner to a fundamental principle for the wearing out of sanskaric energy?

Have you ever forced yourself to stop before acting and reacting in a difficult situation? Try it sometime. It is not easy, as all of one's built-in impulses are to act and react at once. Especially emotionally. But there is a possibility to hold off action and reaction for a brief second, and then even for minutes as one develops the technique and sees the benefits that come from it. Another word that might be used is "reflection." One should not necessarily feel that this period of intensive cogitation or reflection is intended as a dam to any sort of action. It may finally turn out to be just this, but usually all it is intended to be is a temporary stopping of the release into action of all the sanskaric energy that is racing to express itself in the situation at hand.

Meher Baba does not use words lightly, and the manner in which he introduces this phrase should alert us to the possibility that this is intended as a key element in the process of the elimination of sanskaras. Let us pursue it for a few more moments. Try a bit of experimentation that is unlikely to do any sort of harm, of slowing up decision and action for a brief moment. Try deliberately to hold your emotional breath, as it were, for several seconds in an explosive situation. Try not to allow yourself the luxury of even the slightest thought of anger or condemnation of whoever or whatever concocted the ugly situation now facing you. Completely neutral.

Difficult, yes, but it can be done. Then, creep up *behind* the problem, rather than as it *faced* you just now, and look at it for a moment. Next, make a decision on what you feel should be done, and go ahead with your decision. Then when it is all over for now, go back over your emotions as you have just lived them.

Almost certainly, you will discover to your surprise that there was a sharp disarming of the situation during even the short stop you willed yourself to make. And when you went back to the scene of the event and made your decision and carried it out, you felt almost calm about the whole matter. In fact, in all probability you even had a suspicion that you made a much better decision than you would have if you had jumped immediately into action and reaction.

What all this should suggest is that sanskaric energy is a reality, and when the knot is aroused from its sleep in the mental body and passed on down to the subtle body where it is closely connected to the adrenaline supply, there is a swirling tornado of loose energy racing about. There is no concentration of energy in nature at any level that does not have the tendency to dissipate itself. And the usual form of dissipation is into physical and/or emotional action. If it is simply held up in the air at arm's length, even for a short period of time, a considerable amount of that energy disappears. Who knows where? Perhaps one day we will invent a type of needle sensitive to sanskaric energy and find just how and where it goes. But the important thing is that it does dissipate, to a surprising degree, and in an equally unaccountable manner, it tends not to re-collect for another equivalent blow up.

Meher Baba's second discourse on the removal of sanskaras entitled "The Dispersion and Exhaustion of Sanskaras" continues the vein of thought of the importance of the control of one's mental processes.

"The fleeting and evasive thoughts and desires of the mind can be curbed only with great patience and persistent practice.... Control is deliberate and involves effort.... But after the mind is released from the sanskaras, control becomes spontaneous because the mind is then functioning in freedom and understanding. Such control is born of strength of character and health of mind, and it invariably brings with it freedom from fear and immense peace and calmness.... Control is indispensable for the conservation of mental energy and the economical use of thought force for creative purposes."[11]

Note especially the phrase "conservation of mental energy." Throughout his writings Meher Baba brings up the importance on the spiritual Path of the conserving of energy. A very famous dictum of Meher Baba which has spread all over the world states simply, "Don't worry, be happy." But the posters and the folk songs based on the phrase do not go on to quote why Baba has repeated this suggestion almost ritualistically. He gives his reasons very briefly and clearly: "The descent of the grace of the Master is conditioned, however, by the preliminary spiritual preparation of the aspirant.... One of the greatest obstacles hindering this spiritual preparation of the aspirant is *worry*. When, with supreme effort, this obstacle of worry is overcome, a way is paved for the cultivation of the divine attributes that constitute the spiritual preparation of the disciple. As soon as the disciple is ready, the grace of the Master descends...."[12]

And later, on the same subject: "There are few things in the mind that eat up as much energy as worry. It is one of the most difficult things not to worry about anything."[13] Meher Baba lets us know that a key to progress on the spiritual path is the availability of energy which the disciple must have in stock to accomplish the arduous tasks encountered on the Path.

In this same discourse on the exhaustion of sanskaras, a curious

---

[11] *ibid.*, pp. 49–50.
[12] *ibid.*, p. 114.
[13] *ibid.*, p. 357.

line of reasoning leads to the introduction of a very ancient word, "sublimation," but in a new and refreshing context. In cautioning that control of the mind must not become just a negative and dry exercise of repression, Baba suggests that this is possible because each human being contains within himself the base for creative choice. "Creative control becomes possible because the source of light is within everyone.... Spiritual progress is thus characterized by the dual aspect of renouncing the false values of sanskaras in favor of the true values of understanding. The process of replacing lower values by higher values is the process of sublimation, which consists in diverting the mental energy locked up in the old sanskaras toward creative and spiritual ends. When this energy locked up in the sanskaras is thus diverted, they get dispersed and exhausted."[14] (Note the manner that the process is tied back into exchanges of energy.)

Here finally is a context for the exercise of sublimation freed from any notion of the application of moral screws to one's basically bad nature, in order to win through to the shining light of salvation. Instead, as Meher Baba deftly suggests the process, it is a natural one made possible by the fact that each of us has a soul in residence, and even though it tends to be well covered over and neglected, it is still there and gives out instinctive direction signals which are of great help in a sincere search for Truth. Sublimation then becomes a natural substitution process inherent within our own selves and requiring only for its activation a bit of doubting of the final value of our quick desire reactions in the course of living through the challenges of the moment. This is a very possible and even appetizing course to experiment with in daily life.

Continuing in this same discourse, Baba begins his introduction to the very important and complex subject of meditation. Later he devotes eight discourses to the exposition of this subject, more than to any other topic dealt with in the

---

[14] *ibid.*, pp. 50–51.

Discourses. We will not try to go into this technique in connection with sanskaras, considering it in the next chapter in connection with the use of love and surrender as major avenues to God-realization. For the moment, suffice it to say that Baba regards meditation as a potent means for the dispersion and exhaustion of sanskaras, as are also obedience and surrender, and above all else, love.

Regardless of the means or combination of methods used in rooting out sanskaras, Meher Baba reminds us that the final step in the process cannot take place without the intercession of a Perfect One, whether this be a Perfect Master, the Christ Avatar, or God working direct through an agent as described earlier.

It remains now to examine the more fragmentary but important material on the subject that is contained in *Listen, Humanity* and *Sparks*. In the former work, the discourse entitled "Death and Immortality" contains several very intriguing additions to what Baba develops in the *Discourses*. This centers around a reliving in the astral plane of experiences had in the just-terminated lifetime. During the reliving, Baba says there is a very important exhaustion of the sanskaras that takes place due to the intensity of the emotions experienced. He goes on to explain that in physical life, the presence of the physical body acts as a sort of insulator to emotional intensity. When the physical body is dropped and the after-death reliving goes on, the absence of the physical insulator causes the individual to undergo emotional sensations far more intense than those originally experienced during the physical lifetime.

As a consequence, an accentuated dissipation of sanskaras occurs during the in-between-incarnations period. Then, Baba says, just as the sanskaras are about to balance, the drop-soul is drawn to incarnate again into a new physical form. However, the momentum of dissipation of the sanskaras let us say from a negative preponderance towards a net positive balance (of those positive sanskaras not being relived) causes the individual frequently to be born into an almost diametrically opposite situation to that in which he lived in the just-previous lifetime.[15]

This is a fascinating addition to the general subject of sanskaras and their mode of exhaustion. However, there are some undisclosed problems which are not completely clarified in this brief account of reversals, such as Baba's unqualified statement that sanskaras experienced in physical life require counter experiences in another physical lifetime for their balancing.

One further key and unexplained comment from Baba on sanskaras remains to be noted. It is, surprisingly, from the early Discourses:

"The sanskaras deposited by specific actions and experiences render the mind susceptible to similar actions and experiences. But after a certain point is reached, this tendency is checked and counteracted by a natural reaction consisting in a complete changeover to its direct opposite, making room for the operation of opposite sanskaras."[16]

No doubt a future avataric manifestation will continue this fascinating account of the complex story of the role of sanskaras in human living.

A final contour of the portrait of sanskaras within the structure of Creation is added by Meher Baba in his *Sparks*. Whereas the outline he gives in both the *Discourses* and in *Listen, Humanity* emphasizes the negative role sanskaras play in the obscuring of Reality from the focus of consciousness, as well as the complexity of the balancing and dispersion processes by which the sanskaras can be eliminated, in *Sparks* there is a definite further positive

---

[15] *Listen, Humanity*, pp. 93–115.

[16] *Discourses*, pp. 27–28.

contribution that is described. "Bits of relative meaning, locked up in each type of impressionary experience, have to be carefully gleaned."[17] It is not then just a level of consciousness which the individual drop-soul must attain, which is capable of knowing God consciously. There is also a *content* or what Baba calls "individuality" of consciousness that is achieved, which in some way is a further value won in the long process of evolution and involution.

This thought is reinforced as he says a little later, "To put the matter paradoxically, in the Truth-experience of unlimited consciousness, what has been rendered defunct is not the impressions but their binding action. In annulling this binding action, the impressions can perform their true function of yielding their real meaning to the liberated consciousness. Thus, from this point of view, the impressions have been so altered they can contribute their quota to the plus-meaning of a free consciousness."[18]

To these indications of the importance of individuality in the final scheme of God's consciousness of His own divinity, one must add the observation that *God Speaks* refers often to "infinitely individualized consciousnesss." One cannot help but equate this to the concept of an infinitude of drop-souls experiencing an infinitude of different experiences in Creation. This would indicate that Infinity cannot allow one failure or absence in its infinite pattern.

In this same work Baba also gives considerable detail[19] concerning a special kind of sanskara operating in the lives of the Perfect Ones, the *yogayoga* sanskaras, which are non-binding, as contrasted with the strongly binding characteristic of the (*prarabdha*) sanskaras of the evoluting and involuting drop-soul. Still a third further type of sanskara is handled by the Perfect Ones for

---

[17] *Sparks*, p. 70.
[18] *ibid.*, p. 71.
[19] *ibid.*, pp. 77–83.

the benefit of deserving pilgrims on the Path, the *vidnyani* sanskaras which are loosening in their effect.[20]

Although our exposition of the subject of sanskaras has been lengthy, we have had to content ourselves with describing only the tip of the iceberg that exists in the record that Meher Baba leaves in his various works on this subject. If what he says is true of sanskaras, that they, and only they, lie between the consciousness of man and the Reality of God, obscuring that reality from the focus of consciousness until they are entirely removed, then they are of capital importance in the whole process of man's struggles. In addition, they govern the type of body and its characteristics that each human has—in fact there can be no body at all without the underlying base of sanskaras to support it. Moreover, Baba repeats frequently, the nature of the ego is nothing other than the sum composite of the sanskaras. What a tremendous inventory of capital influence in human living!

In this one area alone, Meher Baba has laid out a major new contribution to our understanding of Creation and the problems we face within its confines. It is reassuring to read so constantly in Baba's words, however, that those confines in turn are only in our own imagination, and disappear completely in the realization of Truth.

---

[20] *Discourses,* pp. 288–292 describes the role of these three principal types of sanskaras.

11. LOVE, SURRENDER AND MEDITATION

S t. Francis of Assisi achieved God-realization through his love for Jesus the Christ more than eleven hundred years after the death of the one he loved.

Maulana Jalaluddin Rumi attained the same goal through complete surrender to the Perfect Master, Shams of Tabriz.

Gautama was unveiled and became the Realized Buddha sitting in meditation under the Bo Tree.

All three of these great paths of spiritual progress achieve ultimately the same goal. Which is preferable for the attainment of the objective no doubt depends on the character of the seeker. Meher Baba is one of the few who has given some idea of the dynamics of the various methods.

Baba's viewpoint in this respect came to light through one of those simple, practical situations that arise in daily life. I had been working for some months on a new edition of Meher Baba's *Discourses*. As the project neared its end I was struck by the fact that meditation occupied more discourses than any other subject discussed in this work.

Being a typical intellectual of my time, the numerical fact interested me, and even more, I was surprised on reflection that despite the importance he placed on meditation, Meher Baba had never given me one to perform. How had this happened? I dared not even in my own mind risk accusing him of negligence. But there had to be a concrete answer somewhere, and I was determined to find it.

On my next visit to India, while going over some of the final details with Baba for the new edition, I put the question to him, trying to keep any element of accusation out of my words and my feelings. Fortunately, Baba took the query at its face value and responded by gesticulating, "That is an interesting question, Don. I will tell you the answer. You should know that of the many roads that lead to God, that of love is the high road of all. During the period of Avataric manifestation, the road of love is fully open to all. But that does not mean that it remains open indefinitely. Gradually it begins to narrow and to be less accessible."

"As this occurs," he continued, "the seeker must start to use secondary routes. Of all these, the greatest is that of meditation. Because I am the Avatar, I must provide what is necessary for the aspirant throughout the entire period until my next incarnation. Therefore I have given in great detail instructions for the use of meditation. But during the time that the path of love is open, as it is fully now, it is a waste of time and energy to detract from the way of love by practising meditation."

The immediate question that springs to mind, of course, is "Did Baba say how long the path of love would remain fully open?" He did not. There are many people who have spent much time in Baba's presence who feel they have well-authenticated information that, while not being in physical form, he is nevertheless "present" in Creation for a period of at least 100 years after his death, and that this may continue up to 200 years if the next avataric manifestation is to occur after 1400 years. Oddly enough I had never heard that figure from Baba, nor is it clear how this relates to the high road of love being open. I suspect this may follow a somewhat different formula.

More important than the exact period during which the high road is fully open is that St. Francis was able to follow this preferred route many centuries after the death of the Perfect One he loved so deeply. Certainly this achievement was due to the nature of St. Francis himself, which from all accounts was deeply loving. One might summarize this question by suggesting that if it is one's destiny to find a being who inspires both confidence and deep love, even centuries after his death, then this will doubtless be the paramount factor. Certainly one so graced would have no question of what to do, but would plunge ahead as dictated by deep instinctive feeling, rather than an abstract questioning of whether the gate was still open. I suspect if it were not, one would leap over the barrier and follow the path of love regardless.

While Meher Baba may have left a bit of obscurity on the timing side of the ledger, there is no lack of clarity in his assessment of the efficacy of love. All through his writings he praises constantly love and the results it achieves on the spiritual path. The discourse entitled "Love"[1] gives not only the paramount credentials of love, but also explains why it is so effective in leading the spiritual aspirant rapidly to the goal. Here are some of the pungent words Baba uses to describe this to us:

"Life and love are inseparable from each other. Where there is life, there is love.... The law of gravitation, which all the planets and the stars are subject to, is in its own way a dim reflection of the love that pervades every part of the universe.... In the animal world love becomes more explicit in the form of conscious impulses that are directed toward the different objects in the surroundings. This love is instinctive, and it takes the form of gratifying different desires through the appropriation of suitable objects. When a tiger seeks to devour a deer, it is in a very real sense in love with the deer. Sexual attraction is another form of love at this level.... Human love is much

---

[1] *Discourses*, pp. 110–116.

higher than all these lower forms of love because human beings have fully developed consciousness."[2]

Perhaps Baba's comment on the tiger being in love with the deer it is about to devour may seem a bit shocking, but accustoming oneself to the values discovered along the spiritual path requires considerable flexibility.

In this same discourse, Baba continues by examining the role of reason and the different manners in which it combines with love. The situation in which the individual alternates between the dictates of love and those of reason, with all the unpredictability this entails, rings a familiar bell with those who are honest with themselves. Then Baba continues his classic exposition of the manner in which love manifests in the complexity of human living by describing its admixtures with infatuation, lust and greed. These are his words on this disturbing area of our lives:

"Infatuation, lust and greed constitute a spiritual malady, which is often rendered more virulent by the aggravating symptoms of anger and jealousy. Pure love, in sharp contradistinction, is the bloom of spiritual Perfection. Human love is so tethered by these limiting conditions that the spontaneous appearance of pure love from within becomes impossible. So when such pure love arises in the aspirant, it is always a gift. Pure love arises from the heart of the aspirant in response to the descent of grace from a Perfect Master. When pure love is first received as a gift of the Master, it becomes lodged in the consciousness of the aspirant like a seed in favorable soil; and in the course of time the seed develops into a plant and then into a full-grown tree."[3]

---

[2] *ibid.*, pp. 110–111.
[3] *ibid.*, pp. 113–114.

Meher Baba's description of the poor quality of the usual expression of love does not in all probability surprise the one who introspects honestly on his true relationship with most human beings. But Baba's further insistence that the degree of taint is so deep that true love can only come through the gift of grace from a Perfect Master is no doubt a serious blow to the hopes of many to experience real love during their lifetime. This is important, as despite the disillusionment and cynicism that impregnate modern living, it is nevertheless rare to find a person who does not have real hope to experience the miracle of deep and sustaining love.

Yet Meher Baba states very simply and unequivocally that real love can only come through a Perfect Master. And Perfect Masters, one reflects, certainly aren't found standing on many street corners waiting to help stray pedestrians cross a dangerous passage. Even granting that there might be a small possibility of encountering the Master during the course of one's life, again honesty suggests that one's own stock of good deeds, which must enter into the puzzle in some manner, is likely to be dangerously low. In such case, how can the Perfect One's grace ever be attracted?

These are all reflections that must realistically flow through one's consciousness if one is seriously attracted to an ideal in human relationship, or even more importantly, to the ideal of the search, whatever the cost, for the Truth.

Meher Baba's next words on love and its descent on man are hardly more reassuring. Here they are:

"The descent of the grace of the Master is conditioned, however, by the preliminary spiritual preparation of the aspirant. This preliminary preparation for grace is never complete until the aspirant has built into his spiritual makeup some divine attributes. For example, when a person avoids backbiting and thinks more of good points in others than of their bad points, and when he can practice supreme tolerance and desires good for others even at cost to himself—he is ready to receive the grace of the Master. One of the greatest obstacles hindering this spiritual preparation of the aspirant is *worry*. When, with supreme effort, this obstacle of worry is overcome, a way is paved for the cultivation of the divine attributes that constitutes the spiritual preparation of the disciple. As soon as the disciple is ready, the grace of the Master descends; for the Master, who is the ocean of divine love, is always on the lookout for the soul in whom his grace will fructify.

"The kind of love that is awakened by the grace of the Master is a rare privilege. The mother who is willing to sacrifice all and to die for her child, and the martyr who is prepared to give up his very life for his country are indeed supremely noble; but they have not necessarily tasted this pure love born through the grace of the Master. Even the great yogis who sit in caves and on mountain tops and are completely absorbed in deep *samadhi* (meditative trance) do not necessarily have this precious love.

"Pure love awakened through the grace of the Master is more valuable than any other stimulus that may be utilized by the aspirant. Such love not only combines in itself the merits of all the disciplines but excels them all in its efficacy to lead the aspirant to the goal. When this love is born, the aspirant has only one desire—and that is to be united with the divine Beloved. Such withdrawal of consciousness from all other desires leads to infinite purity; therefore nothing purifies the aspirant more completely than this love. The aspirant is always willing to offer everything for the divine Beloved, and no sacrifice is too difficult for him. All his thoughts are turned away from the self and come to be exclusively centered on the divine Beloved. Through the intensity of this evergrowing love, he eventually breaks through the shackles of the self and becomes united with the Beloved. This is the consummation of love. When love has thus found its fruition, it has become *divine*."[1]

---

[1] *ibid.*, pp. 114–115.

Here then is the factor which makes love the high road of all roads leading to God-realization. It is the capability of pure love to marshal all the energy and concentration of the individual. But this is not all. One objects immediately that all this is concentrated on a human being, whether perfect or imperfect, but how does this help to find God, who is not necessarily identifiable with that particular human being?

The question is central and cannot be ignored. The secret is simply that the focus of all this energy, concentration and deep sincerity is not on oneself. It is no more complex than that. What is normally referred to as oneself is no more than the ego and its vast complex of inbuilt habits and desires. This has already been described here as the great "tragedy" of the development of consciousness, that the consciousness generated always identifies with the *source* of contrast which generated it, and not on REALITY, which is its true goal.

It takes a major tidal wave in life to shake that fixation of the ego. And now it happens, for one of the few resources that possess the capacity to concentrate the energy necessary to blast the tight ties of consciousness to the external object is love.

Suddenly, the focus of attention, if it is true love, which by definition is selfless, is not the ego self and its fixated desire goals. For probably the first time in the long history of the particular drop-soul complex, the center of attention is not ego desires.

It is a physical universe of energies in which we live. Usually, in dissipating the stored energy of a habit-impression (sanskara), a reciprocal tide of energy is generated. The ego attracts this energy, and a new knot of psychic energy is fixed into the mental body storage system. It in turn begs to be let out into expression, and in a manner similar to that in which it was formed. But if the central core of the ego is not there, around which it can again be wound up, it goes off somewhere into creation, but not back into the mental storage bin.

When I think of this process of the rewinding of the
sanskaric energy into a new knot to be stored, I always think
involuntarily of a scene from childhood. It was the day when
the marcel for women's hair was in fashion. I do not know
how prevalent beauty shops were at that time; perhaps our
family just did not have enough money for my mother to use
them even if they existed in our village. In any case, she had
a small curling iron which had to be heated, as the electrical
variety didn't exist then. My mother would heat her curling
iron in the glass chimney of an old kerosene lamp, and at
some mystic point she knew it was at the right temperature, so
she would take it from the glass chimney, spread the device to
catch a strand of hair, roll it up tight, and wait a few seconds.

This, to me, is the wound up sanskara waiting to
unwind. Then the reverse movement occurred, the hair was
unwound, and back the curling iron went into the chimney.
At the right moment, out it came and a new strand of hair
was wound up into a similar tight curl. And so it went on, the
winding up being followed by an unwinding, then reheating,
and the process repeated. For me the curling iron is the
personal ego. Without it, the winding and unwinding cannot
go on. True love removes the curling iron around which the
sanskaric energy is wound and dissipated and rewound.

The point to be clear about is the central role played by the
personal ego in the collection and recollection of the recorded
sanskaric energy. If this observation is valid, then we should find
a similar role being played out in other important means of
Realization, whereby the absence or weakening of the ego allows
sanskaric energy to be dissipated during the period of distraction of
the ego.

Have a caution on one very important point, however. If you are
a spiritual aspirant and longing to make progress on the spiritual

path, the solution is not just to try to go out and find someone to love desperately. Meher Baba suggests the joker when he points out that, with our stock of stored deadly sins, our ability to express true love is vanishingly small, and it takes the intercession of a Perfect One. And that intercession, in turn, has to be earned in a manner that taxes the strength and abilities of even a spiritual giant. It is not a matter of willpower. It is rather one of earning, and sincerity of purpose and continuity of effort are central to its achievement. Nevertheless, a deep, sincere love, even for a very imperfect human being, sets aside the personal ego in some lesser or greater degree, and in this manner even strong sanskaras are markedly weakened.

As one reflects on Meher Baba's declaration of the unique ability of love to propel the aspirant on the spiritual path, there are several observations which tend to clarify why this should be true. Throughout his writings Baba returns constantly to the properties of love; clearly it is an important and, especially to us in the human stage of development in duality, a vital quality of eternal God. Of great interest in this regard, Meher Baba makes frequent reference to the triune Divine Attributes that are experienced by all Perfect Ones: All Knowledge, All Power, and All Bliss. Love is not included by name in the list, and so one wonders if it may not be an aspect of All Bliss. There is no doubt, in any case, that love has a force and an inevitability that give it special effectiveness in dealing with the problems inherent in the fact of duality, when it is combined into human action.

Further, as just noted, the characteristic of God of eternal and absolute **unity**, indicates that when one is truly drawn to be **one** with another, this must follow a road that leads from Illusion to Reality. Inevitably, then, love will embody very powerful capabilities for assisting movement on the Path.

The unbelievable impact of one who knows no separation from others is in part a consequence of this same truth. This was evidenced repeatedly and forcefully in Meher Baba's contact with persons for the first time. Regardless of personal background, they would often dissolve at once into tears, for hours or even days. Frequently the individual so affected would be embarrassed by the uncontrolled emotions displayed. But there they were. No logical reason, the tears just poured out as if from nowhere. I was fortunate to see almost instantly that the depth of my own reaction to meeting Meher Baba for the first time was due to the fact that I knew that he knew and accepted me completely, and that absolutely nothing separated us.

I suspect that one day we must coin a new word for this type of experience. It appears to go beyond what we term love. There is absolutely no sense of wishing or wanting or needing, or even of gratefulness. It is simple unity, and even to feel warmth and affection for the One requires a special effort of separating oneself in imagination and regarding the loved one from a distant point. But in fact that distance is only created in order to dwell on the sense that comes into being when the act of separation is imagined.

"Divine love is qualitatively different from human love. Human love is for the *many* in the One, and divine love is for the *One* in the many. Human love leads to innumerable complications and tangles, but divine love leads to integration and freedom. In divine love the personal and the impersonal aspects are equally balanced; in human love the two aspects are in alternating ascendancy. When the personal note is predominant in human love, it leads to utter blindness to the intrinsic worth of other forms. When, as in a sense of duty, love is predominantly impersonal, it often makes one cold, rigid, and mechanical. A sense of duty comes to the individual as an external constraint on behavior, but in divine love there is unrestrained freedom and unbounded spontaneity. Human love in its personal and impersonal aspects is limited; divine love with its fusion of the personal and the impersonal aspects is infinite in being and expression.

"Even the highest type of human love is subject to the limitations of the individual nature, which persists till the seventh plane of involution of consciousness. Divine love arises after the disappearance of the individual mind and is free from the trammels of the individual nature. In human love the duality of the lover and the beloved persists, but in divine love the lover and the Beloved become one. At this stage the aspirant has stepped out of the domain of duality and becomes one with God; for Divine Love *is* God. When the lover and the Beloved are one, that is the end and the beginning.

"It is for love that the whole universe sprang into existence, and it is for the sake of love that it is kept going. God descends into the realm of Illusion because the apparent duality of the Beloved and the lover is eventually contributory to His conscious enjoyment of His own divinity. The development of love is conditioned and sustained by the tension of duality. God has to suffer apparent differentiation into a multiplicity of souls in order to carry on the game of love. They are His own forms, and in relation to them He at once assumes the roles of the divine Lover and the divine Beloved. As the Beloved, He is the real and the ultimate object of their appreciation. As the divine Lover, He is their real and ultimate savior, drawing them back to Himself. Thus, though the whole world of duality is only an illusion, that illusion has come into being for a significant purpose.

"Love is the reflection of God's unity in the world of duality. It constitutes the entire significance of creation. If love were excluded from life, all the souls in the world would assume complete externality to each other; and the only possible relations and contacts in such a loveless world would be superficial and mechanical. It is because of love that the contacts and relations between individual souls become significant. It is love that gives meaning and value to all the happenings in the world of duality. But while love gives meaning to the world of duality, it is at the same time a standing challenge to duality. As love gathers strength, it

generates creative restlessness and becomes the main driving power
of that spiritual dynamic which ultimately succeeds in restoring to
consciousness the original unity of Being."[5]

Ordinarily when one speaks of love in the context of spiritual
aspiration one places it automatically either in the frame of love for
the Master who leads one on the Path, or the idealized but always
hoped for complete love for another human being which transcends
all selfishness and ego-inspired limitations. In both cases, love is
synonymous with qualities that transcend the usual gambit of
human limitations. The very connotation of the word soars into the
realm of perfection. The constrictions and pressures of ego-based life
are left far behind.

But by now, the seeker of meaning in life has no doubt had to
come to terms with the fact that the Path and those who help one
along its course have not left practicality and problematicalness in a
convenient waste basket along the way. Nor is that the case in the
role of love in leading the aspirant rapidly along the way to the goal.

Once again, I must intrude my own experiences into the
account we are following. I spent 25 years under the thumb of Meher
Baba, followed by another 25 since he left his physical form. I have
already outlined why I do not separate the two into different stages
with different importance. Both, to me, are the continuation of the
intimate guidance of the Master, and his techniques and support
have not changed in the slightest.

Inevitably, after our personal conversation of the values of
meditation and love, I assumed Baba was prodding me along the
latter path. I was constantly astonished by the course of events and
also the speed with which old concepts were junked and new
realizations put in their place. This process has continued to the
present day. And one of the most unexpected realizations of all has

---

[5] *ibid.*, pp. 115–116.

been that the path of love is a moment by moment challenge in all of the aspects of daily life.

The path of love is not reserved at all to the great event of the one true love. It is not limited to the unusual, enlightened relation with very "special" persons. It encompasses each and every human contact, and the glimpse of the breathtaking sunset. But even more surprisingly, as I would never have expected it, the path of love has some of its most valuable and revealing insights within situations of profound upset and rejection of another human being.

How is it possible that rejection of someone can, nevertheless, eventually produce the inspiration that moves one another step closer to God?

I can only recount this story in the manner in which this kind of experience happened to me for the first time. While I was busy rejecting the thoroughly obnoxious and dishonest person standing before me, I noticed inadvertently that he was trembling, not from nervousness, but due to a physical disability. I couldn't help my reaction to this. I was concerned, despite the fact that I disapproved of everything I had come to know of this individual. And yet, there he was–trembling–and I was concerned. The next time I saw him I was more concerned, and less about the money he owed me.

As the episode continued I began to find that somewhere, buried at least two layers deep under his thoroughly disgusting manner of living, there was a human being with all that being's hopes and disappointments and–yes, divinity. I couldn't avoid recognizing its presence, as little apparent as it had been up to that time.

We became, unexpectedly to us both, fast friends. He settled the difference between us in a completely unforeseen manner. To him as well as to me. Did I love him? Yes,

I cannot explain what happened in any other manner. And I know he was as startled as I was by all that occurred from that point on.

This incident was not unique. The Perfect One is always thorough. The episode was repeated on several other occasions with other persons in such a manner that I could not doubt that I was intended to learn a very fundamental lesson about love. Gradually I began to see that love is not limited to the glorious moments of warmth and beauty. It is present in the essence of every moment of time and in every human and even inanimate contact one has in life. It is in everyday living that one encounters it. It does not require a limited and highly special environment for its existence. It just is, and it is everywhere and in everything. This is not melodramatic projection. It is a fact of all Creation, as all of Creation is endowed with divinity.

If one suspects that one's road to Truth is to pass through the avenue of love, then it is of the greatest help to abandon all of one's previous ideas of where and how one will find love. It comes to one's presence from the expected, yes, but it also comes from the completely unexpected.

Is this a surprise? It should not be, if one entertains really the possibility that love is one of the basic eternal attributes of God Himself.

Although I have now read and discussed and dealt with in many manners what Meher Baba has given out on the subject of love for more than a half of a century, still, in the few months that have elapsed since I wrote the foregoing and went carefully over it with other trusted companions, there have been significant deepenings and clarifications that have occurred in my own experiences. It never ceases to astonish me that a real Master never stops the process of helping the devotee. The subject of love has been profoundly reflected upon during these intervening months by several of the most dedicated study groups I have known, and I have watched their process of sucessive discovery with great amazement. I will try in a few short sentences to summarize what has come from our joint pooling of resources. First, however, may I insert a heart-felt word of caution.

There are a great many instances in Meher Baba's written words, plus as many more in personal stories handed down by those who experienced the almost overwhelming warmth and encompassment he projected when one was in his presence, to stoke the fires of a major tradition of the love Meher Baba manifested. This is indeed one of the greatest attractions he projects to new people who had never had the experience of meeting him in the flesh. It is also often the most important recommendation many of his devotees offer to newly interested persons attracted to find out more about him.

For all these reasons one must tread very lightly in trying to put into perspective a more comprehensive picture of the manner in which Meher Baba treated the subject of love over the full scope of his physical life.

The first major aspect that demands reflection was implicit in his very clear statement to me in his comments on the availability of the Path of Love to the spiritual seeker. One cannot brush aside his clarification that the reason he had devoted so many Discourses to meditation was because the present ready accessability to all mankind of the Path of Love was due to the fact that in the future the open gate to love would gradually narrow, until finally the majority of seekers would be constrained to use the secondary but still very important path of meditation. I do not pretend to speculate nor have the ability to perceive relative numbers and width of access, but this statement is of key importance and demands that one reflect deeply and seriously on the role of love in Creation, especially over a period of time, and especially for future generations of seekers.[6]

A second indisputable fact is the different manner and frequency in different parts of his life that Meher Baba referred to the importance of love. His *Discourses* as we have seen are studded with inspiring and heart warming references to the importance of love in Creation and in human relations. These were largely given out in the 30s and 40s. On the other hand, his *God Speaks* is relatively bereft of such comments. This latter work was given by him in the early 50s, and often referred to by him as his greatest work. I personally rarely heard him suggest to a visitor that he read the *Discourses*, but almost everyone who visited him in the 50s and 60s was soon asked if he had read *God Speaks*, and if not, was urged to do so repeatedly. One cannot but reflect that this change occurred as Baba shifted markedly from deep personal involvement in the personal lives and progress of individuals who came to him, into a more long-term approach with far less involvement in the individual's day-to-day life and problems. The rule is not absolute, but the tendency cannot be denied, and here again is a matter that demands reflection when one considers the role of love in Creation and the use of it made by Meher Baba.

A third very puzzling fact as noted before is the absence of the word love in the centuries old list of the triune attributes of God. These have been described classically as All Knowledge, All Power, and All Bliss. One is struck by the absence of any word directly relating to love, unless bliss can be construed as being largely the

---

[6] When two of my most trusted and loved friends, who have worked many long hours to help bring this work to fruition, read the foregoing, they expressed their dismay in the following important words: ...this "seems to contradict the constant emphasis on Love (and its concomitant factors of Obedience and self-sacrifice) which Baba stressed upon throughout His Ministry. He has time and again stressed upon the the supremacy of the Path of Love. To link this only to the generations proximate to His Advent seems contrary to what in all His Advents, past and present, He has bequeathed to humanity for all times. Even in our times we so often find ordinary sincere people of different faiths whose love for the Founder (the Avatar) is the only thing they have clung on to discarding totally the outer crust of traditional religious beliefs."

result of a perfect love. Again, I would not wish, nor am I able, to speculate on this. All I know instinctively is that this also demands considerable honest reflection.

In all, then, it is apparent even from this brief and certainly incomplete listing of major points requiring reflection, that the subject of love in Creation, and especially on the spiritual path, is far more complex and demanding than appears at the first mention of the word. One has too much the tendency to respond with a gut reaction of complete accord and enthusiasm. Certainly this is only the beginning of a long and important road of discovery.

Having suggested that the subject of love cannot be left to a brief reflex reaction of even great affirmation, let us go back now to a short further quotation of direct words from Meher Baba to reestablish the essence of what he has given in so many different addresses.

"There is nothing that love cannot achieve, and there is nothing that love cannot sacrifice. There is nothing beyond God and there is nothing without God, and yet God can always be captured by love. All other essential qualities will come to the aspirant if he follows faithfully the whisperings of the unerring voice of love that speaks from his own heart, shedding light on the path.

"(God) does not listen to the language of the mind and its routine meditations, concentrations and thoughts about God. He only listens to the language of the heart and its message of love, which needs no ceremony or show, only silent devotion for the Beloved.

"The practical way for the average man to express love is to speak lovingly, think lovingly and act lovingly towards all mankind, feeling God to be present in everyone."[7]

---

[7] *Listen Humanity*, pp. 186–187.

"**Surrender.**" "**Obedience.**" Both words are unappetizing; in fact the first, surrender, has many connotations especially repugnant to the Western mind. It is synonymous with defeat, and this inevitably implies either weakness or unpreparedness. Yet, on the spiritual path, the word embodies inevitable challenges that must be met and absorbed.

The act of surrender as encountered on the Spiritual Path is in fact a special and very important case of love. It occurs when another person, and in this case the spiritual Master, is found to be more important than all of one's own desires and goals. It can also be a very dangerous act depending on just whom one surrenders to, as it may lead to the destruction of all one has worked a lifetime to gain. Then again, it may even lead to the greatest goal of all.

The importance of surrender to the Master is a very ancient principle in the Far East. One can say that it has been one of the most important goals taught for many centuries in various mystic schools in the Orient, and more recently increasingly in the West as well. To the Western mind however it may threaten to be a denial of the principle of personal responsibility. What could be worse, many would say, than for an individual to abandon the challenges of life and place them instead on the knees of some vaguely benevolent figure who claimed a mystic ability to deal with them? Unfortunately, in the case of an impostor or a superficially developed "master," this is exactly the situation.

Especially in recent times there have been sensational cases of religious groups which have either committed mass suicide or inflicted grotesque crimes on completely uninvolved people. One wonders at a moral basis that allows such incredible acts to be performed. It seems likely to have come about through the "brainwashing" of the adherents to the sects. Evidently, in the process of this so-called brainwashing, the original moral foundations of the individual have been removed through a complex and continuing indoctrination of new beliefs.

How can this arise? More important, how can the well-intended aspirant avoid the possibility of inadvertently falling into such a trap? For if surrender is an important goal still advocated in major schools of esoteric thought, then how can one avoid surrendering to a potentially dangerous guru?

The fact is that there is no sure way to play safe. But, it must be admitted, this is true not only in the pursuit of the Truth, but in almost any human endeavor. There is always the great danger of going bankrupt when one starts a new business. Or that, once the business is founded, or the administrative position won, there will be possibilities for diversion of funds that are impossible to resist. Similar dangers are present even in such benevolent activities as getting an education, growing crops, planting a garden, and so on and on.

Human progress is subject to possibly tragic eventualities in all fields. It is not just the search for God that may lead to a blind alley or even disaster through wrong choice. This is innate in any enterprise, springing from the very simple fact that when one starts, one does not have the experience and the stature for judging what can come through the intricacies of later developments. A leap into the realm of faith is necessary in almost every type of venture, be it spiritual or material. Even planting a garden or a crop in the fields is an act of faith that climate and markets will cooperate to affect a net gain at the end of the labor. All of life is a constant risk-taking, and often the individual becomes so aware of this, and frightened by it, that he is paralyzed into immobility. This in turn we regard as a failure, but of another sort.

The value at the end of the rainbow in surrender is the possibility of anaesthetizing one's own ego and substituting the ego or enlightened self of the Master in its stead. If it turns out to have been a wise gamble, in other words, that the Master is legitimate and enlightened, then the entire path of inner development is enormously simplified and speeded up. It is a gamble that many people, especially those who have faced great tragedy or hardship in their lives, feel compelled to take.

The most likely danger that may be encountered is that the ego of the master selected may be so enormous that it takes on without real competence the responsibility for directing the life of the trusting searcher. Thus, someone incapable of making sane decisions even in his own life can be oblivious to the fact that he really has no ability, let alone no right, to direct the lives of a group of persons attracted to him. In actual fact, it is a very rare person who is developed to the point of being able to act fruitfully as a guide for another in the complexity of the return to the One.

Having dwelled for some paragraphs on the problem of surrender and the inevitable dangers that beset it, let us go on now to the actual technique which underlies its use.

The personal ego is a very tough and resilient entity. When one begins to have some idea of its persistency and subterfuges, one can hardly believe that one's own self can harbor such a stubborn, destructive resident in one's household. As soon as one becomes aware that there may be a realm of underlying truth in Creation, and that it may be necessary to find it, it takes little time to discover the presence and importance of the ego. In many ways it seems to have a life of its own, as well as a base for decision which has little or nothing to do with one's own conscious ethic.

The ego is capable of doing downright dishonest acts and then blatantly trying to justify them. In fact, some of the most excruciating experiences in life result from battling determinedly with close friends or family, and then finding out quietly after it is all over that one was acting a lie. Meher Baba states the problem of one's ego and its inevitable downfall in blunt terms:

"In the ripeness of evolution comes the momentous discovery that life cannot be understood and lived fully as long as it is made to move around the pivot of the ego. Man is then driven by the logic of his own experience to find the true center of experience and reorganize his life in the Truth. This entails the wearing out of the ego and its replacement by Truth-consciousness. The disintegration of the ego culminates in realizing the Truth. The false nucleus of consolidated sanskaras must disappear if there is to be a true integration and fulfillment of life."[8]

In this second of three discourses on "The Nature of the Ego and Its Termination," Baba continues with some very damning comments on the trickery and stubbornness of the personal ego. Particularly when the individual goes on the spiritual Path, the ego feels itself so threatened that it begins to take drastic measures to continue its existence. This all reads almost like a detective story, but as one pursues Baba's narrative, in some way it all rings true and one begins to realize just what a viper one has accepted for so long, thinking it to be a reasonably civilized member of the family. Finally, Baba describes what he calls the guerrilla warfare phase of the battle:

"In fact, in the more advanced stages of the Path, the ego does not seek to maintain itself through open methods but takes shelter in those very things that are pursued for the slimming down of the ego. These tactics of the ego are very much like guerrilla warfare and are the most difficult to counteract. The ousting of the ego from consciousness is necessarily an intricate process and cannot be achieved by exercising a constantly uniform approach. Since the nature of the ego is very complicated, an equally complicated treatment is needed to get rid of it. As the ego has almost infinite possibilities for making its existence secure and creating self-delusion, the aspirant finds it impossible to cope with the endless

---

[8] *Discourses*, p. 165.

cropping up of fresh forms of the ego. He can hope to deal successfully with the deceptive tricks of the ego only through the help and grace of a Perfect Master.[9]

"In most cases it is only when the aspirant is driven to realize the futility of all his efforts that he approaches a Master. By himself he can make no headway toward the goal that he dimly sights and seeks. The stubborn persistence of the ego exasperates him, and in this clear perception of helplessness he surrenders to the Master as his last and only resort. The self-surrender amounts to an open admission that the aspirant now has given up all hope of tackling the problems of the ego by himself and that he relies solely upon the Master. It is like saying, 'I am unable to end the wretched existence of this ego. I therefore look to you to intervene and slay it.' This step, however, turns out to be more fruitful than all other measures that might have been tried for the slimming down and subsequent annihilation of the ego. When through the grace of the Master the ignorance that constitutes the ego is dispelled, there is the dawn of Truth–which is the goal of all Creation."[10]

En route to the complete and final destruction of the ego the aspirant passes frequently through a very discouraging period in which he observes himself apparently sliding backwards rather than making progress. He finds himself at war internally with conflicting impulses and, often, desires that he may not even know he had hidden within himself. Also, in his external relations he may blow up or have tendencies to disagree and become angry that, on subsequent reflection, he admits to himself were unjustified. I have on quite a few occasions listened to a thoroughly disheartened but deeply sincere seeker pour out his distress. It is best to read what

---

[9] The ancient Sufi Master Jami captures the essence with his famous lines: "Do not boast that you have no pride, because it is less visible than an ant's foot on a black stone in a dark night. And do not think that bringing it out from within is easy, for it is easier to extract a mountain from the earth with a needle!"

[10] *ibid.*, p. 171.

Baba himself gave out on this apparent regression:

"The components of the implicit ego of the subconscious mind have to be brought to the surface of consciousness somehow and become parts of the explicit ego, and then be submitted to the action of intelligent consciousness. If this is to be achieved, there has to be a weakening of the explicit ego in such manner as to allow the emergence into consciousness of these desires and tendencies that could not hitherto find admittance into the arena of consciousness. This release of inhibited tendencies naturally brings about additional confusion and conflict in the arena of the conscious mind rather than by any comfortable easing of them."[11]

Baba comforts the adept by counseling persistence, as the experience of apparent regression is not endless and finally achieves the necessary freeing of the subconscious content. However, it can be very disorienting if the aspirant has no idea of what is really going on.

While Meher Baba describes the elimination of the ego as being the result finally of complete frustration on the part of the aspirant, causing him to surrender to the Perfect Master as being the only way, still Baba weaves through his various discourses another somewhat less crisis-ridden approach. This he terms making the Master the "provisional ego." It is a very unusual technique, and many people have adopted and followed it for long periods. I cannot say that I have observed it to produce to my knowledge a Perfect Master, but that may be due to insufficient time or lack of perception on my part. Here are Meher Baba's suggestions for putting the method into operation:

"To avoid inaction on the one hand and pride of action on the

---

[11] *ibid.*, p. 169.

other, it is necessary for the aspirant to construct in the following manner a provisional and working ego that will be entirely subservient to the Master. Before beginning anything, the aspirant thinks that it is not he who is doing it but the Master who is getting it done through him. After doing the task he does not tarry to claim the results of action or enjoy them but becomes free of them by offering them to the Master. By training his mind in this spirit, he succeeds in creating a new ego–which, though only provisional and working, is amply able to become a source of confidence, feeling, enthusiasm, and "go" that true action must express. This new ego is spiritually harmless, since it derives its life and being from the Master, who represents Infinity. And when the time comes, it can be thrown away like a garment.

"There are thus two types of ego–one that can only add to the limitations of the soul, and the other that helps it towards emancipation. The passage from the limiting ego of the worldly to the egolessness of infinite life lies through the construction of a provisional ego generated by wholehearted allegiance to the Master. The construction of a new ego entirely subservient to the Master is indispensable to the dynamics of spiritual advancement."[12]

The deliberate construction and use of the provisional ego is not the only manner in which surrender can be effected. Either through the exercise of charm and love, of which a Perfect One has a great store, or simply by the sheer force of his projected spiritual authority, the aspirant comes quite naturally to place the happiness and welfare of the Perfect One over his own. It would seem unlikely that as wily a foe as the ego would allow its own death by sheer strangulation, but this is in fact exactly what happens.

Whereas in ancient times this placing of the Master's good before one's own was often precipitated by deliberately fabricated

[12] *ibid.*, pp. 254–255.

tests which the Master concocted, nowadays, this technique appears to have been considerably modified. As the existence of spiritual ashrams has diminished in number as well as changed considerably in mode of operation, meeting the meaningful challenges of daily life has apparently become a more common vehicle.

It might seem that manipulating the circumstances of events in personal life would be too complex and unsure to qualify as a reliable spiritual discipline. And yet there is a great deal of evidence accumulating that the Avatar really does have infinite power and total insight, and that he uses them partially to arrange life in such a manner as to pose to the aspirant in a living situation the kernel of the problem to be unknotted. Caution, though! This does not by any manner of means suggest that the whole proposition is nothing more than the will of the Perfect One. Rather, the aspirant has his own treasury of previously collected sanskaras as well as the karma related to them. The role of the Master is to see these, not fabricate them, and then to devise the combination of external events that will point up the problem to the disciple.

It does not take a great many experiences of learning through incidents in daily life before the seeker, aided by the Avatar, begins to see what is happening, and through this, to develop even greater trust in the Master. This is not to say that the miraculous is used, but rather that complex inner problems begin to disappear, and it is through the aspirant's own observation that the beneficent influence of the Master in his life is established on an unshakable base.

One of the most beautiful expressions of this is an account given some years ago by Charles Haynes, an educator in the United States, to a group in Berkeley, California:

"Many of us in this room tried to keep from going to Vietnam. It was not something that we believed or wanted to do.... So I told

Baba, 'I just can't deal with this, I don't want to go to Vietnam.'

"I tried to get exempt because I was going to seminary. Actually, I was going to seminary anyway but I wasn't going to become a minister. I really didn't want to be a minister in an organized church, so they turned me down.... They turned me flat down saying 'you don't represent a real religion.'

"They turned me down when I was in India. I'd gone to India that summer and I got this cable that I had been classified 1A. I couldn't believe it. 'Baba, I thought I told You, this is something I cannot do. You say You take us only to the edge and then you pull us back. This is the time for a little pulling back.'

"So I went back and, sure enough, I couldn't talk them out of it. The secretary of the draft board said, 'I'm sorry, you're just classified 1A, report to Columbia next week for your physical.' I said, 'This can't be happening to me.' I arrived in Columbia, you know how humiliating that is, you're stripped naked and herded through room after room. Of course, there was nothing in the world wrong with me, which was too bad.

"I'm standing there and I'm beginning to shift on my feet. When I stand a long time my feet hurt, because my feet are sort of flat. But the truth is, this doctor didn't care what your feet looked like.... This doctor goes out of the room, having finished his job and the door opens. A guy comes in, with white hair and glasses, who I'll never forget. He walks up to me, not to anybody else in this line of naked people, and says, 'Do your feet bother you?' I said, 'If I stand for a long period of time I have kind of flat feet.' He said, 'What about when you walk?' I said, 'Well, I can walk for a while, but I can't walk for long distances without feeling uncomfortable.' He said, 'I see.' He grabbed this paper from me, looked at it, made a note on it, gave it back to me and went out of the room.

"So, I was still waiting in line, having lost my place, and a side door in this room opens, the same guy walks out (white hair, glasses), comes over to me, and says, 'Come with me.' I go into this tiny little

cubicle, he sits behind this desk, takes my sheet and starts asking me
my whole medical history.... He took my sheet and started writing.
Then he says, 'Don't get back in line. Go to the door and show them
this. Don't go back through the line.' I went to the door, I showed
the guy this, he read it, he looked at it, he looked around and found
this stamp and stamped it 1Y. 'Out, finished.'

"What it was, was this. On the way back from India, I sat there
and I said to Baba, 'Baba, if You want me for Your work, if it's Your
will that I go to Vietnam, then I will. I know, Baba, whatever You
want I'm going to do it anyway. What I'm saying to You, Baba, is that
I'll accept that, I'll be happy about that and I'll try my best to be
happy about whatever happens, whether I go to Vietnam or whether
I stay home. I'll try Baba, I'll promise that I'll try, that's all I can do.'

"The truth is that that's all Baba is ever interested in, is getting
us to that point. Whatever it is in our lives that is most difficult to let
go of, He will bring us to that point where we say to Him, 'Baba, I
will be happy with whatever happens.' What is going to happen to us
is already there, that's not going to change; but what Baba is
interested in is using the events in our lives, the moments in our
lives, the challenges in our lives, to get us to that point of
surrendering to Him, being resigned to Him, and to whatever
happens.

"Baba's work is not to get us to make the right choices–it
doesn't matter what choices we make, the same thing is going to
happen anyway. No, His work is not to get us to make better choices,
His work is to get us to be happy with whatever happens. A big, big
difference."[13]

It would not be just to leave the subject of surrender without
presenting the safeguard which exists in the selection of the one to
whom the surrenderance is made. Certainly, it is a delicate decision

---

[13] Charles Haynes, "Surrender to Meher Baba" (Berkeley, California: Quarterly Newsletter
Vol. 26, Fall 1996).

and merits the greatest of care. One should not enter into such an act without the most careful attention to its importance and one's own lack of a base of judgment that guarantees results without catastrophe lurking around the corner.

Nevertheless, the ancient tradition in mysticism is that the sincerity of the seeker in making his choice, plus the record of his love and devotion to the one chosen, are the insurance policy for the decision. Perhaps the most famous example of the operation of this principle is the life of Milarepa, the Tibetan founder of one of the great schools of Buddhist mysticism.

Milarepa was born into an affluent family, but had the misfortune to lose his father at an early age. The managing of the family fortune passed to an uncle, who used up the entire inheritance shortly before Milarepa came of age and the right to take over the management of the family assets.

When Milarepa approached the uncle and claimed his inheritance, the uncle admitted there was no longer anything to transfer to him. Milarepa was predictably astounded as well as greatly angered. He vowed to avenge himself and his family, and registered straight away as a student of a well-reputed black magician. Soon he had progressed to the point of being able to handle powerful formulae of black magic, and so the moment had come for him to accomplish his vow of vengeance. This he did, with complete success, and the uncle and his entire family were eliminated.

Shortly after accomplishing his aim, Milarepa had a big dream in which he saw a venerable man to whom he was greatly attracted. Recounting the dream to his black magic Master, the latter told Milarepa at once that the man in the dream was in fact Milarepa's true Master. Finally, one day Milarepa saw the old man of his dreams. At once they approached one another, and Milarepa knew that a great decision must be made. He told the Master of his love for the black magician. The Master confirmed he knew this already, but that by his true love for the magician, he had gained the right not only for himself for the true master, but the same grace for the magician as well.

Milarepa was sent off to find the black magician again and told him at once the story. Both then became disciples of the true Master. The story of Milarepa has been beautifully recounted in our time by the scholar Y. Evans-Wentz, a great modern day mystic in his own right.

Another word of caution. The spiritual insurance policy does not operate unless the aspirant has made his original choice and then followed up in his personal actions with complete fidelity and good faith. Not many persons can pass such a medical examination.

And what about obedience? Meher Baba has summarized the situation by commenting that greater than love for the aspirant is obedience, and greater than obedience is surrender. This leads one to the conclusion that the tests which are met at the stage of obedience are surpassed as one continues on into the challenges of surrender. However, the reader is warmly recommended to read for himself the ample discusssion Meher Baba gives in the *Discourses* on obedience, as well as examples given earlier in this work of the sort of obedience Baba demanded especially in the early phases of his ministry.

Meditation. This is a subject beloved of a great number of modern seekers after the Truth. And rightly so. As Baba said, after love, this is the most important of the secondary roads leading to Realization. Meditation has been the darling of endless great mystics and teachers of esoteric truth since the Path for the return to Reality was christened. Its traditions and the care with which it has been established and passed on for thousands of years confirm a discipline of great authenticity as well as efficacy.

Yet meditation also is not without its dangers. Its aim is to pierce into the subconscious and gradually release its contents. On occasion, that content is explosive. This is for two distinct reasons. The first we know well because of the research done in recent times by the students of psychology who treat man's emotional and even deeper ills. They find on frequent occasion that buried deep in the recesses of the unconscious, and encapsulated by what has become a protective shell, are great reservoirs of psychic energy deposited by earlier experiences which could not be resolved at the time. There they rest, relatively unsuspected even to the individual who has them stored in his own subconscious.

The second stock of very high voltage energy in the subconscious is a more generalized pool of available psychic force, just as one has stores of both physical and emotional energy unless one has depleted them through excessive expenditure. It is this reserve of psychic energy that is most often used by the healer, even though he may believe sincerely that he is using a form of universal or divine energy in his work.

Although the exact manner of tapping into these reserves is still not well understood, there are obviously keys and formulae that exist for their freeing. There is not, however, a safeguard formula to turn off the supply in the event that a high-pressure source is inadvertently tapped.

It is for this reason that the novice is almost always cautioned not to embark on even the most simple exercises of meditation without the supervision of one well qualified to avoid unexpected pitfalls. Unfortunately, it is not incontestably evident at the present time who these qualified people are. Therefore the field inevitably has considerable risks.

In his lengthy and detailed discourses on meditation, Meher Baba lays out two important clarifications of the basic process involved, as well as the distinction between meditation and concentration:

"Meditation has often been misunderstood as a mechanical

process of *forcing* the mind upon some idea or object. Most people naturally have an aversion to meditation because they experience great difficulty in attempting to coerce the mind in a particular direction or to pin it down to one particular thing. Any purely mechanical handling of the mind is not only irksome but is bound ultimately to be unsuccessful. The first principle aspirants have to remember is that the mind can be controlled and directed in meditation only according to laws inherent in the makeup of the mind itself, and not by means of the application of any mechanical or semimechanical force.

"Many persons who do not technically meditate are oftentimes found to be deeply and intensely engrossed in systematic and clear thinking about some practical problem or theoretical subject. Their mental process is, in a sense, very much like meditation, inasmuch as the mind is engrossed in intense thinking about a particular subject to the exclusion of all other irrelevant things. Meditation is often easy and spontaneous in such mental processes because the mind is dwelling upon an object that it is interested in and that it increasingly understands.

"The spiritual tragedy about ordinary trains of thought is that they are not directed toward things that really matter. On the other hand, the object of real meditation always has to be carefully selected and must be spiritually important; it has to be some divine form or object or some spiritually significant theme or truth. In order to attain success in meditation, the mind must not only get interested in divine subjects or truths but must also begin trying to understand and appreciate them. Such intelligent meditation is a natural process of the mind; and since it avoids the monotonous rigidity and regularity of mechanical meditation, it becomes not only spontaneous and inspiring but easy and successful.

"Meditation should be distinguished from concentration. Meditation is the first stage of a process that gradually develops into concentration. In concentration the mind seeks to unite with its object by the process of fixing itself upon that object; whereas meditation consists in thorough thinking about a particular object to the exclusion of every other thing. In concentration there is practically no movement of the mind, but in meditation the mind moves from one relevant idea to another. In concentration the mind merely dwells upon some form or a pithy and concise formula, without amplifying it through a succession of ideas. In meditation the mind tries to understand and assimilate the object by dwelling upon diverse attributes of the form or various implications of the formula. In concentration as well as in meditation, there is a peaceful intermingling of love and longing for the divine object or principle on which the mind dwells; and both these activities are very different from the merely mechanical processes that have rigid regularity and unrelieved monotony."[14]

Meher Baba then continues with various suggestions on the mechanical aspects of going about meditation, such as the importance of silence and seclusion as well as the value at times of complete darkness. Posture has its role also, as well as habits of timing and place. And a welcome admonition, that meditation should be joyous! Group meditation has its advantages, up to a certain point, when inevitably the branching of the road occurs and thereafter it continues on an individualized path.

The most common problem encountered in meditation by almost everyone is the intrusion of personal thoughts and worries. These are virtually uncontrollable, and the novice reacts with impatience or even anger. "It is useless to waste energy by trying to combat and repress disturbing thoughts *directly*.... It is best to ignore them and turn to the object of meditation as early as possible, without attaching any undue importance to the disturbing factors."[15]

---

[11] *Discourses*, pp. 202–203.
[15] *ibid.*, p. 206.

Associative and dissociative meditation are products Meher Baba says of the first of three basic principles underlying all meditation. The important one of these two is associative, for this is the manner in which one links oneself with truth-bearing factors. Before this can be productive, however, it is first necessary to dissociate oneself from the delusionary and valueless components of the world in which one lives.

The second major principle of meditation refers to the part of the individual personality which is brought to bear in the act of meditation. The first brings the intellect into operation. The second involves the activity of the heart. The third, which Baba has discussed on many occasions and evidently is to be a favored principle in the New Age of the New Humanity, is the action principle. This might be renamed "meditation in action," which has become increasingly a platform for many young people to launch into the practical pursuit of spiritual development. Its prime assumption is that in an important manner the daily life situations are imbued with meaningful lessons for the spiritual path. This will be considered in greater detail at the end of this section.

The third principle of meditation concerns the items of experience that meditation tries to understand. Here, completely, the base is the belief that the experiences of living are deeply meaningful and must be understood for the aspirant to make progress. Baba points out that it is in this third principle that it is necessary that the course of meditation be designed by a true Master, as it is only he who knows what the course of progress of the aspirant is to be, and therefore can intelligently assign and direct the relevant course of meditation.

Even meditation has its habit patterns. The student frequently becomes enamored of a particular type of meditation, and so remains tied to this course. The presence of a real Master is then absolutely necessary to untie the habit of the student and get him off into the next process necessary for his further development.

Assuming that all progresses properly and that the student has been guided by one who knows, eventually the principles lead to the experience of *nirvana*. In this state one is absorbed in divinity. It is important, however, to note that this does not involve the adept in seeing God. This is such a key point that it is worthwhile quoting exactly what Meher Baba says on the subject.

"*Nirvana* is that state where apparently 'God Is Not.' This is the only state where 'God Is Not' and 'Consciousness Is.' This experience of the first stage of *fana* is what Buddha emphasized, but later on it was misinterpreted as Buddha having emphasized that there was no God. The reality, however, is that God Is; but in the absolute vacuum state of the first stage of *fana* only consciousness remains, experiencing absolute vacuum.

"As it can never happen for God not to exist, in the state of *nirvana* God plays the part of consciousness itself, which consciousness is sometimes termed super-consciousness or *mahachaitanya*."[16]

Baba continues his systematic explanation of the various forms and modes of meditation by considering hearing as a basis for meditation, and also reading. Hearing is limited ordinarily both by physical absence from the one who gives the spoken word, and also by the rarity of the speaker being a truly enlightened individual. However, there is a great literature available, of which certainly portions have been given out by individuals of more or less high degrees of attainment on the spiritual path, or even Realized. Regardless of the enlightenment of the originator, there is a progression that is observed as the meditation shifts from the original reading, to the mental recollection, and finally to the spontaneous perception of the Truths involved in the original writing.

In this discourse, the fourth under the general heading of "The

---

[16] *God Speaks*, p. 136.

Types of Meditation." Meher Baba gives an outline of the original course of Creation and the mechanisms of evolution and involution. Baba suggests this brief treatise as a reading meditation for the student.[17] It is simply and concisely put, and has the advantage of being almost free of puzzling and obscure concepts that cause the mind to stumble, and disturb therefore the course of meditation.

The fifth discourse on meditation is an enlargement detailing the basic principles of meditation outlined above. At the end of this[18] Baba gives more precisely the manner in which the dedicated disciple practises the meditation of action, referring all deeds and goals to the Master (who becomes the provisional ego), thus cutting out entirely his personal ego from the process. Needless to say, if this can be accomplished, it has a very powerful effect in dispersing the sanskaras of the aspirant.

It must be said, however, that Meher Baba clearly advises that meditation, including the meditation of action, be practised under the immediate guidance of a real Master. The process is so personal and matched to the highly specialized needs of each individual, that the presence of the Master on frequent occasions is obligatory. This would seem therefore to suggest the conclusion that the meditation of action in which the Master is visualized as the beginning and the end of all action cannot be practised after the lifetime of the Master.

No doubt this suggestion will cause great distress to many persons whose Master has departed the physical body, but it appears to be an inevitable conclusion. The implication then is either that one find another Master living in the flesh, or that one assume that in some manner one may follow the path of love, with both its uncertainties as well as its great attractions. A very important possibility in this regard is that of using internal links formed with other aspirants for the truing of one's intuitions of the content of daily life.

---

[17] *Discourses*, pp. 222–227.

[18] *ibid.*, p. 232.

The Avatar uses many methods to help us along the path, some adapted to one type of complex of personal problems, others to different situations. Some necessitate his presence in physical from, others are adapted to periods when he has abandoned physical form. But at all times, in all states, the Avatar is responsible for Creation and he always has the means to fulfill that responsibility. However, it remains for the aspirant to be open to the fact that certain methods used even frequently under certain conditions and states may not be applicable in others.

At the end of the sixth discourse on meditation, Meher Baba makes a very powerful statement which should act as a beacon for all those traveling determinedly on the Path:

"The disappearance of mental operations of all types contributes toward making the mind absolutely still without allowing consciousness to fall into abeyance. All thoughts that appear in the mind of the aspirant are forms of perturbation and have their origin in the momentum of stored sanskaras. The agitation of the mind can disappear only when the aspirant can so control his mind that all thoughts can be ruled out at will. Only in complete internal silence is Truth found. When the surface of the lake is still, it reflects the stars. When the mind is tranquil, it reflects the nature of the soul as it is."[19]

One of the most difficult personal disciplines to undertake, above all in the present state of civilization, is to erect a barrier around even a few moments in the day in order to be inwardly quiet. And yet Baba says that this is a prerequisite for Truth to be found. It will not happen by itself. The aspirant has the responsibility for creating the situation within which the goal can manifest.

---

[19] *ibid.*, p. 239.

Meher Baba's remaining discourses on meditation are devoted entirely to the higher states of attainment. Here the soul knows itself as God and is completely absorbed in this experience (*Nirvikalpa Samadhi*). A rare one returns to a state of simultaneous consciousness of Creation, becoming thereby a Perfect Master experiencing the state of *Sahaj Samadhi*.

Before leaving the subject of meditation it is of interest to return to the type Baba terms meditation in action. While he goes into some detail in his discourses on the special type of meditation in action devoted entirely to the being of the Master, and which is directed by the Master, there is a somewhat less restrictive form which clearly was set into motion by Baba during his lifetime. We have already mentioned above that there is a good deal of evidence for a much more detailed use of the events in daily life as a major school of spiritual experience. Often during his lifetime Baba spoke of the spiritual lessons embedded in the experiences of daily life. In his New Life also, it is noteworthy that much of the differentiation between the Master and the devotee was leveled, except for obedience, which continued as a requisite.

In place of many of the old, classic forms of observance of guru-aspirant relationship, a newer form termed companionship was observed. This the mandali participating in the New Life regarded as perhaps the greatest joy they knew with Baba. It is a persistent term, and it seems increasingly to be a key element in proceeding along the spiritual Path, apparently intended for the next era of those seeking the Truth.

Another important ingredient in the newly emerging pattern has to do with the gift of intuition that Baba said was his boon to humanity. This seems for the first time to make generally possible the continued contact with the Christ-Avatar after he leaves his physical body. Thus an entire new realm of potential for spiritual search appears to come into being. Daily life, more keenly tuned to the individual's needs for growth, with insight imparted increasingly by intuitive means, and companionship with its inner links of real strength between aspirants as a corrective tool for possible misdirected or thwarted intuition–all this has a lot of very exciting possibilities.

If this is to be, even in part, a practical mechanism for spiritual growth, then deliberately regarding daily life as charged with spiritual meaning is a necessity. A further requisite is to develop the habit of being able to stop dead in one's tracks when one senses an important event about to happen, or as just having happened. Stop the emotional reactions invited by the event! Reflect, quiet the mind, refuse to react, go internally and listen quietly for even a moment to the inner voice! Decide, act and trust, and look for the spiritual lesson. These may well be signposts for a new manner of going about meditation in action.

12. THE OCCULT

There are "occult forces" present in creation[1] that embody enormous energy. While these forces and the experiences they are capable of producing can be of considerable benefit at a certain stage of traversing the spiritual Path, they can also lead to some of the most difficult and even disastrous situations encountered during the entire journey to Realization.

Most of the 20th century has seen a continuing fascination on the part of a great many students of mysticism with miraculous experiences, control of supernatural forces and, among a wide variety of other hidden studies, a major continuing fascination for the very ancient science of astrology. More recently there has been added to this list the use of hypnosis to regress to memories of previous lifetimes.

The attitude of aspirants usually falls into one of two extremes, either of profound attraction by the forces and events of the occult, or total rejection of the entire subject. Meher Baba describes the reasons for these commonly observed contrary reactions.

[1] Although a commonly used term, "occult force" is not easily defined and, certainly at present, is almost impossible to measure. Without risking writing a separate treatise on this one term, let us say for the moment that, as already described, Creation constitutes an extremely broad spectrum of forms of wave energy, certainly extending far beyond the range currently measured and manipulated with various instruments available both to science as well as the technician. Beyond these reaches certain "gifted" individuals apparently are sensitive to other spectra of energy and the phenomena they produce, and also manage to direct and control these bands of energy to affect results impossible to achieve with commonly known forces and instruments of control.

"The spiritual path leading to the emancipation of consciousness brings with it an unfoldment of many psychic capacities, which are latent in the human soul. This unfoldment increases the scope and range of human consciousness. These new elements often play an important part in helping or hindering the spiritual emancipation of consciousness. Therefore, the aspirant not only has to understand the value of such experiences as unusual and significant dreams, visions, astral journeys, and glimpses of the subtle world, but he also has to learn to distinguish real occult experiences from hallucinations and delusions.

"Although it is customary to exaggerate the importance of occult experiences, it is not uncommon to doubt their validity and to treat them with the contempt usually accorded to all forms of mental aberrations and abnormalities. The attitude of unqualified contempt for occult experiences is of course most pronounced in those who are not even abecedarians in direct knowledge of the occult. It hurts the ego to admit and feel that there might be vast unexplored fields of the universe that are accessible just to a limited number of persons, and from which one happens to be excluded. The undeserved contempt that occultism at times receives is almost always the outcome of profound ignorance about its real meaning. This attitude of contempt is of course different from a cautious and critical attitude. Those who have a cautious and critical approach and who are endowed with humility and openness of mind are ever ready to recognize and admit occult phenomena when they occur.

"An aspirant is usually helped by a Perfect Master through ordinary means, and the Master prefers to take him veiled along the spiritual path. But when there are specific indications, he may also use occult techniques to help the aspirant. Special types of dreams are among the common methods used for touching the deeper life of the aspirant. Masters have not infrequently first contacted aspirants by appearing in their dreams. Such dreams, however, have to be carefully distinguished from ordinary dreams. In ordinary dreams the subtle body is active in exercising its functions of seeing, tasting, smelling, touching, and hearing; but the soul is not using the subtle body with full consciousness. As these experiences in ordinary dreams are received subconsciously, they are in most cases purely subjective, relating to physical activities and concerning the gross world, and are the creations of nascent sanskaras stored in the mind. In some cases, however, a dream that is indistinguishable from ordinary dreams may be the reflection in the subconscious of some objective experience of the subtle body and not merely a product of fancy."[2]

Such completely contrary reactions to occult experiences are not uncommon, given the diversity of human nature. Baba's comment serves however to alert the importance of a very careful analysis of this area, whether one is attracted or repelled by it. Above all, those mesmerized by occult phenomena should be aware of the fact that almost certainly they will need eventually to refocus on more important avenues of endeavor. Correspondingly, however, those who reject outright the realm of the occult must make the opposite adjustment of gradually accepting this realm for the value that is finally to be embodied in such experiences.

Let us return for the moment, however, to Baba's words, "An aspirant is usually helped by a Perfect Master through ordinary means, and the Master prefers to take him veiled along the spiritual path." Baba explains that this procedure is preferred because of the almost inevitable fascination of the aspirant for the unusual nature of occult happenings. He develops frequently a great desire for repetition, and more repetition, and this can become a serious detraction from real progress.

Even this reasoning does not however plumb the real importance of Baba's words. The first implication is that if one is

---

[2] *Discourses*, pp. 179–180.

studying with a Master who provides a constant diet of supernatural experiences, then the level of development of the Master is probably not very high. Baba is not so blunt as to state this in so many words, but progress on the spiritual path is highly dependent on honesty, and it is best to face such a fact early rather than after having spent long years in fascination for that which is virtually meaningless.

The second aspect of the importance of the subject lies in the concept of "being led under the veil." An adept on the spiritual path often finds early in his efforts various allusions to "the veil." Perhaps the most common employment of the term is in the advent of the Avatar into Creation. He is born without conscious knowledge of the role he is to fulfill. He is also completely unaware of his quality of spiritual perfection. All this is termed as being "born under the veil." Later, it is the duty of one of the Perfect Masters in Creation to lift this veil, although the timing of the advent of the Avatar has been dictated by a joint decision and action of all the ruling Perfect Masters.

But it is not only the Avatar who is subject to the veil. Baba's words indicate that a Perfect Master finds it more efficient to lead the spiritual aspirant through the necessary course of development without the aspirant being in the least aware of where he is in his ongoing. This has the advantage that no time is wasted in useless astonishment at the marvels characteristic of the ascending planes, and also almost complete freedom from starting up wrong turnings or bypaths, or of endless comparisons with fellow seekers on the Path. The Perfect One guards against all of this when he leads the novice under the veil.

All this is not easy psychologically for the aspirant, however, for as a consequence he never knows just what he has accomplished; his only assurance lies in his complete trust in his guide. The product is a sublimely developed individual, but completely unable to tell another seeker what he has gone through, and virtually devoid of tales of miraculous experiences. It can be hard on him, as this is inevitably a test of his devotion to and faith in his Master.

A far more serious problem arising from the availability of supernatural forces comes well along the Path, starting in the late third plane and especially present on the fourth. Meher Baba describes this in ominous terms:

"Therefore the subtle-conscious human soul at the stage of consciousness of the fourth plane is fully conscious of the first, second and third planes and experiences in full the subtle world, and so is completely conscious of the tremendous energy of the subtle world. Thus this human soul on the threshold of the mental world, commanding the energy at its height, is now nearest to the domain of Mind, which is the mental world, and thus is much more susceptible to the overpowering forces of the aspects of the mind, *viz.*, the thoughts, desires and emotions. And although this subtle-conscious human soul on the fourth plane consciously makes use of the subtle world's energy at its zenith, it is still unconscious of Mind. It therefore unconsciously makes use of the aspects of Mind, which are now too overpowering and thus most alluring for this soul which, so to speak, has to face and bear the full blast of the aspects of the mind (thoughts, desires and emotions) at their highest.

"This situation for the human soul on the fourth plane is extremely dangerous, since it is extremely treacherous. Here the soul, equipped with highest energy, which can be put to use either for the best or for the worst, has to maintain a sort of equilibrium of two forces at their zenith, *i.e.*, the height of the energy of the subtle world and the overpowering height of aspects of the mind of the mental world. If this human soul on the fourth plane, while unconsciously using the aspects of Mind, is overcome by the overpowering allurements of these aspects (thoughts, desires and emotions), he then cannot resist using energy at its climax for the worst by performing powerful miracles such as raising the dead, curing the blind, the sick and the maimed, etc., just to satisfy his own overpowering desires. He is even capable of creating the whole

world of forms with all of its creation, so great is the power obtained
from the energy at its height of which this subtle-conscious human
soul is conscious.

"Thus this misuse of energy at its zenith, through the medium
and the overpowering allurements of the aspects of mind, also at
their zenith, creates a sort of tremendous, irreparable short-circuit
in the two fundamental supernatural forces—of energy at its zenith
in the shape of stupendous power, and of mind at its zenith in
the shape of irresistible desire—resulting in an unimaginably
tremendous clash and explosion in the advanced consciousness of
the subtle-conscious human soul of the fourth plane. Absolute
disturbance is thus created in the consciousness of this human soul
resulting in downright disintegration of the advanced consciousness
of this human soul. Thereupon this subtle-conscious human soul
invariably falls to the lowest level of consciousness, which is the most
finite type of consciousness of the crudest form. Therefore this
human soul has to take the form of stone and has again to go
through the process of evolution."[3]

There is not another danger on the Path that Meher Baba
describes in such sober words. He repeats the warning virtually
throughout his works. He does reassure that such a fall to the stone
state is extremely rare, as one of the important functions of the ever-
present five Perfect Masters is to guard against this type of danger.
But it can happen, and the implication is that even getting close to
such a possibility is in itself an experience that may require a
considerable effort by the aspirant to win back to relatively safe
ground again.

In a previous quotation of Meher Baba's words he observed that
dreams are often used by the Master for initial contact with the
aspirant. There is no reason to doubt the verity of this statement.
Many times deeply sincere persons recount their experience of

---

[3] *God Speaks*, pp. 64–65.

having seen their spiritual guide first in a dream, and of seeing him physically only later. For some reason, this gives an added confidence in the credentials of the Master when he finally appears in the flesh. And why not? We are completely mortal and so often deceived that we sometimes need a little extra help to move us along a route we recognize as special and perhaps beset with dangers.

After cautioning that one must learn to differentiate between dreams that are spiritually significant and those of little value, Baba proceeds into the realm of other beginning occult experiences (always bearing in mind, of course, that a Perfect Master, if he is at the helm, may well be leading the aspirant totally under the veil; in such case, there are few unusual beginning occult experiences). Baba describes these initial occult happenings as those of "significant visions, lights, colors, sounds, smells, or contacts." Presumably the last are with individuals. Or it might even be with one's guardian angel.

Among these beginners' experiences, the loveliest as we have already suggested is that of sounds, what is called in ancient mystic tradition "the music of the spheres." When one first hears this, it seems so lovely and natural that one sets it down as being nothing more than a result of the natural creativity of one's own subconscious mind. After a time, and a bit of reflection, one decides that it is very special and in a way "beyond."

Baba says quite simply of such occurrences, "The beginner is apt to exaggerate the importance of his glimpses into the inner worlds and to develop an ungovernable craving for repetition of these experiences, or he tries to treat them as abnormal phenomena and underrates their significance. Of these two alternatives, the attitude of exaggerating the importance of occult experiences is the most common, because the novelty and rarity of occult experiences are factors that contribute to charging them with overwhelming importance."[1]

---

[1] *Discourses*, p. 181.

An even more important misuse of these occult experiences that Baba points out is to come to depend on them as a "goad" to action. The aspirant refuses to budge unless he has a divine portent indicating the way. It is especially in such instances of over-dependence that it is important to be under the direct guidance of a real Master. "In order to avoid this pitfall for the aspirant, the Master takes good care not to cater to his new craving for occult experiences. Such experiences are vouchsafed to the aspirant if and when they are absolutely necessary for spiritual purposes and not when he wants or asks for them....

"The introduction of the aspirant to occult phenomena is necessarily a very gradual and prolonged process. The Master is never anxious to expedite it, as few persons are really qualified to stand the expansion of their experience in this new dimension."[5]

It is especially desirable to reflect that the proper supervision of the aspirant who is commencing to have spontaneous happenings of an occult type, according to Baba, must be effected by a Master. Also, while Baba does not always spell it out, in the *Discourses* the usage of the word "Master" is in almost all cases in the sense of the Perfect Master. Granted, it is a relatively rare student on the Path who has the good fortune to be under the guidance of a Perfect One (Perfect Master or the Avatar). Realistically, therefore, progress without the peril of severe accidents or prolonged hang-ups, which is afforded by the presence of a Perfect Master, rarely occurs. Consequently, passage through this thicket is bound to be very accident-prone, and so the aspirant must be careful to do his best to guard against misuse of as well as enchantment by the phenomena that occur.

Meher Baba rarely referred to "occult phenomena" and miracles in closely connected passages. There is no ready rule to differentiate one from the other. Often, the word miracle is used

---

[5] *ibid.*, pp. 181–182.

simply in a polite context in discussing a happening associated with religious exercises or experiences. The best clarification would possibly be to suggest firstly that most events which cannot be explained through any established physical laws are caused by occult forces, and secondly that events termed as miracles are on the white magic side and never on the black.

This is by no means intended to belittle events established through the centuries, especially by the Catholic Church. There is every reason to believe that the events themselves, as well as those who caused them or participated in them, involved in most cases individuals of spiritual stature. The only point we are suggesting is that the forces involved are virtually impossible to differentiate from what are termed in esoteric literature as occult forces. Indeed, there is even a tradition that when Jesus Christ was about to perform a miracle, he deliberately established himself on the fourth plane, where the infinite divine forces are readily and naturally available.[6]

It is singular that Meher Baba repeatedly made a strong point of his declaration that he did not perform miracles. And yet many of those closest to him during his lifetime love to recount stunning tales of the most miraculous nature. If Baba was accosted with such a story, at least in his later years, he normally said simply that he had not consciously participated in the event being described.

For a definitive clarification of this puzzle one is referred to an intriguing passage at the end of the "Supplement" of *God Speaks*:

"The miracles wrought by Saviours and Perfect Masters have a divine motive behind them and may be either voluntary or involuntary. The voluntary miracles of a Saviour or Perfect Master

---

[6] Although not clearly defined and differentiated, Meher Baba leads one to understand that "supernatural" forces used on the fourth plane are universal, thus partaking of infinitude, while those used on the third plane are a composite, probably involving a considerable component of one's own psychic, and therefore limited, store of energy. Below this level any manifestations almost certainly are predominantly or wholly drawn from one's personal supply.

are those that he deliberately performs by the force of his **will**, and the involuntary ones are those that occur independently of the will of the Saviour or Perfect Master and are wrought by means of the ever-active force that surrounds these great beings. In the latter type of miracle the Saviour or Perfect Master is unaware of the incidents of the miracle of which he himself is the source and prime cause. Both voluntary and involuntary miracles of these Perfect Ones are nevertheless always directed towards the spiritual awakening of the world."[7]

Once the pattern of clarification starts it often continues. As I read these words recently and really focused on them for the first time, one of the close ones to Baba remembered Baba's own words given one day to a small group about him. He compared the circumstances to a great emperor who invites someone to be his guest. After greeting the invited person and assuring that all is in order, he leaves the guest for some moments, but without having attended personally to some of the details for his needs and comfort. These he has confided to the care of others in the palace who know and are accustomed to follow through on such occasions. In this way the guest has his every need provided, but the emperor is not personally conscious of certain of the needs which have nevertheless been cared for.

Thus, Baba's frequent comment I heard him make on many occasions when some miraculous event was claimed to have occurred through his intercession was that he had not consciously had anything to do with it–a very accurate and honest representation of the facts. I wonder if we should not call these the minor miracles of the Perfect Ones, and realize that they often happen as an automatic consequence of the force those Perfect Ones embody. They are not consciously willed, but are simply the natural outcome of the power and the capable sources of aid that surround them.

---

[7] *God Speaks*, p. 224.

Leaving these exceptional incidents aside for now, let us continue to examine the record which Baba himself set out on the use of miracles by a Perfect One. There is a considerable amount of pertinent material on the subject contained in the *Discourses* that he gave out, especially during the 1930s, when there was a fairly large group of Westerners residing either with or within easy "commuting" distance of him.

"...where there is no love, there is no bliss or beauty of being. In fact, God's nature as the Ocean of Love cannot be grasped by the mind. God has to be known through love and not through an intellectual search for miracles.

"That is the reason why I do not perform miracles for those who are the closest and dearest to me. I would rather have no following than use miracles for convincing others of my divinity. It is true that, while loving me, people often do have spiritual experiences that were hitherto unknown to them; and these experiences help them in the further opening of their hearts. But they are not meant to feed the mental craving for intellectual conviction, and they should not be regarded as the goal."[8]

In this section Meher Baba points out the necessity for the Master-aspirant relationship to be based on love, and that the performance of miracles makes no contribution (in fact, the implication is that it may even retard such a development) to this vital connection. In a later passage in the same work, Baba makes a generalized statement on the manner in which great Masters use their powers. He has been recounting a story of how Ghausali Shah, one of the Masters of Rumi, had appeared in two places at the same time—sitting with the circle of disciples, while at the same time appearing to one of them sent to fetch water from a nearby stream.

---

[8] *Discourses*, p. 96.

"These stories show how the Masters may use their powers on rare occasions to break down the ego of their disciples or help them further along the path. As a rule the Masters are very sparing in the use of their divine powers, and they never use them unless it is absolutely necessary for spiritual purposes. Ordinarily they secure their purposes through normal, mundane ways. While doing so, they not only exhibit great understanding, a keen sense of humor, unending patience, and consummate tact, but they also take great trouble to help their disciples and adjust themselves in numberless ways to whatever might be entailed by the needs of the situation."[9]

A personal incident that occurred in my life in the 1950s was especially enlightening to me in this field. It was a glorious reencounter with the Gospel of St. John after many years of not having been near it. A distant relative nearing the completion of his college degree had to write a term paper on any one of the books from the New Testament. When he got stuck and called for help, I found myself immersed for the first time in some years in St. John. What a superb adventure it was to read again after all those years the sensitive words of John describing the actions of the Christ.

But one thing became rapidly apparent: how often Christ tried to arouse the interest of an individual directly in an important spiritual principle. But almost always, the individual's approach to what Christ was saying was a very unimaginative and very literal interpretation of the surface of the words. Christ would try again, and even again, and when all else had failed, as St John describes it in this particular happening in his Gospel, he told the woman a tidbit or two from her love life. Then she really paid attention, and in fact, brought all her friends running to see this man who knew things that he couldn't possibly know. How horribly disappointed Christ must have been to have to use a bit of magic to get the person

---

[9] *ibid.,* pp. 155–156.

addressed to listen to a few words of simple spiritual principle.

As one reflects, it becomes clear that in the Christian tradition there has been a long and increasingly marked emphasis placed on the performance of miracles. One is tempted to speculate that there has been so much attention paid to the miracles performed by Christ that this has often tended to outshine the beauty and force of the spiritual teaching he has given. Is it possible that the attitude adopted by Meher Baba in his mid and later years was a process of leveling the ground to make it more likely that this time mankind would not concentrate on the unimportant actions of the Master rather than on the truly magnificent truths that God gives us through him?

Meher Baba did not, however, avoid all contact with the unusual or even the virtually impossible. The lore of his life abounds with extraordinary events, but in almost all instances, Baba plays them with a completely poker-faced serenity. He does not get trapped into underpinning a new era of spirituality built on phenomena.

It is not the Perfect One who does things in an incomplete or unbalanced manner. It is our recollections and later handling of the interpretation of those events which is frequently lacking in balance. We are the ones who produce the flaws. In this instance in considering the miracles performed by Jesus one comes gradually to suspect that he did exactly what had to be done in order to awaken those around him to a few of the necessary seeds of Truth. He planted those seeds in such a manner that they might be tended properly and produce the spiritual results for those who were around him at the time. It has been us, who come centuries later, who begin to place such emphasis on the miracles themselves that, finally, they have all but obscured the spiritual lessons that Jesus placed before those around him. While this is principally our fault, nevertheless part of this is a natural process of degeneration, and in fact is instrumental in precipitating a fresh dispensation of the Truth.

One of the central responsibilities of the Avatar is to rebalance major working principles in Creation, which are tending to get out of balance, especially among humanity. He does not do the job simply by applying a miraculous charge of spiritual energy. Rather, it appears that he says words to us and gives directional shoves in the manner needed to rebalance gradually the mechanism involved. If miraculous happenings have tended to get out of hand by being considered more important than spiritual truth itself, then the Avatar will in some manner start up the processes needed to rebalance the situation. So far, however, they seem to this writer to be going still further out of balance, as there is nowadays a fascination with occult forces and happenings that takes up a vast proportion of the attention of many of the honest seekers after Truth.

For now, it is apparently up to us to begin to suspect that right here within the domain of the miraculous there is an important factor on the spiritual path that needs careful attention. Otherwise we will be slowed, and many others will be also.

Once having had a great experience, often the student has an overwhelming urge to discuss it with other comrades on the Path. Or else, contrarily, if he has always shown the Doubting Thomas temperament, he goes into a bout of questioning the subject of spirituality from every angle. Was it all an illusion? Is he misreading what he thought he had learned and experienced? Is it all perhaps the product of malevolent forces trying to build up his ego again? The train of possible faults and failings is endless. Meher Baba comments on this:

"Even when real occult experience can be clearly differentiated from illusion, it suffers in its power and efficacy if it becomes the object of doubt. This can happen when the person who has had the experience discusses the matter with others who, because of their incapacity to understand such things, throw out contrary thoughts and shake his conviction. For this reason, the Master usually requires a disciple to maintain strict secrecy about his experiences. Even a deep experience is likely to become weak through the contradiction and skepticism of others, unless the aspirant has learned to follow his own inner experience irrespective of what others might think or say. If the aspirant is to make quick progress and to profit most from the Master's help, he must develop immense and unshakable confidence in himself and the Master. He must not look to others for guidance, because those who will understand his problems or his experiences are very few. The aspirant must indeed be prepared to face the possibility of not being completely understood by any of his friends or relatives, for they may be in the dark about the grounds for his ideology and course of action.

"If at the time of its occurrence an occult experience has served the purpose of giving new momentum to spiritual endeavor, it often does not matter if the aspirant considers it in retrospective analysis and thought as being a form of delusion. However, there are some occult experiences that are deliberately vouchsafed to the aspirant in order that they should be standing sources of inspiration and guidance. With regard to these special experiences, it becomes necessary that the aspirant cease doubting their validity and importance.

"The general attitude of seeking endless corroborations of occult experiences is definitely unhealthy, and the Master gives corroborative confirmation only when he considers it necessary. Further, he takes the initiative in the way he judges best in the situation. Whatever he does arises from his unfettered discretion and is in no way related to or dependent upon any expectation developed by the aspirant. But when it is spiritually necessary, the Master does increase the efficacy of occult experience by confirming its validity and authority through some direct or indirect corroboration from the aspirant's normal range of experience."[10]

Meher Baba finishes off this aspect of the subject with a final prod for the aspirant not to neglect his own inner effort in the intoxication of having had some supernatural experience:

"The harnessing of occult forces is not to be regarded in any way as a substitute for the inner effort the aspirant must make to advance further. When occult experiences are gifts from a Perfect Master, they serve the purpose of unveiling much of the hitherto obscured intuition, removing some of the difficulties leading toward the spiritual path, and filling the aspirant with the great confidence and enthusiasm that are necessary to cope with new requirements at each stage. But the aspirant makes real progress by putting into practice the best intuitions of his heart, not by being the merely passive recipient of occult experiences."[11]

The second discourse on occultism is entitled "The Relationship with the Master in the Spiritual Life" and details the great value of intimate contact with the Master, including the act of touching the feet of the Master. While this may connote subservience to the Western mind, Baba explains that this is a very significant act which actually lays the burden of individual sanskaras on the Master.[12] I was overwhelmed one late afternoon when Meher Baba asked me to massage his feet. I wondered if the great sense of the lightening of life which occurred about this time represented just such an assumption of the emotional load of my sanskaras by Baba. Rumi was given enlightenment at the end of a chess game with his Master. Is it too much to dream that I might have been given the

---

[10] *ibid.*, pp. 183–184

[11] *ibid.*, pp. 184–185.

[12] *ibid;* pp. 187–188.

grace of some lifetimes of lessened emotional struggle after a foot massage? Or is it perhaps rather a path being opened that results in lessening of inner conflict while leaving the real burden of effort where it originally lay: right on my own shoulders?

The final of the three discourses devoted to occultism by Meher Baba is entitled "Occultism and Spirituality." Baba points out here that occultism is a branch of knowledge, just as the sciences as we know them are concerned with specific areas of material phenomena. Baba notes the long-term existence of societies formed to study occult phenomena in the same manner as the sciences. He makes no negative or belittling comment on such effort. In fact, why should they not exist and perform a positive function?

The Masters themselves over thousands of years have given out specific knowledge on such subjects as reincarnation, karma and the existence of the different personal bodies and the planes. These, Baba says, help by giving the "right sort of background for spiritual aspiration." On the other hand, there is always the constant warning not to misuse the occult powers. "Even the slightest misuse of occult powers causes a binding for the soul. Sometimes it may retard the progress of the aspirant and may even lead to a considerable setback."

The following paragraph suggests very briefly that one of the reasons for the sparing use of occult powers even by a Master (always in the sense of a Perfect Master) has to do with possible interference with karma.

"In the hands of the Masters of spiritual wisdom, occult power is not only safe but has immense capacities that can be harnessed in the service of humanity; yet even they are very sparing and economical in its use. By its very nature, occultism as an art has its own natural limitations. It cannot be widely used for helping the material needs of humanity or helping it in its mundane purposes. The introduction of an uncertain and incalculable factor, which the free exercise of occult power would involve, is bound to create much confusion and disturbance in the ordinary pursuits of man, who must be left to his own limitations, resources, and possibilities for the equal and uninterrupted working out of the law of karma. The use of occult power, therefore, has to be strictly restricted to the furtherance of spiritual purposes."[13]

You will recall from the earlier section of this work Meher Baba's careful reminder so frequently repeated that he did not remove the karmic weight from the follower, but that, because of the love of the individual for him, he would lower a specific karmic burden from the top of his head to his shoulders. There have been exceptions, apparently, but as suggested, the apparent elimination of a grave problem is more likely to be a postponement to a later date and a set of circumstances which may allow the resolution of the burden more readily. To give more substance to this conjecture, one should recall that both space and time are accepted nowadays as having little reality outside of an ambience of separate bodies; in other words, since duality as duality is a fleeting dream and not part of Reality, then time and space also do not exist in Reality. This suggests at once that a Perfect One no doubt has considerable or perhaps total latitude in handling both time and space flexibly in dealing with even the karma of those who love him. I do not suggest this as a proven principle that I have unearthed, but it may well provide a key to some of the seeming contradictions between principles and actual happenings that one observes in the life of a Perfect One.

Finally, however, in this very important and complex subject, one should recall the short and clear statement Baba makes in the "Supplement" to *God Speaks:* "The *Avatar* never takes on the *karma* of individuals but His Godhood functions universally."[14]

---

[13] *ibid.*, p. 195.

[14] *God Speaks*, p. 269.

Meher Baba terminates his exposition of the subject of occultism with the following admonitions:

"There is a very clear and definite distinction, however, between occultism and mysticism, spiritualism and spirituality; and any failure to grasp the full import of this difference can only lead to confusion.

"All miracles belong to the phenomenal world, which is the world of shadows. As phenomena, they are subject to change, and nothing that changes can have lasting value. Realization of the eternal Truth is an initiation into the unchangeable Being, which is the supreme Reality; and no acquaintance with the occult world or capacity to manipulate its forces can really amount to realization of the Truth. Occult phenomena are as much within the domain of false imagination as are ordinary phenomena of the gross world. From the spiritual point of view, the only important thing is to realize Divine Life and to help others realize it by manifesting it in everyday happenings. To penetrate into the essence of all being and significance and to release the fragrance of that inner attainment for the guidance and benefit of others–by expressing, in the world of forms, truth, love, purity, and beauty–this is the sole game that has intrinsic and absolute worth. All other happenings, incidents, and attainments in themselves can have no lasting importance."[15]

Astrology. Earlier we noted that in this century there has been a constant and widespread interest in astrology. As is true of Sufism, the origins of this science are lost in antiquity. There are fascinating traditions about the nature and purpose of astrology thousands of years ago. At that time, one story goes, astrology was actually the religion of mankind based on natural science. Of course, there are no concrete records remaining to give corroboration of this belief.

---

[15] *Discourses*, pp. 199–200.

There is also another intriguing concept which is fundamental to the ancient base of astrology. This is that the entire universe is in fact a macro-man, within which there is a typical living structure and interdependence of the organs. If this were true, it would not be astonishing to confirm the interrelationship between vastly separated parts of the universe which is intrinsic in astrological principles.

All this is beside the point in modern usage of astrology. Nowadays it is frequently used for the study of the character of individuals. However, even more importantly for many of those attracted to it, astrology represents a means of predicting the future, and thereby being able to avoid painful or even catastrophic events that are to arrive in one's life.

The use of astrology to study the character traits of the individual is similar to that targeted by much of modern psychology. Its use, however, to predict and thereby avoid undesired happenings in one's life gets into a far more sensitive area of human progress. At once one must start by questioning the accuracy of such predictions. Then, if this point is favorably resolved, one faces the further question of what then are the consequences in relation to one's karma, which is inevitably deeply enmeshed in the course of the events predicted astrologically?

It is not my aim to try to establish myself as a master of astrology or, for that matter, of the life and words of Meher Baba. I can nevertheless present certain happenings from my own life which relate to these fields, and this is what I have attempted to do. I am on far more fragile underpinnings in the realm of astrology, as I studied it assiduously for only something over a year shortly after having graduated from the university. A close personal friend with a mentality similar to mine, Katherine Ahlstrand, had become fascinated with the art of astrology as a young university student in Uppsala. After her matriculation she was accorded the singular privilege by the Vatican to study their resources on the subject. It became apparent to her shortly that there had been some fairly serious errors in transmission of concepts and data in recent centuries. When she corrected modern practice to correspond more closely to the ancient bases, then a very striking correlation could be seen between the observed nature of the individual and that portrayed in their natal chart.

I found similar correspondences when I had studied enough to draw up horoscopes for several close friends, and the picture I obtained was more than astonishing. It was exact. When I progressed and regressed the charts by changing the birth hour, it was as if I saw my friends go into focus and then out of focus. I could not doubt, from my own observations, that astrology as I had been taught it by Mrs. Ahlstrand was an exact science, astounding as that might seem. Oddly enough, that completely satisfied my original interest, and so I left astrology aside.

Although the character side of the horoscope was the more interesting to me, I could not avoid seeing that the predictions of future events and problems was also remarkable. But rather than fascinating me, this repelled me. I do not want to give the impression of a moral judgment here, but instinctively I have always been put off by what seemed a morbid interest in knowing the future. Later I began to suspect that this had been an early warning signal of the complications that attempts to delve into the future could produce in the spinning out of one's personal karma.

Again and again it may be seen clearly that the universe is a vast complex of different categories of energy. The path of return to the One appears equally constantly to be a similar great complex of balancing out of the various energies as well as the plus and minus accounts associated with each individual soul-plus-bodies. In Creation natural processes are set in motion in a natural manner for the balancing of those accounts. This is what is referred to as karma. However, the needs that arise in this balancing finally surpass the resources normally available to the individual. This is where the importance of winning the attention of a Master arises, his help being critical to final success.

Enter at this point the aspirant who has become obsessed with drawing up astrological charts predicting future events, and all this he judges predominantly from the standpoint of personal pleasure and pain. It is a very restricted point of view, and not necessarily at all what is required to balance the accounts of numberless previous lifetimes. Therefore, a very "successful" reading of a chart may well allow one to avoid a painful circumstance, but what is the end result in relation to karmic law and the final balancing of the account? It may very well go in exactly the opposite direction.

It does not take a genius to see that astrological tampering with the course of life's events may well produce a far greater regression than advance in life. Far better, if available, to find a Master and face the crisis of surrender to him, than trust one's own poorly based judgment of what is desirable in life, which may prove finally to be only retrogressive in its end results.

One of Meher Baba's closest and most constant mandali was Meherjee Karkaria, a Parsi from a priestly family near Bombay. The Parsis often use astrology; it is classic among them. After having discovered Baba and surrendered completely to him, Meherjee was off somewhere in Iran selling rugs. Then, on a subsequent visit to Bombay, a friend proposed to have his astrological chart drawn up by a specialist whom he knew. The astrologer in vigorous terms told Meherjee that his rug business was threatened by immediate disaster, and advised him to sell it at once. That night Meherjee sent a cable to his assistant in Iran with instructions to liquidate everything without delay.

The next morning while visiting Baba, who happened to be in Bombay, Meherjee was asked by Baba how his affairs were progressing in Iran. Meherjee recounted the incident with the astrologer the previous day. Baba tweaked Meherjee's ear sharply and demanded, "What do you need an astrologer to do for you? I am your astrologer. Send a cable at once countermanding your order of yesterday. But when I tell you to sell the affair, then do it at once."

This Meherjee did, and the upshot of the entire matter was that there was in fact a slight dip for some weeks in the economy in Iran, but it rapidly recovered and Meherjee's business broke all records. Then one day he had the command from Baba, and without hesitation he sold the shop at once.

There is still another fact to consider. While I had deserted astrology instinctively, several of my close friends continued their studies. We never tried to convince each other of anything, so I followed my non-astrological bent and they followed their love for the charts. But they began to notice something. If an old and loved friend met Meher Baba and came under his spiritual guidance, the astrological predictions went completely awry. The Great Astrologer had obviously trumped the heavenly relationships. This became so evident that the usage of astrology among many of those who loved Baba fell into disrepute. And yet, believe it or not, those same persons continued out of fascination to draw up the charts of their close friends.

Should we hazard a summary of this closely cherished arena? It might read something like the following. Astrology in its original versions is apparently an exact science, as are chemistry, physics and biology. There are laws and principles which, when properly followed, accurately delineate both character and future happenings. Before using astrology, especially for predictive reasons to avoid unwanted incidents in one's life, one must consider very carefully how this affects the karmic balances in life's experiences and the long-term wisdom of such avoidance. Even more importantly, if one has the grace to find a real Master, it is almost certain that his analysis and agenda for help will outweigh the astrological forces.

One should look at the question of astrology with great care before using it in any manner that may importantly affect one's spiritual aspirations.

Hypnosis. The second subject mentioned earlier as being of great interest at present is that of the use of hypnosis to regress into previous lifetimes. This has been a natural outgrowth of the observance by Sigmund Freud that a spectacular improvement occurred in the state of emotional balance of patients when they were able to regress in memory to a specific traumatizing incident, usually in early childhood. Freud's description indicated that the cure was nothing short of immediate and miraculous.

Although one is justified in wondering if the simple fact of recall itself resulted in such a major release from the problems resulting from the original experience; still, it is possible that the defining of the original incident allowed a more direct approach to an eventual cure. However, a student of the path would wonder what could be done if the traumatic incident happened in a previous lifetime, and therefore beyond the power of simple recall. This in fact was what a number of psychologists, who were at the same time mystics, began to reflect upon.

It was not long before the idea of the use of hypnosis suggested itself as a possible means of jumping the memory barrier between lifetimes. Soon the literature began to fill with various incidents of such use of hypnosis. It seemed that not only an extremely valuable psychological tool had been discovered, but also a realm of fascination to the general public had been opened as well.

When nature reveals a naturally existing barrier, it is almost always wise to proceed with caution before destroying it. The atomic scientist is conversant with the kind of a protective "dike" that surrounds the enormous energy content of the nucleus of an atom. This prevents that energy from being released spontaneously. In fact, it took a great deal of study before the means were found to destroy the barrier and release the nuclear energy content. The result was both the atom bomb and the atomic energy plant.

There is a natural safeguard that protects the conscious self from automatic access to the memories from previous lifetimes that are stored in the mental body. The one who tries deliberately to leap over that protection tampers with forces whose consequences he cannot predict. Although quite long, the manner in which Meher Baba deals with the realities and the dangers in this field merit detailed quotation.

"Those who have direct access to the truth of reincarnation are even fewer that those who have direct access to the truth of immortality of the individual soul. The memories of all past lives are stored and preserved in the mental body of the individual soul, but they are not accessible to the consciousness of ordinary persons because a veil is drawn over them. When the soul changes its physical body, it gets a new brain; and its normal waking consciousness functions in close association with the brain processes. Under ordinary circumstances, only the memory of the present life can appear in consciousness because the new brain acts as a hindrance to the release of the memories of those experiences that had been gathered through the medium of other brains in past lives.

"In rare cases, in spite of the resistance offered by the brain, some memories of past lives leak into the present life in the form of dreams that are completely unexplainable in terms of the present life. An individual may see persons in his dreams whom he has never seen in his present life. It often happens that those who appeared in the dreams were persons whom he had met in his past lives. But of course such dreams, when they are of the ordinary type, cannot be treated as a *memory* of past lives. They merely indicate that the imagination at work in the dreams was influenced by information taken from past lives. The real memory of past lives is clear, steady, and sure like the memory of the present life. When it comes to an individual, he no longer has any doubt about his having existed in several previous lives along with many other individuals. Just as he cannot doubt his own past life in the present incarnation, he cannot doubt his life in past incarnations.

"The number of persons who can remember their past lives is very small compared with the vast majority, who are so completely bound to the gross sphere of existence that they do not even suspect supersensible realities. The release of such memories is severely conditioned by the limitations of the brain, as long as consciousness is entangled with the physical body and its brain processes. When consciousness is emancipated from the limitations imposed by the brain, it can recover and reestablish the memories of past lives, which are all stored in the mental body. This involves a degree of detachment and understanding that only the spiritually advanced can have. The memory of past lives can come with full clarity and certainty, even to those who are still crossing the inner planes of consciousness but have not yet become spiritually perfect.

"The memory of past lives does not come back to a person, except in abnormal and rare cases, unless he is sufficiently advanced from the spiritual point of view. This provision made by the laws of life secures unhampered spiritual evolution of the individualized soul. At first view it might seem that the loss of memory of previous lives is a total loss, but this is far from being so. For most purposes, knowledge about past lives is not at all necessary for the guidance of the onward course of spiritual evolution. Spiritual evolution consists in guiding life in the light of the highest values perceived through intuition, and not in allowing it to be determined by the past. In many cases, even the memory of the present life acts as an obstacle for certain adjustments demanded by the spiritual requirements of the changing situations of life. The problem of emancipation may in a sense be said to be a problem of securing freedom from the past– which, in the case of those who are bound to the wheel of birth and death, inexorably shapes the present life.

"Life would be infinitely more complicated if one who is not spiritually advanced were burdened by the conscious memory of numberless past lives. He would be dazed and unsettled by the diversity of settings in which persons would appear to him in the light of his memory. He is not called upon to face such confusion, however, because he is shielded from the resurrection of the memory of past lives. Things and persons come to him in a limited and definite context and setting, with the result that he finds it easy to determine his actions and responses in the light of what he knows from the present life.

"This does not mean that his actions and responses are *entirely* determined by what he knows from his present life. All that has happened in past lives also has its own unconscious but effective share in determining his actions and responses. In spite of the actual influence of past lives, the fact remains that since he is shielded from the resurrection of conscious memory, his consciousness is not subject to the confusion that would result if the conscious memory of past lives were among the data he had to consider for the purpose of determining his actions and responses.

"The resurrection of the memory of past lives can be faced without confusion or loss of balance only when the person has become desireless and has lost all feeling of 'mine' and 'thine.' "[16]

Meher Baba's explanation of the positive and negative values of recall of past lifetimes could not be clearer. It does not follow necessarily though that this will cause the curious and enthusiastic adventurer to abandon his searches in the field. It should, however, at least caution him as to the possible consequences. Above all, it should act as a brake on the guru who is tempted to create sensations by toying with forces that he may not be fully able to handle wisely.

There is still a further factor that must be dealt with in the case

---

[16] *ibid.*, pp. 314–316.

of regression into the memories of previous lifetimes. It is the phenomenon of what in previous decades has been called "coloring," a term principally employed in the receipt of messages through mediums, automatic writing or other semi-trance states. The word coloring was used to identify a specific problem that those seriously involved in the field took into account in their exchanges with the disincarnate realm. It was a very simple and quite reasonable concept. It indicated merely that all "messages" received from the "other side" by a receiver in physical form had to pass through the subconscious of the receiver, and therefore were inevitably subject to an unknown quantity and quality of influence resident in the unconscious of the receiver. Anyone familiar with the basic principles of Newtonian physics will find this understandable and even inevitable.

Simply put, and no doubt to be argued at great length, the problem is that our unconscious is a storehouse of myriads of past experience, not only of this lifetime but also of previous lifetimes. The principle of coloring states very simply that there is no way that material can be retrieved from this elaborate storage system without coming into contact with both similar and dissimilar occurrences. The resultant train of mental impressions transmitted to the conscious mind may therefore be a mixture of materials from quite varying origins.

Hence the memories stored from a specific incarnation may be either little or very much modified as they pass through the unconscious by contact with these other events which are not necessarily connected at all in original time and space. It is something like our experience of dreams. Parts may be quite lucid and connected to events similar to those we have already experienced and remember from our present lives. Then there are other parts fused intimately together which make no sense and may even seem wildly fantasist.

The fact of coloring is present and can be of overwhelming

importance. That hypnosis may have been used is beside the point. It cannot guarantee in the slightest that the other compartments of memory have been shielded off from the resultant train of recollection. There is nothing mystic nor special about hypnosis that controls the circuits of the deep unconscious. It is just as open to the problem of coloring as were the perhaps more romantic or even dangerous excursions into the unconscious of the mediumistic transmission so popular in the past and still a part of our modern era.

One might summarize the viewpoint of Meher Baba in regard to the occult by saying that it is an area of great importance, both constructively and potentially destructively, on the spiritual Path. Generally, each element of occult power and experience has a natural timing and place in the progress of the aspirant on the spiritual path. It is far better to allow those natural forces and timing to bring about their own natural opening rather than risk delays or even serious accidents by trying to control these phenomena prematurely.

13. THE INDIVIDUAL

Very few things are more important to the human being than his individuality and, in the event of the disappearance of the physical body, the fate of that individuality. What is the position of Meher Baba in regard to this paramount question?

Oddly enough, despite his insistence that the only Reality is indivisible, eternal God, and all else is a dream or imagination, there is a striking sequence throughout his works of considerations of individuality as we know it, and even in some cases the permanency of the compact and differentiated entity we call the individual.

It is a complex issue, and nowhere does Baba clarify it with the sort of brief, crystal-clear statements that characterize the large part of his expositions on Creation.

But first, let us go back and recapitulate the references already given above concerning the origin of Creation and the drop-souls that evolve into human beings. It all started with God in His original state in the Beyond the Beyond as being infinite, indivisible and completely unconscious, but with the innate potential of the Whim to know His divinity consciously. Then, for reasons that Baba says cannot be explained intellectually, and hence must await for understanding upon our own achievement of God-realization, the Whim began to manifest.

At the "location" of the surging of the Whim, which Baba clarifies to be the Om Point of Creation, there is a turbulence which causes portions of indivisible God to become as if isolated and encapsulated in the form of a bubble or drop-soul. This is all in imagination, for in reality, God is indivisible; but the dream is so realistic that the drop-soul itself imagines that it is completely isolated and separate. Thus the long adventure of the drop-soul within the grand dream of Creation starts its course.[1]

Within the dream the first iotas of consciousness are produced, along with impressions or sanskaras. Consciousness inevitably and automatically focuses on the illusion of manyness within which it was produced,[2] and this is mistakenly called Reality. Even in the earliest generation of primitive consciousness, it automatically and completely identifies with the "out there" of manyness and action.

The increasingly higher levels of consciousness are produced through the interaction of the external environment of imagined separateness with the increasingly complex physical, subtle and finally emotional bodies that are associated with each drop-soul. So the process of generation of consciousness goes on until finally, in the last animal form of evolution, consciousness reaches the level necessary to fulfill the original Whim of God to know His own divinity consciously. Then only the misdirection of consciousness towards the external environment, which has been considered Reality all during the previous history of the drop-soul, is capable of being corrected, and matured consciousness can finally come to know the true nature of God as Reality.

Here is where it is necessary to pause and spin out some of the details that are important in considering individuality.

How is it possible to reconcile individual existence with the statement that Reality is infinite and indivisible?

---

[1] Meher Baba gives a detailed description of these origins and the basic mechanisms especially in *God Speaks*, pp. 80–89. For a vivid accounting on the dream of Creation given by Baba to one of the Four Language Group Sahavas, see *Listen, Humanity*. pp. 36–38.

[2] In my own mind I term this "focusing on the scene of the crime."

Intellectually and rationally, there seems no way to harmonize these two opposite concepts. The two words used by Meher Baba, and often employed by other Masters of the Path, are "imagination" and "dream." Meher Baba spends considerable time in pointing out the *seeming* complete reality of intense dreams. In them, we have the total sense of experiencing something tangible and continuing. It is only when we have awakened from the vividly realistic dream that we say to ourselves, "Ah, it was a dream after all." Sometimes we also add, "Thank goodness."

Meher Baba's point is simply that if there are dreams that absorb us so completely as we dream them that we take them for continuing tangible reality, then it has to be admitted that there is a possibility that what we term waking life may in turn be another, bigger type of dream. Baba says very simply that one day we will awaken from it, in the process of coming to God-realization, and then we will know completely clearly that what we had experienced was in truth just another, bigger dream. But it had no base at all of continuing reality and so has finally disappeared forever.

Such an explanation may well leave the inquiring mind of the searcher for Truth more exasperated than satisfied. And yet, it has to be admitted as being a very possible and final description of actuality. Above all, though, even granting the validity of such an analogy, where does it leave the central problem of the fate of the individual, who has undergone countless crises and trials in the long succession of events within which individual consciousness was developed?

Certainly, to be very honest, the parallel of the dream as a description of the true nature of all Creation does not seem to offer any concrete comfort to the individual who is asking, by this time rather plaintively, "But what about me?"

In no attempt to postpone the confrontation of this central problem, let us go on a bit further to examine the record of the individual existence during its sojourn in Creation. It is long and detailed. There is the complex history of the incarnations throughout the long course of physical evolution, which stretches just as far as Darwin had envisaged it. The one point to bear in mind, though, is that Darwin had certainly never entertained the idea that it was a continuing entity, the drop-soul, that persisted throughout this long saga. Or had he, perhaps? He was an uncannily bright and also intuitive individual, and it is hard to believe that he could have pierced to the heart of a riddle of the development of form so fruitfully without having also had some intimations of the further less tangible base that underlay it. But that is for Darwin to untangle and perhaps one day establish what he actually perceived. No doubt he is still busily at work on some continuation of his epic contributions.

The question that we must pose now is whether the experiences in the dream of Creation are unique in the case of each drop-soul, part unique and part repetition of experiences undergone by other drop-souls, or largely or even totally repetition of what has been passed over countless times by other antecedent entities.

The one clue from Meher Baba that reads on this was a brief reference one day to the infinitude of God's consciousness, and the fact that it could only be produced from an infinitude of different challenges met in an infinitude of different physical experiences by an infinitude of different drop-souls. There is also Baba's statement that God's consciousness is infinitely individualized. This is a pronouncement of primordial significance.

"As desires aim at self-satisfaction, the whole consciousness becomes self-centered and individualized. The individualization of consciousness may in a sense be said to be the effect of the vortex of desires."[3] And then later, as Perfection is achieved, "The limited individuality, which is the creation of Ignorance, is transformed into the divine Individuality, which is unlimited.... Individuality becomes

---

[1] *Discourses*, p. 18.

limitless by the disappearance of Ignorance."[4]

A mathematician observing the complexity of Creation and assuming that there are interconnecting means of existing forces to affect all other existing forces in one manner or another would have to conclude that it would be impossible for one center of force and experience to repeat the precise conditions for a given moment that another center of experience was undergoing, or had experienced, or would experience. Enough, then, for the possibility of an infinitude of different experiences.

But not so fast. It is necessary to add that Baba says that the dream of Creation, being underlain by the infinitude of God, also extends infinitely. If the original is infinite, then why not the dream as well? The mathematics follow quite simply.

There is also a considerable background of mystic literature which describes each drop-soul as being unique, and that its development and finally its course of perfection is similarly unique. Thus there is no way for even a great teacher to lay down a single unique and universally valid course for the return to God. The Path of perfecting consciousness is completely and uniquely individual. This may not constitute complete proof for the non-repetition of pattern from one soul to another in the total complexity of consciousness developed, but such agreement for so many centuries by so many different schools of thought should indicate that almost certainly there is a basic truth here.

In a number of schools of mysticism it is fairly common for the guru to give certain instructions to an entire group, but more individualized details are given to the individual aspirant in private. Often as well, the student is warned not to discuss with others his personal spiritual experiences. It is a characteristic of human nature to want to have the same experiences as the person at one's side. Otherwise, one feels left out and inferior. But if the course of

---

[1] *ibid.*, p. 21.

development and the path of return were identical, it would imply that the consciousness produced was the same. In such case, when the first man had developed and perfected his own consciousness, the entire coming to consciousness of God would have been completed for all time. The end of the purpose of Creation would have been achieved and presumably it might as well disappear.

But obviously Creation goes on, and all the evidence is that the reason is in the basic importance of diversity. This is what is meant by Divine or Infinite Individuality. It has the connotation of total diversity and yet without in any way being divided or separated.

If this is true, then one has a truly inspiring picture of the final role of the individual. It is that each drop-soul is charged with a section of the infinite consciousness of God as its responsibility for development. In infinitude, there is no such thing as repetition of the same unit. Each drop-soul has a unique and individual function. Each contribution is unique and irreplaceable. Each part of the infinitude must be realized and perfected, free of any and every flaw. Only completely freed consciousness is then left and becomes the eternal individualized contribution of that drop-soul.

This last does not mean that there are no problems and that everything gets done without delay or accident. This is apparently an inherent property of the system of Creation. There does seem to be a flexibility and a choice and a slower and a faster and an easier and a tougher aspect to Creation and all within it. But, finally, it all has to get done, and to come back home. This is evidently why, amongst others, there is always a small contingent of Perfect Masters about, and periodically, the presence of the Christ-Avatar as well to get through particularly complex aspects.

The basic fact underlying individuality is that of infinitude, which allows infinite individualization through the contributions of an infinitude of drop-souls through the passage of an infinitude of time within the infinite dream of Creation. That is the key. In fact, in Reality there is no such thing as time or space, so the stretching out only exists within the scope of the dream being dreamed within a dream.

The reason it is so difficult to conceive an individual existing within infinite indivisible Unity is because of an almost universal confusion between the personal ego and the quality of being individual. The ego is definitely separate and exists within the dream of separation and contrast. This is the heart of ego life, and we mistake this role as being the central reality of individual life as well. But just as consciousness can exist without being focused on any one thing, so individuation can and does exist after the termination of the ego. The two are not identical and coexistent.

To try to take this from the realm of the abstract and into the world of beings and events, I will need to describe again a personal observation in daily life that has been very important to me, although very slow to develop. It has to do with desires and their attachment to certain specific aims. As is true of many human beings, I have long been aware of the manner in which my desires fix themselves on certain objects or achievements. I have also come to know that the manner in which Meher Baba defines this process as being the typical rolling out of a sanskaric desire pattern is a very accurate and important description of what occurs.

For many years I tried to wear down several of the more troublesome of these sanskaric patterns in my own life and frankly found myself getting nowhere. Needless to say, this was very discouraging. Finally I had to content myself with realizing that probably as it had taken many incarnations to deposit the core of these sanskaric forces, so it would undoubtedly take many more incarnations to wear them out. I had hoped originally that there would be a shortcut, either through great effort on my part to understand and block, or if not that way, by allying myself with a Master who knew and would help.

Personal effort obviously had not produced observable effects in any reasonable period of time. Then the Master entered the picture, and although he was completely trusted and loved, oddly enough the sanskaras still did not seem to budge. Having made this sad observation, I reverted to my earlier conclusion that just as the formation had been long, so the dissolution would also be long, even with the best available help from the Master plus my own stubborn efforts. I had always been conditioned to believe that life did not give one something for nothing, and so I reconciled myself to the long haul.

Meanwhile, as this story was spinning itself out, I heard quite a good many of my companion aspirants commenting that they worried about what life would really be like when they managed to get rid of a large package of desires. In their minds, personal life is built on wanting and accomplishing. If there is no wanting, then what will motivate, and if there is no motivation, then what can life possibly be about?

Obviously I could not negate their argument, but for some reason it rang false to me. Then one day I had it. For the first time, a small desire pattern disappeared, and what did I note? I still functioned in that domain, and I still had intense interest and energy within it, perhaps even more than before. But I just was not compulsed. Life within the arena now freed did not grind to a halt, nor even lessen its speed, and without question there was great reality and interest in it. I continued to see things that had to be done there, but I was no longer internally tied to and affected by the course of events related to it.

On reflection, my mind turned to my own observations of Meher Baba in action. He, I knew from long experience of sensing his inner moods, was completely free from the most upsetting or attractive happenings. I had seen repetitively the instant freeing characteristic in him when he had accomplished whatever had to be done in a given situation. And yet, his participation in the events of life was the fullest and most joyous I had ever known. Here must certainly be found the ultimate truth concerning the "juice of life" if and when parts or all of it were freed from desires and needs. Instead of removing the zest from living, being freed from habit, desire, and compulsion merely increases the joy of participation.

Once this was clear to me I never again had any concern for the future and the possible effects of the spiritual path on participation in daily living.

It seems clear on reflection that the secret of individuation is a parallel situation. Individual experiences and the flavor of the individual within them are produced by the ego. It loses itself almost totally within the individual happenings because of its identification with them as the reality, and it lives each second as if it were all one's own and to be defended as a right of absolute personal possession. The ego is identified with the happening, and we assume therefore that the happening is identified with the ego.

This just is not so. The stamp of personal flavor is there, but it is not identical with, or dependent for its existence on, the ego. The ego can disappear, just as I found it could disappear from living situations, without divorcing the focus of personal interest from the event. And similarly, an experience can retain the pattern of the original taste and efforts infused into it, and still conserve those patterns when the ego has finally disappeared from it.

Can we anticipate in words what Meher Baba appears to indicate to us? Once the ego is removed, the dream of separation and duality disappears, but the flavor of individuation does not leave the consciousness developed and imprinted within the original experience. This is the secret for the continuation of individuated experience within the indivisible unity of the final Reality.

The words of Meher Baba in this domain are suggestive, but as said before, do not have the same crystal clarity that characterizes his description of the greater part of the route traversed by the drop-soul in Creation. Meher Baba does however carry the story of the conditions of the retention of individuality one step further in his *Sparks:*

"The Truth-Individual (the term used in this work for the God-realized one) who descends into the world of illusory duality is referred to as the Qutub, which literally means 'the center.' The Perfect Master becomes the center of the universe.... This core of identity becomes the nucleus of affirmative divine individuality of the Truth-Incarnate, without blurring or limiting his oneness with the all-inclusive Truth."[5]

And in another passage from *God Speaks* he states very simply that the consciousness of God of His own divinity that is brought into the fully developed state through the dream of Creation is infinitely individualized.[6] This means that in all of divine consciousness there is developed pattern (one of my friends prefers the term "flavor," which also seems excellent here), which has emerged from the potentiality already innate within God. This patterning has emerged from the realm of potentiality through the dream process of separation and contrast. This is the contribution of the individual drop-soul, and this contribution is eternal.

This in itself might be considered quite a success story. But it does not end there. The second and even more important fact in Reality is that the ugly duckling finds at last that it is the great emperor. This is not just a prince or a princess, or even the ugly duckling become the swan. It is that, in reality, it is itself none other than the Infinite One. What more could one possibly aspire to? Not even just a part, but the entire being of Reality. This, the individual pattern developed through long lifetimes, is preserved in its clear

---

[5] *Sparks*, p. 49.
[6] *God Speaks*, p. 152.

definition, and also the real being of the drop-soul is found finally to be none other than the entirety of indivisible Infinity. Perhaps this all sounds too good to be true, but there is no other way to interpret the words of Meher Baba. And he is not the only one to define this eventual truth. Many other great expounders of the truth of Creation through the ages have given the same final verdict.

There remains only the curious situation set out in the final quote above from *Sparks* to consider. This is that, depending upon the degree of participation of the individual in the manyness of Creation after having arrived at God-realization, the composite individuality of the being may be kept in a singularly intact state. This fact may be of some importance during the stages of involution when the ego is still intact, but in Reality it becomes evidently just another curious philosophical fact among a multitude of others concerning the manner in which God and His innate Whim spin out the incredible dream of Creation.

> *The preceding has been concerned almost exclusively with what happens to individuality eventually in God's scheme. It would not be just to omit entirely from these speculations the responsibility of the individual to God, and even to his own individuality. There are many of those ties of "duty," and if we have been conscientious and honest, some of these have already made their appearance here and there. There is another that I would like to introduce, again from a personal standpoint. This is the imperative to establish priorities as one follows the challenge of the search for Truth. One of the first things I became aware of was that I had too many things to do to get them all done. Then the realization dawned that this is not an abnormal situation, but inevitable. Creation is crowded with necessities and imperfections crying out to be remedied. Every human being who looks honestly at*

himself and his surroundings with a moment of detachment is aware of this. It is not new nor extraordinary.

As I was sitting on the terrace just now relaxing after a California salad and some nice French wine and cheese, and also enjoying very much the Côte d'Azur sunshine in the late fall, I found that my mind was completely preoccupied with calculations having to do with the rent for the apartment. And so, why not? But on the other hand, why?

I began to examine where I was, and I was a bit shocked to note that it was a rare afternoon, and while I was sitting relaxed in the sun, my mind was somewhere near the North Pole. There was a great gap between the two foci of attention and presence.

I went inside the apartment and recounted this to the computer, who is my friend to whom I entrust these thoughts. Then I went back onto the terrace and determined I would enjoy the sunshine that God had provided on this occasion. This is my thought for today on the necessity of establishing priorities in the responsibility of the individual to Reality.

14. THE MASTER

The "master" is the one who is in command of the mechanics of what is being lived through. It may be oneself who is the master, or it may be someone on the outside, even far on the outside. Having started with a relatively simple definition of the word, the subject rapidly becomes more complex. For instance, the word has deep implications of command, but there is an equally strong content in the word's meaning which suggests control that comes through deep knowledge of inner workings. This implies that control is not arbitrary, but inevitable, because of the intimate understanding of the mechanics underlying the situation on the part of the "master."

Thus, on one hand the master is the one who commands, and is generally obeyed. In turn, he may be benevolent or a despot.

On the other hand, the master may guide, because he knows not only how it all works but also where it is intended to go. This is a very different understanding of masterhood from the previous one.

In mystic thought, the real Master is the one who knows both how events function as well as the intended end of the entire process. Clearly such a Master is a very powerful and valuable ally.

The Master of mystic development is often thought of as being principally of value because of his knowledge. This is in part a misconception. His real value lies in the fact that he is the personification of divine Love and has mastered its application. On this depends largely his value within the problems that humanity encounters in Creation. It is the evident and, even more, the hidden strength of that love which is irresistible. This is what accomplishes the impossible in an impossibly short time. What is removed with the help of this flood tide of perfect love is the accumulated product of countless ages of ego-centered living. What the master assists to remove is harder than diamond, and yet it is cut away in a fraction of the time in which its deposition and hardening took place.

In addition, the process of removal is incredibly sweet and excruciating, as well as more exciting than the greatest mystery story ever written. It not only captures the imagination but explodes it too. In the shortest time, continents are passed by and one enters into a garden full of exotic blooms as well as vicious thorns, which one might have dreamed of but never thought really to exist.

If this is the true base of reality, how does it happen that everyone in Creation is not on board the Master's train? It is quite simple, although tragic. It is because the ego says very flatly that reality and value lie elsewhere. And where? In the ego's parlor. But have a care about trying to get on that train. If one tries to board it without real effort to prepare for the trip, one may slip, or simply jump off, scared by the first appearance of the thorns along the wayside. Nevertheless, make the try, as it may well be your time to make the all-important leap into the great adventure despite the objections of the ego.

Who is the Master? The real one is he who has completed the journey and knows absolutely the end. Others guess and often make a big mess in the process of doing. But the guarantee to find the real Master is maturity and sincerity. Along with sincerity inevitably comes honesty, and with honesty impregnating every moment and every action, an enormous sorting out is inevitably accomplished.

Through this, the seeker prepares the ground for the Master, who knows which passengers are to be taken onto the train. And so he stops the train for a moment and hitches the aspirant aboard. This one often doesn't know that he is now on board the most important conveyance he has ever encountered.

In an earlier section we described some of the key forces and techniques open to the aspirant: love, surrender (obedience), meditation. These all are open to the searcher for Truth. This is all very important, as the student on the Way has his own part of the game to fulfill. The other part is outside his control, but earned by him as he searches for clues.

Should one risk an all-inclusive definition of the work the Master is destined to accomplish? It would be presumptuous to pretend to know, but why not make a try? Perhaps the words would run along somewhat in the following manner:

The seeker has only one problem, his own desires. These are the clay from which the form of the personal ego is built. The Master has only one problem, how to get the seeker to act without holding the image of his own desires before himself at every moment. The Master has one unbeatable resource, his own infinite love.

If this presumptuous definition has some truth in it, then one should see unrolling in the relationship of the Master with the seeker a constant story with only one theme, the substitution of the ego of the seeker in action, by the love of and for the master.

Let us see if the scenario holds up. Meher Baba sets the stage by outlining the basics of the relationship between the Master and the disciple in his discourse on "The Ways of the Masters:"

"Masters are absolutely impersonal and universal in their consciousness, but for spiritual purposes they can limit the scope of their work and also allow their manifest personality to become the center of the aspirations of their disciples. They use personal relationships as well-defined channels to pass on their help to those aspirants who become connected with them. The masters are always on the lookout for those who need and deserve their help, and the faintest gleams of spiritual yearnings are not overlooked by them. They foster and promote the advancement of all aspirants in multifarious ways that are unfailingly effective, although they might not necessarily be completely intelligible to others.

"The help of a Perfect Master consists in making the spiritual journey of the aspirant sure and safe, as well as in shortening the time he might otherwise take to arrive at the goal. The aspirant may go a long way through independent search, but he is unable to cross the sixth plane without the help of a Master. Even on the intermediate planes of involution of consciousness, the help of a Master is extremely valuable because he prevents the aspirant from getting stuck on the way and protects him from the pitfalls and dangers with which the spiritual path is beset. Kabir, the Perfect Master, has compared the three stages of the path to the three phases of fire. Just as first there is only smoke and no fire, then there is fire enveloped in smoke, and lastly there is only fire without smoke, so the beginnings of the path are enveloped in thick ignorance, midway there is confused perception of the goal, and finally there is realization of Truth without the slightest alloy of illusion. Since the path lies through illusions of many kinds, the aspirant is never safe without the guidance of a Master, who knows all the stages of the path and can take him through them."[1]

Later, in the same discourse, Baba starts to develop the manner in which love enters significantly into the relationship:

---

[1] *Discourses*, pp. 153–154.

"The Sadguru takes infinite pains to contact and win over the disciple for spiritual life. Since the progress of the disciple is secured only if his love for the Master is not allowed to dwindle, he takes every care to remove all obstacles that might be standing in the way of the wholehearted devotion of the disciple. If sometimes he is seen to humor the individual nature of the disciple, it is only to keep those obstacles from creating a serious impediment in his way. Sometimes he might even seem to feed the ego of the disciple, but all this is just allowing full scope to the ignorance of the disciple. It is only a preparation for the final extinguishing of his ego, just as animals to be offered in sacrifice are carefully nurtured before their annihilation. The Master is himself beyond good or evil and is not perturbed by the failings of the disciple. He tolerates them with unfailing patience and infinite capacity to wait, knowing full well that once the disciple gets established on the path these failings will be swiftly washed away.

"Once the Master is satisfied that the disciple is firmly established on the path, he is keen to cleanse the mind of the disciple of all blemishes. Often he achieves this task even at the risk of appearing ruthless, just as when a surgeon, completely disregarding the protests of the patient, is active with the knife. Ultimately the disciple cannot fail to see that all such measures are really in his interest. Therefore he is never pushed away from his Master but is drawn closer to him in the very process of the cleansing that might have appeared irksome or painful.

"The usual method of the Master, however, is as sweet and agreeable for the disciple as it is effective. The Master is very pleased when the disciple shows any real progress in the spiritual life. By conferring well-merited praise on the disciple, he confirms in him the spiritual qualities he is in the process of realizing and arouses in him the confidence that will enable him to cope with any situation. The glow of noble emotion, a gesture of self-denial, a heroic sacrifice, or an incident revealing extraordinary patience or love or faith—any one of these is sufficient to make the Master happy and evoke his approbation. The usual method of the Master to encourage the good qualities in the disciple is plain and unconcealed appreciation of his attainments. The disciple soon begins to value the Master's approval and delights in it more than in anything else. He is ready to resist the greatest of temptations and undergo the most trying ordeals, which would otherwise have seemed impossible to him, if only he knows that this will make the Master happy."[2]

Reflected clearly in Meher Baba's words, it is evident that through the deepening close relationship between the disciple and his Master, the attention of the disciple is drawn increasingly to the happiness of the Master and how he can best discern and promote this. It is essential to recognize that the deepening tie of the aspirant to the Master occurs in the complete absence of any ego-motivated desire on the part of the Master to become the center of such attention. If it were aimed at feeding the ego of the Master, which of course a Perfect Master does not have, then the results produced in the disciple would be seriously flawed. Nevertheless, Baba has made it clear on several occasions that the essential above all is that from the very start, there must be a "connection" between the master and the disciple. It is the master himself who knows if this all-important tie exists. If not, then there can be no basis for the profound relationship on which the journey must be established.

Throughout the establishment of this deep tie, and repeatedly even after, Meher Baba admonishes the aspirant to hold onto his daaman. While this is literally the garment worn by the master, Baba has extended the understanding of the intent of the word by clarifying that this is really the feet of the master onto which the disciple must hold fast. This admits that even the advanced aspirant is not free of discouragement at times when taxed to the limit by

---

[2] *ibid.*, pp. 157–158.

hurdles that absolutely must be cleared. Then it can become a challenge of doggedly holding on despite all.

Someone who assumes the role of Masterhood without being Realized must face this test constantly, as the quality of results achieved is directly related to the guru's selflessness. It is possible nevertheless for a very deeply sincere aspirant to avoid in large part the failings of the master by the sincerity of his devotion. This then results in the appearance of the true Master, who assumes the guiding role.

The importance of the complete focus of the student on the chosen Master is brought out by Baba further on:

"The supreme claim of the Master cannot be challenged or limited even by the spontaneous reverence that the disciple is bound to feel for Masters other than the one who has accepted him. All Perfect Masters are *one* in their consciousness, and it is absurd to imagine any grades between them. Though one Master is not greater than another, the disciple must, for his own purposes, place the claim of his own Master over and above the claims of other Masters–until he transcends the domain of duality and realizes the unity of all life. Mental energy would be dissipated unless there arose a supremely imperative claim among the many conflicting claims of life.

"Exclusive concentration upon one Master is therefore usually indispensable for the gathering up of the dispersed mental energy of the disciple. In very rare cases, owing to special circumstances, the Masters themselves might decide to share the spiritual work in relation to a particular disciple. There are therefore exceptional cases of disciples who have had to affiliate themselves to two or more Masters. This is an exception rather than the rule; and where there are more Masters than one, they arrange the distribution of their work so carefully that they do not set up conflict of claims."[3]

---

[3] *ibid.*, pp. 158–159.

Listen now to the account of how a group devoted to Baba greeted him on one of the mornings during the week they were to be in the presence of their Master:

"As Baba came into the hall that second morning of the first week—or was it the second week, or the third or the fourth?—there were more garlands, and insistent chorused shouts of 'Avatar Meher Baba–ki-jai.' First one cohesive knot would give the cheer, and one or two more garlands would be placed about Baba's neck. Then another group in another section of the hall would chorus out like a cheering section at a football game, and more garlands would be hung.

"After this had continued for some minutes, and several slight diplomatic pressures on Baba's part had not served to quiet the enthusiasm, it became apparent that he had made up his mind to firm action. He raised both arms high in the air and at once the hubbub subsided.

" 'Compared with the essentials for the path, the three most unimportant things are to garland me, to bow down to me and to sing in my praise or perform an *arti*. These are not necessarily the signs of love for God.

" 'I know well that you garland me with love. This is a good idea when we first meet. But why do it every day? I have only two coats of the color (pink) I like most, and one is already spoiled by repeated garlanding.

" 'Do not waste any more time in garlanding me tomorrow. Let us not waste money, and let me not be burdened with garlands.

" 'Don't shout "Avatar Meher Baba–ki-jai" every time I come in and go out of the hall. What is the use of that? Keep shouting, but do so within your hearts so that only you and not others may hear.'

"Like abashed schoolboys the group sat looking straight ahead, unwilling to catch a glance from the corner of a neighbor's eye.

"Momentarily the air hung tense with the light reprimand,

while Baba looked keenly over the hunched heads and forward-leaning shoulders.

" 'Did you sleep well last night?' he asked.

" 'Yes, Baba,' was the general reply.

" 'Who did not sleep last night?'

"Slowly one man stood up near the door, heavy brown scarf wrapped tightly about throat and head, eyes inflamed, nose running. His diagnosis was promptly read by almost three hundred pairs of eyes.

"Another, and then another, and then several, rose to their feet.

" 'Why didn't you sleep last night?'

" 'Because I was so happy to be near you again, Baba.'

" 'And why didn't you sleep?'

" 'My stomach was upset, Baba, I think I ate too much dinner because I was so glad to see all of my old friends again.'

" 'And you?'

" 'Some of the Parsis were playing cards and I couldn't sleep. I do not think they should play cards when they are here to learn of God from you.'

Baba was prompt with his reply.

" 'What has playing cards to do with one's love and longing for God? Playing with cards is better than playing with the whole of life. Shams Tabrezi and his famous disciple Moulana Rumi were both very fond of playing chess. Shams' greatest work was done at the end of a game of chess with Rumi.

" 'When Rumi lost the game he could not help crying out to Shams, "I have lost".

" 'Then and there, with the words, "No, you have won," Shams gave Rumi instant God-realization.' "[4]

In the afternoon of the same day, among many other things

---

[1] *Listen, Humanity*, pp. 29–30.

discussed by Baba, he offered the following practical suggestions:

" 'The best way to cleanse the heart and prepare for the stilling of the mind is to lead a normal, worldly life. Living in the midst of your day-to-day duties, responsibilities, likes, dislikes, etc., will help you. All these become the very means for the purification of your heart. This natural, normal method depends for its success upon a clear idea of the forces behind your thoughts, and the facts underlying your actions....

" 'The fire of divine love alone can destroy all impressions once and for all. However, remembering me can keep down the impurities in the impressions in your mind, as alum catches hold of (flocculates) dirt in a vessel of turbid water. Therefore, when you feel angry or have lustful thoughts, remember Baba at once. Let my name serve as a net around you so that your thoughts, like mosquitoes, may keep buzzing around you and yet not sting you. In that manner you can prevent unwanted thoughts from turning into unwanted actions, and thus eventually bring your heart to the purification required for me to manifest therein.' "[5]

Here is a very simple but very clear method for using the love of and faith in the Master as a means of control of the actions of the ego. In such a method, the desire-impulse is not confronted and suppressed, but distracted by a higher value within oneself–the love for the Master. In the action, the sanskaric energy is not repressed but allowed to swirl about, and at least some of it is dispersed.

The challenge to be met is simple and clear. The barrier to the realization of Truth consists of the vast accumulation of sanskaras in previous incarnations. The most efficient way to remove this barrier is to find the magic value that can distract the ego during each

---

[5] *ibid.*, pp. 43–45.

personal act. Beyond such a discovery, however, there is still another very important ingredient that enters constantly into the game. This is the conservation of energy by the disciple.

A great many of the strong suggestions the Master makes concern the guarding of energy by the aspirant. Perhaps the Master also in some manner makes a contribution to the storehouse. Baba often calls attention to how necessary these resources are to overcome the tremendous obstacles encountered on the Path. His words on this are definitive, and he repeats them in many contexts. Here is a brief but strong example:

"In order to help the disciple achieve this difficult task the Master has to become the nucleus of all the spiritual idealism of the aspirant, because intensive concentration of mental energy is necessary if the aspirant is to break through the many barriers that lie between him and his goal."[6]

There are indications in both Baba's writings as well as generally in spiritual literature that under certain circumstances the Master may grant the deserving aspirant a balancing of accounts of considerable importance. But one also gains the impression that such a gift may be limited to the final accounting processes, when the aspirant has already earned and traversed a large part of the course. Just what the formula may be, I have never seen precisely described by any great spiritual leader.

On the contrary, there are many indications that a large part of the job of conserving and directing spiritual energy must be shouldered by the disciple. We have already drawn attention to Meher Baba's words of the importance of mastering the tendency to worry, which he characterizes as being one of the greatest causes of needless expenditure of vast amounts of the psychic energy needed

---

[6] *Discourses*, p. 158.

for the Path. In this regard, another very impressive description is given by Baba in *God Speaks* on the necessity of mastering the technique of "forgetfulness." This is a higher quality principle aimed at the same goal as control of the worry habit. Here is what Meher Baba advises:

"The whole philosophy of approaching and realizing the Truth hinges on the question of what we may call forgetfulness. The word 'forgetfulness' used here must not be associated with its commonly accepted meaning of forgetting to post a letter, or of a state of mind that is simply dull and blank. Forgetfulness in this special sense is an attitude of mind that develops gradually into spiritual experience. External renunciation is not forgetfulness, because it is mostly physical and partly mental; but internal renunciation, when it becomes purely mental, does assume the quality and dignity of forgetfulness. Thus one may renounce the world, but it is not so easy to forget it.

"Forgetfulness in this special sense thus explains the secret that lies behind all happiness, spiritual or otherwise, that human beings experience....

"Positive forgetfulness, then, is the cure, and its steady cultivation develops in man that balance of mind which enables him to express such noble traits as charity, forgiveness, tolerance, selflessness, and service to others. One who is not equipped with this positive forgetfulness becomes a barometer of his surroundings. His poise is disturbed by the slightest whisper of praise or flattery, and by the faintest suggestion of slander or criticism; his mind is like a slender reed swayed by the lightest breeze of emotion. Such a man is perpetually at war with himself and knows no peace.

"In the exercise of this positive forgetfulness, not only is non-reaction to adverse circumstances essential, but also non-reaction to favorable and pleasurable circumstances. Of these two the latter is the harder and is less often described, although it matters just as much.

"Positive forgetfulness, although it lies at the very root of happiness, is by no means easy to acquire. Once a man attains this state of mind, however, he rises above pain and pleasure; he is master of himself. This forgetfulness, to be fully effective for the spiritual life, must become permanent, and such permanence is only acquired through constant practice during many lives."[7]

It is tempting to suggest that a large proportion of the disciplines and strong suggestions made by the Master are divided between methods for distracting the ego during action (whether physical, emotional or mental) and various manners of conserving spiritual energy. It may seem repulsive on first hearing to suggest that the spiritual process functions somewhat like a great machine which follows certain laws governing the use and conservation of energy. But why should this not be so?

The history of sanskaras from beginning to end is traced within Creation, and it is a vast complex of constellations and transformations of different classes of energy. Hence, inevitably, the disestablishment of the sanskaras in turn must transpire within similar complexes of energy. It would be foolish to assume that, in some manner, on the stroke of the chiming of the clock denoting the start of the unwinding process, an entirely different order of causal law starts to operate.

All of these sanskaric and karmic activities operate within the domain of Creation, and certainly Creation is anchored in principles of energy. They cannot be neglected. They control in fact the manner in which the necessary operations occur, hence a healthy respect for the basic principles of energy is paramount.

How many times have I seen the manner in which clearly, but usually unobtrusively, Meher Baba precipitated an aspirant's awareness of his own energy level? If it had been seriously depleted,

---

[7] *God Speaks*, pp. 211–214.

Baba stopped his review right there and gave the disciple a loving but very clear description of what could reasonably be asked of the body and the nervous system, and what could not.

To carry all this a step further into the realm of spiritual effort and forces required to maintain it, we had noted in Chapter 10 that Meher Baba has spoken of the sanskaric deposit in the mental body as being a kind of "solidified might." In his discussions of the manners of the dispersion and exhaustion of the sanskaras, he has noted that in the process of the sublimation of sanskaric desires, the energy associated with the sanskara is held up from expressing itself through the desire pattern associated with the sanskara. It is then utilized instead as a positive force for progress along the Path.

All of these references make it clear that energy is a fundamental factor in traversing the road towards enlightenment, and that the aspirant must be conscious of its importance. Further, he must attempt certain disciplines aimed at the preservation and consolidation of this energy.

When all is said and done, however, one comes back to the side-tracking of the personal ego as being the key objective to be achieved. Without it, the ego goes on ad infinitum constantly recapturing the energy of habit patterns and staying in robust, strong health. Needless to say, God and Reality, in such case, remain distant; however, without one's being aware of it, the tightness of the sanskaric knots is almost certainly beginning to lessen. Hence, even if it be long in the future, the days of the ego are now numbered.

One must go back to Baba's constant theme of the unique ability of love to concentrate and utilize to the maximum the psychic energies required on the Path. It is impossible to confuse the logic which indicates that the most effective course that can be followed is to have a Perfect One at the center of the concentration. It is not that he needs that love. It is also not that he is seeking thereby to direct the aspirant towards some goal outside the intrinsic nature of the aspirant himself. In real fact, the Perfect One is seeking to achieve nothing more or less than to bring the seeker to his real Self.

The Master, being perfected, is beyond all desire. And yet it has been ordained that after his own long labor of perfecting consciousness has ended, he will return for a time into the swirl of the world to help others on the way. This he does in a completely free and dispassionate manner. The secret, though, is that one of the divine attributes which impregnate him totally is divine love. The seeker drawn to him finds himself caught up in a force which cannot be resisted, even if he had wished to. Inevitably he is propelled along his way in the most efficient and rapid manner possible. And his own greatest contribution is achieved to the degree that he too can experience and express the resources of his own capacity to love.

All this panorama of great tides of deeply personal love flowing back and forth between lover and beloved, when viewed from the sidelines by an uninvolved spectator, can be very alarming, especially to the western mentality. Almost certainly this will create an increasing crisis in the future as growing numbers of advanced souls are present who are capable of being true centers for aspiration. Yet such a dichotomy is inevitable as awareness of the depths and the powers of love are perceived more and more by an awakening New Humanity in the New Age of human fulfillment of God's wish to know His own divinity consciously.

15. Who Is He?

This book has been about Meher Baba, whom I and many others consider to be the Avatar of this New Age. The high points of his life and philosophy have been given to the best of my ability, and personalized in many instances by my own experiences. Now it seems appropriate to summarize a number of the high points covered.

Creation is the result of the Whim of infinite God in His most original state to know His divinity consciously. In the complexity of the Creation which results from the surging of this Whim there is a fundamental and important characteristic of "wearing out" or, to put it dramatically, "decay." This is true not only of physical objects, such as our bodies, but even such a psychic factor as "Truth," as understood and manifested by humanity.

It is in this area of wearing out that the Avatar, the first human being to complete the long itinerary of evolution and involution to God Realization, takes on as God's direct representative in Creation the key responsibility of renewal. This is an enormous role, covering not only the human aspects, but reaching back to the simplest manifestations of form. This the Avatar fulfills basically himself, and it is only the details that are filled in by others who have or are near to achieving a conscious knowledge of their own Godhood identical to that of the Avatar.

The most complex perhaps of the Avatar's responsibilities lie in the realm of the manifestation of Truth at the human stage, as well as the taking on of the direct responsibility for the completion of the Path to God Realization for a surprisingly large number of human beings. It is specifically in this latter domain that the dramas unfold which are largely the subject matter of the chronicles of the various lives of this unique representative, the God 6Man, on earth.

Much of this book has been concerned with what we have observed of the manner in which the Avatar handles those he has chosen to help along the advanced stages of the spiritual Path. But we would do well to remember that, dramatic and appealing as this is to us, it is only one component, although an important one, of his total charge of responsibilities in Creation.

One would also do well to become conscious *now* of the saga of the Avatar, as it is now that the force of his mission is at full strength, and therefore most accessible to those ready to profit by it.